DEC - 3 2012

Spring Wildflowers of the Northeast

Spring Wildflowers of the Northeast

A NATURAL HISTORY

Carol Gracie

WITH A FOREWORD BY ERIC LAMONT

PRINCETON UNIVERSITY PRESS — PRINCETON AND OXFORD

Published by Princeton University Press, 41 William Street,
Princeton, New Jersey 08540
In the United Kingdom: Princeton University Press, 6 Oxford Street,
Woodstock, Oxfordshire OX20 1TW
press.princeton.edu

Library of Congress Cataloging-in-Publication Data

Gracie, Carol.
Spring wildflowers of the Northeast : a natural history /
Carol Gracie;
with a foreword by Eric Lamont.
Includes bibliographical references and index.
ISBN 978-0-691-14466-5 (cloth : alk. paper) 1. Wild flowers—
Northeastern States, I. Title.
QK117.G68 2012
582.130974
[23]
2011023958

British Library Cataloging-in-Publication Data is available

This book has been composed in Minion Pro

Printed on acid-free paper ∞

Printed in Singapore

1 3 5 7 9 10 8 6 4 2

For my sons, Jon and Geoff Gottlieb

Contents

Rarely does a modern natural history book seamlessly combine the elements of exhaustive fieldwork by the author with extensive scholarly research. *Spring Wildflowers of the Northeast: A Natural History,* by noted author and accomplished botanist Carol Gracie, does just that. Gracie's vision of weaving "science, culture, and beauty" into the framework of her book has been splendidly achieved.

In her pursuit of observing and photographing wildflowers in the Northeast, Gracie has traveled as much as anyone, if not more. For her earlier book, *Wildflowers in the Field and Forest,* coauthored with the late Steven Clemants, she drove more than 27,000 miles in search of wildflowers to photograph. Additionally, years of observing plants in more than forty foreign countries and territories has provided unique and insightful experiences that are shared with an eye for detail.

During the past forty years, I also have been lured by the wildflowers of the eastern United States and beyond. Most, if not all, readers of this book have likely embarked on the same pilgrimage, and we are fortunate to have before us a collection of detailed observations and intimate experiences with wildflowers by one who shares our passion. Every reader, from the professional Ph.D. botanist to the amateur nature lover, will learn something new and fascinating about each of the thirty-plus species covered in this book.

Gracie combines historical elements of botany like the Doctrine of Signatures and the observations of Henry David Thoreau with cutting-edge, modern research to present a comprehensive story of the natural history of each species covered. Twenty-three pages of references are a testament to the extensive research involved in preparation of this treatise. Descriptions of plant characteristics, reproductive strategies, related species, habitat preferences, and ranges of distribution are presented in a narrative that captivates the reader. Throughout the book, essays are embellished with quotes from past botanists including, among others, Carl Linnaeus and his student Peter Kalm, André Michaux, Mark Catesby, Asa Gray, and Thomas Nuttall. Also included are legends and accounts of ethnobotanical uses of plants by the Iroquois, Huron, Ojibway, and Cree Indians, and the Inuit of Alaska, with follow-up discussions on the validity of those uses today.

As noted by the author, plant taxonomy has been turned on its head during the past two decades based, for the most part, on molecular data. The author presents a detailed history of plant names, both common and scientific, and patiently explains the reasons for recent name changes. Gracie has a gift for clarifying difficult taxonomic concepts and sometimes shares her frustrations: "there is generally good reason for such taxonomic changes, but it can drive one crazy."

Often her discussions of plant names end in stories from far away lands, as in the case of the genus *Mertensia* and the naturalist who circumnavigated Russia collecting jellyfish. Her plant stories take on a life of their own and include places like the north coast of Greenland, Antarctica, and the Himalayan Mountains.

Gracie has documented the pollination strategies for each wildflower in her book, sometimes supplementing little or no previously published information with her own observations. She reports on a native andrenid bee as a visitor to the flowers of purple trillium, a first-time published report for that species of *Trillium.* Even Frederick and Roberta Case, authors of the book *Trilliums,* state: "We have seen little published information on pollinators of trilliums."

Among many other topics, Gracie discusses the negative effects of deer on spring wildflowers and the devastating effects of alien earthworms. She explains why plants have been called virtual "chemical factories" in their war against ravenous insects and other herbivores. Human activities are largely responsible for the elimination of many native wildflowers, and disapproval of negative human impacts subtly enters into some of her essays: "It is perhaps poetic justice that those who pluck these orchids from the wild may suffer an irritating skin rash."

One of the strongest aspects of this book is the photography that accompanies each species, and once again seldom does a modern natural-history book include such detailed documentation of the life histories of plant species. Inquisitive observations captured through the camera lens illustrate discussions within the text and reveal an extraordinary world rarely experienced by most people.

The purposes of *Spring Wildflowers of the Northeast* are manifold, but ultimately it is a personal account of one woman's intoxicating obsession with flowering plants and their connection to the rest of the natural world. As such, it becomes a valuable contribution to our knowledge of the flora of the Northeast and an aesthetic presentation of the beauty and intricacies of these captivating wildflowers.

Eric Lamont

~ *Preface* ~

I have always loved wildflowers. As a little girl I picked wildflower bouquets for my mother, including as many different species as I could find. My mom was a former city girl and not familiar with flowers that grew in the wild, so she was usually not able to tell me their names. However, she did teach me the names of our garden flowers, among them *Coreopsis, Dianthus,* and *Gladiolus.* At the time they were just flower names to me; I did not realize until many years later that they were also the generic names of the plants. My father, on the other hand, had done a lot of camping and hiking as a boy and young man, and it is from him that I inherited my love of the outdoors and nature. Pop's interests lay more in the realm of trees, birds, and snakes than wildflowers, and it was not until I was an adult that a friend introduced me to my first Peterson field guide, and I began to learn the names of wildflowers. Identifying plants has since added much pleasure to my time in local woods and fields.

Just knowing the *names* of wildflowers was soon not enough; I wanted to know more about them: why they lived where they did, what insects visited them, how they got their names, etc. I have since spent many happy years observing and learning about wildflowers, and I have come to appreciate the rich and interesting life histories that underlie their beauty and connect them to the rest of the natural world. As with people, plants become both more interesting and more memorable once you get to know them. I find that it is easier to remember plant names, both common and scientific, if you can associate the name with something that you know about the plant; for example, knowing that bloodroot has red sap allows me to easily remember its scientific name, *Sanguinaria* (pertaining to blood in Latin).

While photographing plants for a field guide to northeastern wildflowers (Clemants and Gracie, 2006), I had the opportunity to spend long hours in the field observing not only the flowers but also their visitors. My curiosity about insect-plant relationships grew, and I was prompted to question not only what was taking place, but why. What were the floral visitors doing? Was it beneficial to the plant—or harmful, or both? Why was the flower shaped the way it was? Some of what I write about in this book was learned

by this firsthand observation. I occasionally digress from the subject of the plant itself to tell something of the lifestyle of a pollinator or a seed disperser because I feel that this added information makes for a more interesting and complete story. In some cases I have roamed beyond the geographic scope of the book in order to compare and contrast species in our northeastern flora with those from other parts of the country—or even other parts of the world. To supplement my own observations, I have scoured scientific journals, books, and the Internet for additional information, much of which is not readily accessible to the general reader. Since I am a visual learner, I am a strong believer in the value of images to impart information. Thus, I have attempted, whenever possible, to show in photographs what is being discussed in the text.

This book is written for all who share an interest in wildflowers. To make the subject matter accessible for even the neophyte wildflower lover, I have arranged the plants alphabetically by common name (but always with the scientific name and family given as well). I have done my best to avoid the use of scientific jargon, but when I found it necessary to use a term that might not be familiar to the nonprofessional, I have defined it either within the text or in the glossary at the end of the book. I have not included formal citations or footnotes within the text because the book is intended for a general audience. However, references used for each species are provided under the relevant species divisions in the reference section at the end of the book so that the reader may go to the original sources for further information.

The scope of the book encompasses the entire northeastern portion of the United States as well as adjacent Canada, in agreement with the most widely used flora for the area, the *Manual of Vascular Plants of Northeastern United States and Adjacent Canada*, by Gleason and Cronquist (1991). The common names used are those that are most generally used in my own area of the greater Northeast, that is, in New England and the Tri-state area (New York, New Jersey, and Connecticut). However, many of the plants are known by a dozen or more common names throughout their range, and some of these alternate names are mentioned within the text. The information at the beginning of each species treatment includes both scientific and common names of the species and its family. When blooming times are given, they are based on those of plants in my geographic region, both because I am familiar with the plants of that area and because southern New York lies more or less in the center of the latitudinal range of this book. The same species are likely to be in flower earlier in the southern part of their range and later in northern areas.

The most recent system for summarizing plant family relationships, including the currently accepted family names and lists of the genera presently included in each family, is provided by the Angiosperm Phylogeny Group (APG) and is based, for the most part, on molecular data. It is the system that is used in this book for family designations and names. The new system may cause some confusion for readers who are familiar with long-standing family names. For example, the Scrophulariaceae (figwort family) has had most of its northeastern members placed into other families, primarily the Plantaginaceae (plantain family) and the Orobanchaceae (broomrape family), with only a few genera remaining as "scrophs." The Liliaceae (lily family) has been similarly segregated into several, more narrowly defined families. Molecular studies at the generic and specific levels have also resulted in changes to what had previously been well-known accepted names, for example, all of our native "asters," formerly in the genus *Aster*, are now placed into five different genera. If a species has already been treated in the ongoing, monumental work on the flora of the United States and Canada, *Flora of North America*, I have used that designation of the species. Otherwise, I have followed the names accepted by TROPICOS, an online resource for nomenclature of New World plants provided by the Missouri Botanical Garden (http://www.tropicos.org).

A brief explanation of how plants receive their scientific names and the various levels of plant classification should help to alleviate any fear of using Latin-based names, as well as provide an understanding of the relationships among species, genera, and families of plants. In 1753 Carl (Carolus) Linnaeus, the founder of the system we use to name plants and other living organisms, published his monumental work, *Species Plantarum*, in which he provided names for all the species of plants then known to European botanists. Linnaeus sought to simplify and standardize the naming of plants by giving each species a unique combination of two names (termed a binomial) to designate the genus (plural, *genera*) and its modifier, the species (used for both singular and plural). Individual species that shared many characteristics in common were grouped into larger categories called genera, and the genera, in turn, were grouped into families based on similar characteristics. Today, family names have been standardized to always end in *-aceae*.

Botanists may choose to give generic or specific names to a plant using a descriptive term (e.g., a large-flowered plant might be named *grandiflora*: *Magnolia grandiflora*), or a geographical locality (e.g., a plant originally collected in Virginia might be named *virginiensis* or *virginica*: *Claytonia virginica*). The species part of the name, called the specific epithet, varies such that it agrees in gender (masculine, feminine, or neuter) with the genus name; thus *alba* (the feminine form of "white") agrees with *Baptisia*, a feminine genus name, but *albus* (the masculine form of "white") agrees with *Asphodelus*, a masculine genus. A genus or species may also be given a name that commemorates a person, perhaps the first one to collect the plant or someone of importance, for example, *Kalmia latifolia* (mountain laurel), was named by Linnaeus to honor Peter Kalm, a student of Linnaeus who collected many new species in North America (*latifolia* indicates that the species has broad leaves). *Potentilla robbinsiana*, the rare Robbin's cinquefoil, known only from New Hampshire, was named by William Oakes to honor his fellow botanist and physician, James W. Robbins (*Potentilla* is the diminutive form of *potens*, meaning "powerful"—from the reputed medicinal powers of one species, *P. anserina*). It is not permitted for the person who describes and names a plant to name it for him- or herself, even if he or she was the one to first discover the plant. Scientific names are always italicized, and the names of genera are always capitalized, but those of species are not, even if they are based on a proper noun. Species may be further subdivided into subspecies, varieties, or forms. Although the binomial system of nomenclature was meant to provide a single definitive name that was recognizable worldwide for each species, there is sometimes disagreement among botanical taxonomists (those who classify plants), and alternative names may be found for some species. A strict code, the International Code of Botanical Nomenclature, governs the naming of plants, but botanists may petition the authorities to use another name, especially if there is a long history of common usage for a well-known species, and if a change to an earlier, technically correct name would only cause greater confusion. Such decisions are made at an international meeting convened every five years. When writing a scientific name, it is accepted practice that once a plant has been referred to in a written work by its full scientific name (genus and species), subsequent mentions of the plant may abbreviate the genus by using just the first letter followed by a period.

Traditionally, flowering plants (angiosperms) have been divided into two main categories: monocotyledons (monocots)—plants having one seed leaf (cotyledon) within their seeds, generally narrow leaves with parallel veins, and flowers with their parts in threes or multiples of three; and dicotyledons (dicots)—plants with two cotyledons, broad leaves with branching venation, and flowers with their parts in fours, fives, or usually some number other than three. Today, this simple system has been supplanted with one that is more complex but more finely defined. New methods of studying plants and their relationships (e.g., cladistics and DNA sequencing) have allowed systematists (those who study evolutionary relationships) to clarify evolutionary relationships that were poorly understood, or misunderstood, previously. Although the monocots are still viewed as a natural and intact group, various groups within the original dicots have been shown to have evolved from a common ancestor at different times, some before the monocots were separated from them and some after. The current overall classification of plants has four categories: the monocots (described above); the eudicots (meaning "true dicots"), which have the characters mentioned above for the earlier classification of dicots; the magnoliids, which consist of dicots that are for the most part woody plants (with some members of the Piperaceae [pepper family] and Aristolochiaceae [birthwort family] having an herbaceous habit) and that have retained characters that are considered to be more primitive, for example, numerous, spirally arranged

stamens and carpels, superior ovaries, and seeds with minute embryos and copious endosperm (e.g., *Magnolia*); and a still more basal group, the ANITA (an acronym from the five families or orders that compose the group: Amborellaceae, Nymphaeales, Illiciales, Trimeniaceae, and Austrobaileyaceae) grade, which branched off from the original angiosperm ancestor early in the evolution of angiosperms. Many members of this group lack water-conducting vessels or have vessels that resemble those of gymnosperms and are viewed as the most primitive angiosperms (e.g., *Nymphaea*, water lilies).

I have chosen to focus on the life histories of only a few dozen of the spring-blooming wildflower species found in the northeastern United States. Some were selected because of their beauty, and others are included because they have compelling natural history stories, historical or medicinal uses, or interesting interactions with insects. Both common and less well-known species are included. In addition to our native species, I have included a few that have been introduced from afar if they are found commonly naturalized in our area. For the most part, our native spring wildflowers are found in woodlands. They have evolved to take advantage of the early spring sunlight that reaches the forest floor before the tree canopy has leafed out. Thus, to see them you must deliberately seek them out by going into the woods in early spring; with few exceptions, they will not be found along roadsides or in open fields.

Medicinal uses and purported edibility are mentioned in many of the descriptions, but I in no way endorse any such use; rather, I strongly discourage it. Certainly many of our local plants have medicinal properties, but rarely have they been thoroughly studied or scientifically tested for efficacy or negative side effects. In many cases, reports of medicinal properties are based on the use of plants by Native Americans before and during Colonial times. Native peoples, of necessity, experimented with a vast variety of plants in their attempts to treat disease, sometimes with disastrous results. If the patient recovered, the recovery might be attributed to the plant(s) used in treatment, when, in fact, the "cure" might have been unrelated to the treatment. Early colonists, in attempting to find substitutes for medicinal herbs that they had used in Europe, sometimes followed Indian methods or substituted plants that resembled those they knew from home. Herbal remedies sold in today's market do not undergo the standardization and certification necessary for medications approved by the United States Food and Drug Administration and thus might vary in strength, or even ingredients.

It is my hope that as you learn more about local wildflowers, your appreciation of them will grow, and you will enjoy becoming a better observer of nature. There is still much to learn about even our "common" wildflowers. You will find a 10× magnification lens to be extremely useful for observing the fine details of floral structure; it does for flowers what binoculars do for birds. With such a lens and a good field guide, you are on your way to discovering a new and fascinating world. I urge you to follow your interests because serendipity can lead to interesting discoveries in the study of nature. Do remember that in nature, there is always variation: you may encounter a normally purple flower in its white form, or one with more or fewer floral parts than is "normal." I am certain that as you become more familiar with the natural history of wildflowers, you will want to become an advocate for their protection and conservation. Many of our once common wildflowers are now rare due to habitat

destruction, competition from invasive species, over-browsing by a white-tailed deer population that is out of control, and the degradation of forest soils by introduced worms. You can help to preserve our wildflower heritage for future generations by becoming involved in and supporting local and regional conservation organizations. The New England Wildflower Society, based in Framingham, Massachusetts, does much to promote wildflower conservation throughout New England and is a reputable source of native wildflower species; its lovely Garden in the Woods is a showplace for native wildflowers throughout spring and summer. Other regional centers known for their native wildflower displays are Bowman's Hill Wildflower Preserve, in New Hope, Pennsylvania, and the Mt. Cuba Center, near Wilmington, Delaware. Local organizations whose mission it is to promote and protect native species include local garden clubs, nature centers, land trusts, and the Native Plant Center in my home county of Westchester, New York. In addition, national conservation organizations such as the National Audubon Society and the Nature Conservancy (and local chapters of both) are advocates for our local flora and fauna.

Acknowledgments

I am indebted to many people for assistance with the various aspects of producing this book. First, my thanks to Robert Kirk of Princeton University Press, who was enthusiastic about the book from its inception and patiently waited until I had time to devote to the project. I am sincerely grateful to the four people who read the entire manuscript in progress: Ed Hecklau, Rob Naczi, Ginnie Weinland, and my husband, Scott Mori. All made valuable comments and suggestions that helped to improve the final product. The above reviewers also provided congenial company on several field trips. In addition, Ed and his wife El were delightful hosts for several Adirondack botanical excursions, Rob shared information on localities of interesting plants and took me to a wonderful featherfoil site in Delaware, my long-time friend Ginnie continued to provide inspiration, and Scott offered love, encouragement, support, and understanding throughout the process of preparing this manuscript.

Various members of my walking group kept me informed of new plant sightings and blooming times as well as provided delightful companionship in the field: thanks to Diane Alden, Alice Ballin, Brooke Beebe, Anne Carter, Joan Coffey, Vivian Frommer, Polly Goodwin, Ursula Joachim, George Johanson, Francesca Jones, Zell Kerr, Sophie Keyes, Carol Levine, Roz Lowen, Yvonne Lynn, Joanne McAuley, Jane McKean, Sondra Peterson, Janet Townsend, Phyllis Tortora, Ginnie Weinland, and Rena Wertzer; in addition, Phyllis Tortora twice welcomed me to her Adirondack home for some northern botanizing. Many other friends and associates responded to my e-mail requests for locality information when I needed to photograph particular species at certain stages of their life cycles and sometimes also took me to the sites: Dan Aitchison, Alison Beale (who also alerted me to the commencement of the spring nesting activity of andrenid bees), Charles Day, Andy Greller, Roy Halling, Becky Hrdy, Taro Ietako, Gail Jankus, Linda Kelly, Wesley Knapp, Tait Johansson, Eric Lamont, Paul Lewis, Irene Marks, Barbara Morrow, Nannette Orr, Vi Patek, Jody Payne, Michael Penziner, Helle Raheem, Sam Saulys, Mike Slater, and Lew Sparks. Others providing companionship and good humor in the field were my son Geoff Gottlieb and friends Paul and Jean Lewis and Joep Moonen.

Special thanks go to my husband, Scott, and our good friend Paul Lewis, who spent three strenuous hours on a muggy spring day digging up a skunk cabbage plant so that I could photograph the roots (while Paul's wife Jean and I supplied cold drinks and encouragement). After reading about the tenacity of the contractile roots, I just *had* to see them for myself—and show them to you, the reader. Thanks to Sue Moga for facilitating my visit to the site.

Others who deserve thanks for their contributions include Fred Battenfeld, who invited me to his greenhouses to photograph sweet violet (*Viola odorata*); Ana Berry, who decades ago taught me to identify wildflowers using Peterson's *Field Guide to Wildflowers*; Barbara Brummer of the Nature Conservancy in New Jersey, who made it possible for me to see New Jersey's yellow-flowered spring beauty; Bill Buck, who identified the mosses in my photos; Steven Cook at the Pequot Museum in Connecticut, who granted access to the museum's wonderful collection of Indian artifacts, especially those that utilized plant materials; Tony Ianniello, who informed me that the sports teams of his alma mater, New York University, were called the Violets (the male football team has subsequently dropped the Violets appellation in favor of the somewhat more intimidating Bobcats); Linda Kelly, who was of invaluable help in locating rare or interesting species in New Jersey, in addition to providing pleasant accommodations; Mike and Kim Kerner, who graciously allowed me to visit their New Jersey property to photograph wildflowers; Jim McClements, who opened his species-rich wildflower garden to me on several occasions; the New York Botanical Garden, whose rich library resources were the source for much of my research; Margaret Ordonez, who provided information on Indian artifacts and an introduction to the staff at the Pequot Museum in Connecticut (my thanks again to Phyllis Tortora for establishing the contact with Margaret); Jim Reveal, who provided thoughtful insights about botanical nomenclature; Meredith Vasta, the collections manager at the Pequot Museum, who facilitated my visit there; and Matt Wilson, an excellent trainer at the Danbury (and later Greenwich) Apple Store, who resolved all of my technical issues.

Amy Litt's skill in simplifying the definitions of molecular terms and providing answers in layman's terms to rather esoteric molecular questions is much appreciated. Several people took the time to look at my photos to confirm what was depicted and/or to provide additional information about the subject: Janis Antonovics, Tom Croat, Theresa Culley, Elizabeth Elle, Peter Groffman, Guy Gusman, Roy Halling, Susan Kalisz, Job Kuijt, Jody Payne, and Richard Stokes. Thank you all. And special thanks to Juliet McConnell and Mark Spencer at the Natural History Museum in London for facilitating the permission process to allow me to use an image of a specimen from the John Clayton Herbarium (*Claytonia virginica*) and to Eric Lamont, April Randle, and David Wagner for allowing me to use their images (featherfoil plants in ice, a bumblebee visiting blue-eyed Mary flowers, and a *Calyptera canadensis* caterpillar on early meadow-rue, respectively).

I have great respect for the many researchers whose long years of study and resultant publications served as an inspiration for this book. If they are not mentioned within the text, their work is cited in the reference section at the back of the book. I hope to bring some of their interesting discoveries to the attention of a broader audience who might not have access to the scientific literature but who would find the subjects of their research fascinating when distilled for a more general audience.

And finally, I am especially grateful to two prepublication readers, Garrett Crow and Eric Lamont, both exceptionally well versed in the botany of the Northeast; their careful reading of the manuscript and thoughtful comments helped to eliminate errors and improve the text. All those on the staff of Princeton University Press have been most helpful throughout the production process; their professional expertise has resulted in many refinements of the text; my thanks to Alison Anuzis, David Campbell, Beth Clevenger, and especially to Gail Schmitt, whose skillful copyediting is greatly appreciated. Of course, I take full responsibility for any remaining errors.

Spring Wildflowers of the Northeast

Buttercup Family

Fig. 1. A plant of red baneberry in flower. Note the loose arrangement of the inflorescence and the filamentous pedicels (flower stalks).

Fig. 2. A fruiting stalk of white baneberry. The white fruit with a dark spot at the apex (a remnant of the stigma) is responsible for the common name "doll's eyes." Note the thick pink pedicels (flower stalks).

White Baneberry and Red Baneberry

Actaea pachypoda and Actaea rubra

Buttercup Family (Ranunculaceae)

Both white baneberry and red baneberry are poisonous plants native to the Northeast. They are most easily distinguished from one another when in fruit because the leaves and flowers of the two species are similar.

Habitat: Both species of baneberry are commonly found in deciduous forest but may also occur in mixed forest with conifers, particularly the red baneberry. Red baneberry may also inhabit swamps.

Range: White baneberry—parts of the Canadian Maritimes and the southern border of eastern Canada south along the East Coast to northern New Jersey, continuing inland along the southern Appalachians and then west to eastern Minnesota and northern Mississippi. Red baneberry—more extensive, reaching north well into Canada, west to Alaska, and south only to northern New Jersey and Pennsylvania in the East. Across the northern United States, its distribution extends irregularly south in the Midwest and the Mountain States and from the Pacific Northwest into California in the Far West.

It is difficult to tell the two species of baneberry apart when they are not in flower or fruit. Both are perennials inhabiting deciduous woodlands, and both are similar in overall appearance and in the shape of their compound leaves with sharply toothed leaflets (fig. 3). However, when in flower, there are small but detectable differences: first, the inflorescence of white baneberry is cylindrical with the flowers densely congested on the raceme (fig. 4), in contrast to the inflorescence of red baneberry, which is more pyramidal with its flowers less densely arranged (fig. 1); second, and probably more important for identification purposes, is that the stigma of the white baneberry flower is sessile and is as wide as or wider than the ovary, sometimes appearing even to extend down the sides of the ovary (fig. 5). The stigma of red baneberry is just slightly elevated and, while large, is narrower than the ovary and never extends down its sides (fig. 6). Looking carefully at the flowers will result in the additional observation that the 4–10 petals of the two species differ in shape. The tips of the petals of white baneberry appear either as though they had been bluntly cut off or that they are bilobed at the tip, almost as if anthers

Buttercup Family

Fig. 3. A plant of white baneberry showing the overall habit and leaf type, which is similar in both species of baneberry.

Fig. 4. A cylindrical inflorescence of white baneberry, with densely crowded flowers.

were affixed to the apex of the petals (some botanists consider the petals to be staminodes rather than petals; indeed some consider the petals in all Ranunculaceae to be derived from stamens) (fig. 7). In contrast, the petals of red baneberry have an apex that is either acute or obtuse, but never bilobed (fig. 6). Both species have petals that are more or less clawed (sharply narrowed) at the base.

When the inflorescence is just beginning to flower, it is not always easy to discern that the pedicels (flower stalks) of the flowers of white baneberry are thicker than those of red baneberry. However, as the inflorescence matures, and especially when in fruit, this feature becomes more pronounced. In fruit, the two species cannot be mistaken. In white baneberry, the raceme and individual fruit stalks will be nearly as thick as the main stalk of the inflorescence and deep pink to red in color (fig. 2). The inflorescence stalk of red baneberry is more delicate and is greenish-brown with filamentous pedicels (figs. 1, 6).

Berry color should not be used as the sole means of identifying the two species, since fruit color can be variable. White baneberry typically has white fruit, but very occasionally red-fruited forms do occur

(called *A. pachypoda* forma *rubrocarpa*, or even *A. ludovicii*, if viewed as a distinct species). These red-fruited rarities are probably the result of hybridization with red baneberry and do not contain viable seeds. Red is the typical color of red baneberry fruits (fig. 8), but plants with white fruits are not uncommon (known as *A. rubra* forma *neglecta*) (fig. 9), particularly in certain geographic regions. Thus, it is important to always look at the form of the raceme and the width of the pedicels when making an identification. A noticeable black spot at the apex of each fruit, whether red or white, is the remnant of the stigma; it is markedly larger in white baneberry fruits, giving rise to another common name for the species—"doll's eyes" (fig. 2). *Actaea spicata*, a black-fruited European species, has a red-fruited variety, *A. spicata* var. *erythrocarpa*, which is considered by some taxonomists to be the same species as *A. rubra*. Further investigation is needed to make a valid assessment of the relationships between the various members of this circumboreal group of species.

The generic name, *Actaea*, is from the Greek *aktea*, an ancient name for elderberry (*Sambucus*), although there is little resemblance in the plants. The specific

Fig. 5. (Left) A close-up of a newly opened flower of white baneberry in which the stigma is receptive but the anthers have not yet dehisced to release their pollen. Note that there are already pollen grains from another flower on the stigma. **Fig. 6.** (Right) A close-up of flowers of red baneberry. Note the slender pedicels, stigmas that are not as wide as the ovaries, and petals that are acute at the apex.

Fig. 7. A close-up of a flower of white baneberry. Note the thick pedicel, the stigma that is wider than the ovary, and the petals with small, bilobed structures on their blunt tips.

epithet, *pachypoda*, from the Greek meaning "thick foot" (*pachy*, "thick"; *poda*, "foot"), refers to the thick stalk of the mature fruit in white baneberry. Red baneberry's epithet, *rubra*, of course, denotes the usual color of the fruit of that species, and the term "bane" refers to a source of harm or death, because these plants are known to be poisonous. *Actaea* is a genus originally described by Linnaeus in 1753. Linnaeus' genus *Actaea* included two species having a single carpel: one with dry, dehiscent fruits (the North American black cohosh), which Linnaeus called *Actaea racemosa*, and one with fleshy berries, a European species, which he called *Actaea spicata*. Linnaeus also included in *Actaea* another species with dry fruits comprising four carpels, a Siberian species that had been described previously in the genus *Cimicifuga*

and was recognized as such by Linnaeus in his *Genera Plantarum* in 1752. By 1753 he had decided that carpel number alone was not a sufficient reason for separating the two genera and transferred the *Cimicifuga* species to *Actaea*. Linnaeus based his decision on the similarity in inflorescence type, flowers, and seeds of the two genera. However, he was to change his opinion once again in 1767, returning *A. cimicifuga* to the genus *Cimicifuga* as *C. foetida*, again distinguishing the genera based on the number of carpels.

Later taxonomists defined the two genera differently—by fruit *type*; species with berrylike fruits were placed in *Actaea*, whereas those with dry, dehiscent follicles were placed in *Cimicifuga*, including black cohosh (*C. racemosa*), the only single-carpelled member of that dry-fruited genus. That classification system was still in use when volume 3 of the *Flora of North America*, which includes the Ranunculaceae (buttercup family), was published in 1997. However, the following year, John Compton published his definitive work on the systematics of *Actaea* and *Cimicifuga*, showing the two genera to be so closely related that it was necessary to "lump" them into a single genus. Compton and his colleagues felt that separating two morphologically similar genera based on a single (but obvious) feature (fruit type) was not a justifiable reason for maintaining the two as separate genera. They cited examples of other genera that include species with both berrylike and dry, dehiscent fruits (e.g., *Aloe*, *Hypericum*, and *Lobelia*), and they demonstrated that a set of less obvious morphological features, along with DNA analysis of two different

Buttercup Family

Fig. 8. (Left) A red baneberry plant in fruit. Note the slender pedicels. **Fig. 9.** (Right) A white-fruited red baneberry plant. Note the slender pedicels and black stigma remnant at the tip of each fruit; the black spot is smaller in this species than in white baneberry.

genes, all indicated that members of the two genera should, in fact, be consolidated into a single genus—*Actaea*, the earliest name applied to this group. Compton's work is recognized by the APG. This long history of taxonomic changes offers some insight into the reasons behind the name changes that cause confusion for amateur and professional botanists alike.

The genus *Actaea*, as described in the *Flora of North America*, has eight species, two of which are found in North America. As previously noted, one, *A. pachypoda* (formerly known as *A. alba*), is confined to the eastern part of the continent, while the other, *A. rubra*, occupies a range that extends across the entire northern expanse of the continent, with fingers extending irregularly south in the Mountain States and the Far West. However, at the time of publication of this family treatment in *Flora of North America* (vol. 3, 1997), *Cimicifuga* was still considered to be a separate genus of about 12 species (6 in North America). Thus, if one combines the total number of species in the two former genera, there would now be about 20 species of *Actaea* worldwide.

Sweet aromas produced by the petals of both white and red baneberry flowers attract insect visitors. Analysis of the roselike fragrance of red baneberry petals indicates that the primary constituents responsible for producing the aroma are a mixture of monoterpenes and related compounds. The fragrance of white baneberry has not yet been analyzed, but it differs from that of red baneberry in that it is more citruslike. Rosy and citrusy scents are attractive to many types of insects, but they are also very similar to compounds that deter herbivory by insects. Olle Pellmyr and his colleagues

hypothesize that the aromatic compounds originally produced as deterrents also served as cues for female insects to find flowers that provided copious, nutrient-rich pollen and ovules to feed on. This chemical signature also signaled to male insects that mating opportunities existed at the site (because of the profusion of visiting females). The insects then carried pollen to other plants of the same species, thereby enhancing the plant species' reproductive success to a point where it outweighed the detrimental effects of the pollen feeding. In baneberry, the natural selection that benefited the insects (and thus the plant species itself) led to an enhancement of the aroma used to attract the insects. Pellmyr proposes that in this way, compounds originally designed to deter insects subsequently underwent modifications that allowed flowering plants in general to evolve to their present state of insect attractiveness, with the result of enhancing successful pollination. Many species of ancient lineage, such as *Actaea*, have a strong fragrance that attracts insects, possibly indicating that floral aroma, rather than color, was the original insect attractant. In *Actaea*, aromatic compounds, including geraniol and nerol, have been shown to affect the behavior of insect visitors. Nerol, which has a sweet "rosy" odor, is found in many essential oils and is an important ingredient in perfumery.

The flowers of *Actaea* offer no nectar reward, only pollen. Strangely, the current principal pollinator of both species of baneberry in the Northeast is an introduced weevil, the European snout beetle (*Phyllobius oblongus*) that arrived in the United States sometime prior to 1923. The European snout beetle does not visit the flowers for pollen; rather, it favors

Fig. 10. Fruits and seeds of white baneberry. Note the thick, red pedicels, large black spot at the tip of each fruit, and wedge-shaped seeds.

the inflorescences of baneberry as mating sites. The ensuing activity results in the beetles being covered with pollen, which they then transport to the receptive stigmas of nearby plants. Baneberry stigmas are receptive to pollen immediately upon anthesis (the opening of the flower) and throughout the flower's life, but the anthers do not elongate and release pollen until four days after the flower opens, a partial barrier against self-fertilization (see pollen grains on the stigma of a flower in which the anthers have not yet dehisced, fig. 5). Reproductive success is high in both eastern species of baneberry, which have nearly 100% fruit set. Investigations of the gut contents of the introduced weevils revealed that they do not feed on the pollen; instead, they are known to feed on the leaves of deciduous trees, leaving telltale notches along the leaf margins in spring. Obviously, before the alien beetles arrived, pollination must have been carried out by other insects, and in the Michigan study by Pellmyr, it was shown that native beetles are responsible for pollination in *A. rubra* in that area. However, in the later-flowering *A. pachypoda*, pollination is carried out principally by solitary bees and syrphid flies, insects that emerge at the same time that the white baneberry blooms but later than the flowering peak of red baneberry. In areas where both species coexist, *A. rubra* always begins flowering earlier, with the flowering periods of the two species overlapping by just three to five days. There is, therefore, a small window of time during which pollen from one species might be deposited on the stigma of the other, with the rare result of a hybrid. The Michigan study provides a look at the original reproductive system of the

two species of baneberry, which has become obscured by the introduction of an alien beetle in the Northeast.

Although highly toxic, baneberry fruits are consumed by a wide variety of birds (including robins and yellow-bellied sapsuckers) that generally digest the pulp and excrete the tan-to-brown, wedge-shaped seeds (fig. 10); ruffed grouse also eat the fruits, but the seeds are destroyed in the process. Small mammals, such as mice, squirrels, and voles, eat baneberry fruits, with most fruits disappearing at night. The rodents sometimes remove the pulp and eat just the seeds and thus do not serve as dispersal agents (unless they cache some seeds for future use and then forget to retrieve them). Larvae of geometrid moths attack a high percentage of the fruits of both species while they are still green, burrowing into the seeds and destroying them.

The berries are the most poisonous part of the plant, but all parts of the plant are toxic, and ingestion can cause respiratory paralysis and cardiac arrest. Despite this known toxicity, white-tailed deer are known to browse the plants. The browsing does not kill the plants, but it does prevent them from flowering, thereby curtailing their ability to reproduce. Baneberry plants have long been used for medicinal purposes. Peter Kalm (see the chapter on skunk cabbage) reported in 1770 that both species were used by Native Americans and colonists to treat rattlesnake bite. Native Americans also used red baneberry for the treatment of menstrual problems, as a purgative, to treat syphilis, to increase milk flow, and as a gargle. Yet the juice from the fruits was reportedly also used as an arrow poison!

Poppy Family

Fig. 11. Bloodroot flowers close at night and on rainy days, protecting their pollen when the likelihood of visitation by pollinators is low.

Fig. 12. Two typical flowers of bloodroot, each with eight petals. The still-expanding petals of the flower on the right give it a square appearance due to the alternation of broad and narrow petals.

Bloodroot

Sanguinaria canadensis
Poppy Family (Papaveraceae)—Poppy Subfamily (Papaveroideae)

Bloodroot is a monotypic species, meaning that it is the only species in its genus. Both the scientific name of the genus, *Sanguinaria* (from the Latin *sanguis*, meaning "blood"), and the common name, bloodroot, refer to the reddish sap found in the underground stem, the leaves, and the flower stalk.

Habitat: Rich woods.

Range: Nova Scotia to Ontario and Manitoba, south to South Dakota, Florida, and Oklahoma.

Fig. 13. Two bloodroot plants emerging from the soil in early April.

Bloodroot pushes its way up from the still-cold soil before one can count on frost-free nights (fig. 13). It grows in rich forests, often on hillsides. The leaves and flowers of bloodroot emerge at the same time, having developed underground a year before.

A single leaf envelopes the flower, protecting the delicate pink flower stalk from wind and conserving warmth (fig. 14). The flower stalk elongates above the protective leaf and, if the weather conditions are favorable, opens its single flower (fig. 15). On overcast days and at night, the flowers remain closed, protecting their pollen during a time when pollinators are inactive (fig. 11). Reopening of the flowers is dependent

Poppy Family

Fig. 14. (Left) Flower buds pushing their way above the enshrouding leaves.

Fig. 15. (Right) Two recently opened bloodroot flowers that have grown taller than the leaves that still surround their stalks.

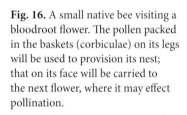

Fig. 16. A small native bee visiting a bloodroot flower. The pollen packed in the baskets (corbiculae) on its legs will be used to provision its nest; that on its face will be carried to the next flower, where it may effect pollination.

on both temperature and cloud cover. On sunny days the flowers will open when the temperature reaches 8°C (46°F). However, the native bees that are the main pollinators of bloodroot are unable to fly at temperatures below 13°C (55°F). Thus, the job of pollination often falls to flies, insects that are capable of flying at slightly lower temperatures and that serve as secondary pollinators during these cooler periods. The highest pollinator activity occurs when temperatures reach 17°C–20°C (63°F–68°F). A microclimate of warmer

air exists just above the leaf litter, providing the low-growing bloodroot with a slight advantage over its taller associates. Pollen is the only reward offered to the pollinators, because the flowers produce no nectar. Bees and flies eagerly seek the pollen (figs. 16, 17). The flowers open first in the female phase, during which pollinators, attracted by the contrasting white and yellow colors, may transport pollen acquired from another flower to the receptive stigma of a flower in the female phase and effect cross-pollination (fig. 18).

Bloodroot

Fig. 17. A fly visiting a bloodroot flower. Note the pollen on its antennae. Flies serve as secondary pollinators of bloodroot because they are active when the temperatures are too cool for bees to fly.

Fig. 18. (Middle left) A native solitary bee leaving a bloodroot flower covered with pollen.

Fig. 19. (Middle right) A dark, hairy, native andrenid bee—bloodroot's principal pollinator.

Fig. 20. (Bottom left) An iridescent green, native halictid bee visiting a bloodroot flower.

Two to three hours after the flower has opened, some of the stamens begin to dehisce and release their pollen. The flowers close in the evening, but the already-opened stamens do not come into contact with the stigma. More stamens open on the second and third days. The principal pollinators—small, solitary bees in the genus *Andrena* (fig. 19)—have dark, hairy bodies that allow them to absorb warmth from the sun and thus fly in cool temperatures. Additional visitors include syrphid flies, bee flies, halictid bees (fig. 20), and honeybees. Within 12 hours of the pollination of the flower, the stamens wither, and the petals fall soon thereafter (fig. 21). However, if by the third day after opening the flower has not been cross-pollinated by insects, some of the stamens bend inward toward the stigma, enabling the plant to self-pollinate.

Poppy Family

Fig. 21. (Left) A bloodroot flower with withered stamens and only two remaining petals.

Fig. 22. (Right) A bloodroot bud with one sepal still attached.

Only a few stamens must contact the stigma to ensure pollination. This backup reproductive system allows bloodroot to produce seeds even if weather conditions have not been favorable for pollinator activity. Petals last only three to four days but may extend their longevity by a few days if the temperatures have been below the level necessary for pollinator activity. I have missed their fleeting beauty in my own garden by failing to check the plants diligently each day in early to mid-April.

Bloodroot flowers commonly have eight petals and two quickly deciduous sepals (fig. 22). Before the petals are fully expanded, the flowers appear almost square shaped, the result of an alternation of shorter, narrower petals with longer, broader ones (fig. 12). Most members of the poppy family have four petals, and it has been shown (by looking at the embryology of the flower) that the additional four (innermost) petals in bloodroot are derived from stamens. Occasionally you may find flowers with 10–20 petals, a naturally occurring variant called *S. canadensis* 'Plena' or 'Flora Plena' in the horticultural trade (fig. 23). A positive correlation between the number of petals and stamens and the number of ovules produced has been observed; thus 'Plena' flowers are capable of producing more seeds.

Sometimes, however, the number of petals is *greatly* increased, resulting in flowers that look like miniature peonies, which are given the name *S. canadensis*

Fig. 23. 'Flora Plena' bloodroot flowers have more than the usual eight petals.

'Multiplex' (fig. 24). In this case, *all* of the stamens and pistils have been converted into petals. The 'Multiplex' variant was found in the wild only once, in Ohio in 1916. The owner of the land where it grew gave divisions to two friends in 1919. One resulting plant died, and the location and fate of the other was unknown. 'Multiplex' plants began appearing in gardens, but their origin was not known. Ultimately, Henry Teuscher, the director emeritus of the Montreal Botanical Garden, disclosed that he was the second friend who had received one of the original divisions and that he had subsequently distributed divisions of his plant widely. Clones from divisions of that original plant are perpetuated in gardens today. The widow of the discoverer of the plant said that the original plant had died by 1966. Because the flower has no reproductive parts, it is unable to reproduce sexually and thus holds its petals for many days, an attractive feature for gardeners. However, I much prefer the simple, though ephemeral, beauty of the original species with its contrasting bright yellow stamens.

Following pollination, the ovary develops rapidly into an upright, spindle-shaped capsule that remains hidden beneath the now enlarged leaves (fig. 25). Each seed has an attached oil-rich outgrowth called an elaiosome (from the Greek *elaio*, "oil," and *some*, "body"), which is a favorite food of ants. Ants gather the seeds that drop from the split fruits (fig. 26) and carry them away to their nesting site, where they consume the fleshy appendages. Charles Robertson first

Fig. 25. (Top) Fruits developing beneath the expanding leaves of bloodroot. **Fig. 26.** (Above) Ants attracted to a bloodroot seed, which bears a fleshy elaiosome.

Fig. 24. A group of 'Multiplex' bloodroot flowers, with many petals.

reported on this behavior in bloodroot in 1897; he later noticed ants carrying the appendaged seeds of other species as well. It was not until 1940 that mymecochory (the dispersal of seeds by ants) was mentioned again in a scientific publication. Subsequently, Burton Gates found that the seeds had been removed from the fallen fruits of *Trillium grandiflorum*, and he noticed a black ant in one of the capsules. In further

Poppy Family

Fig. 27. (Above) Bloodroot seedlings growing from seeds that have germinated directly under the fruits from which they fell, without having been dispersed by ants. **Fig. 28.** (Top right) Bloodroot leaves beginning to senesce in late summer. **Fig. 29.** (Right) The shadow of a bloodroot flower on its leaf. Note the lobing and prominent veins of the leaf.

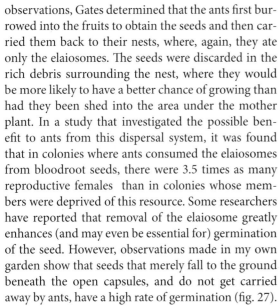

observations, Gates determined that the ants first burrowed into the fruits to obtain the seeds and then carried them back to their nests, where, again, they ate only the elaiosomes. The seeds were discarded in the rich debris surrounding the nest, where they would be more likely to have a better chance of growing than had they been shed into the area under the mother plant. In a study that investigated the possible benefit to ants from this dispersal system, it was found that in colonies where ants consumed the elaiosomes from bloodroot seeds, there were 3.5 times as many reproductive females than in colonies whose members were deprived of this resource. Some researchers have reported that removal of the elaiosome greatly enhances (and may even be essential for) germination of the seed. However, observations made in my own garden show that seeds that merely fall to the ground beneath the open capsules, and do not get carried away by ants, have a high rate of germination (fig. 27).

Unlike many other spring woodland wildflowers, bloodroot is not a true ephemeral. Its distinctive leaves remain long after the fruits have matured, and they continue to increase in size well into August before they finally turn yellow and then die back by early fall (fig. 28). The irregularly lobed, kidney-shaped leaves and the prominent network of veins on their undersides make this species easy to recognize

(fig. 29). Break one of the veins gently with your fingernail (fig. 30), and you will see the red-orange sap that gives this plant its common name, bloodroot, and its scientific name, *Sanguinaria* (referring to blood). Puccoon, an early name given to several unrelated plants that yield a red dye, was also applied to bloodroot in the southern part of its range. In 1622 Captain John Smith, writing of his journeys in Virginia, noted that the natives had "their heads and shoulders painted red, with oil and Pocones [*sic*] mingled together which scarlet-like color made an exceeding handsome show." The red sap is plentiful in the thick underground storage rhizome (fig. 31), often erroneously referred to as the root of the plant. Bloodroot was used by Native Americans as both a dye and a medicine. The bright red-orange sap provided the Indians with a colorful, long-lasting component in their palette of natural dyes, which they used for body decoration as well as for dying plant fibers, quills (fig. 32), and other materials used in basketry

Fig. 30. Red sap exuding from a damaged leaf vein.

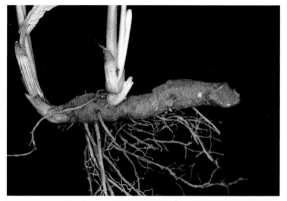

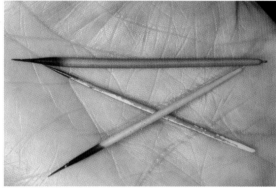

Fig. 31. (Top) A cut rhizome with red sap. Note the roots growing from rhizome. **Fig. 32.** (Above) Porcupine quills dyed with sap from bloodroot rhizomes.

and clothing. Early colonists quickly adopted both the medicinal and the dye properties of bloodroot. The dyed color varied from yellowish to red according to the metal of the pot that was used in preparing the dye bath. Cherokee Indians harvested the rhizomes in spring or summer and stored them underground to maintain their freshness. I have found that dye made from fresh rhizomes with no mordant added yields an orange color.

Colored or milky sap is a common characteristic of members of the poppy family. Although the sap of bloodroot has been shown to contain several toxic alkaloids (as do many other members of the poppy family; e.g., the white sap of Eurasian poppies is the source of opium and heroin), Native Americans used the "root" of the plant medicinally to treat bronchitis, asthma, sore throats, and other ills and as an emetic. Its caustic properties have been used in treating warts, skin cancers, and other skin conditions. The alkaloid propotine, also found in the opium poppy, is responsible for another common name for the plant, sweet slumber. The sap is said to have hallucinogenic properties and is considered by the FDA to be an unsafe herb. Dr. James Duke, an ethnobotanist who investigates medicinal plants, described his personal encounter with bloodroot as one in which he experienced tunnel vision after ingesting just a small portion of the rhizome.

A more contemporary use of the alkaloid sanguinarine, which is also found in the sap of bloodroot, was discovered in the 1990s. Sanguinarine was widely touted in magazine advertisements as effective in preventing the buildup of dental plaque and resultant gingivitis. Advertisements for toothpaste

and mouthwash prominently featured illustrations of the bloodroot flower or its "root." The emphasis was on using a natural product (implying falsely that products from nature are inherently safer). However, by the late 1990s, evidence of adverse side effects had been detected. Products containing sanguinarine had been linked to an almost tenfold increase in the incidence of whitish, oral mucous membrane lesions, termed leucoplakia, which have the potential to become cancerous. Sanguinarine was subsequently removed from the formula and replaced by another antibacterial agent. Laboratory testing of secondary compounds in the plant have shown antimicrobial, anticancer, and antifungal effects that might be of value in modern medicine. However, because bloodroot requires well-drained soil in a forest environment, growing it in commercially adequate quantities has not been successful.

Barberry Family

Fig. 33. An inflorescence and leaves of blue cohosh. Note the yellowish flowers. Blue cohosh flowers vary in color from yellow to greenish to purple (see flowers in fig. 34).

Fig. 34. A close-up of flowers of blue cohosh. Note the purplish flowers (compare with those in fig. 33). The petallike organs are sepals, and the glistening, fan-shaped organs between the sepals and the stamens are reduced petals that secrete nectar.

Blue Cohosh

Caulophyllum thalictroides
Barberry Family (Berberidaceae)

Blue cohosh is perhaps best known for its deep blue "fruits" that ripen in late summer. The flowers, though interesting, are small and dull in color and thus inconspicuous. The plant is toxic but has a long history of use in herbal medicine.

Habitat: Rich woods, particularly on limestone slopes and alluvial soils.

Range: Most of eastern North America other than Florida, Mississippi, and Louisiana in the United States and Newfoundland and Labrador in Canada.

The generic name of *Caulophyllum thalictroides* is derived from the Greek *caulos*, for "stem," and *phyllos*, for "leaf," referring to the fact that the stem of the plant can be perceived to be the stalk of the sessile leaf. The specific epithet indicates that the leaves of blue cohosh (fig. 35) resemble those of meadow-rue (*Thalictrum*). "Cohosh" has its origin in the Algonquin word for "rough," a reference to the knobby rhizomes of this species, and the "blue" in its common name is descriptive of the "berries." Blue cohosh is also called papoose root or squawroot for its reputed use by Native Americans as an aid in childbirth and for regulating menstrual problems.

The uses of this plant by Native Americans to treat a wide spectrum of conditions (rheumatism, gallstones, fevers, toothaches, etc.) is an example of the willingness of people in the days before modern medicine to try almost anything and everything readily available in an attempt to cure disease and alleviate pain. The most common early use of an extract from the rhizomes of blue cohosh was as an aid to speed and ease childbirth. This use has been perpetuated to this day in both Europe and the United States. A survey of American midwives found that 64% reported

Barberry Family

Fig. 35. The newly unfolding leaves of blue cohosh. Note that the leaf shape is similar to that of meadow-rue (*Thalictrum*) leaves.

Fig. 36. The purplish stem and leaves of a blue cohosh plant that has just emerged. Note the light-colored flower buds of the inflorescence.

using blue cohosh to treat women before or during childbirth. Yet, the herbal preparation made from blue cohosh has not been evaluated for its effectiveness or safety by the FDA, and studies have shown that the use of blue cohosh may be risky to both mother and infant. In one case study published in the *Journal of Pediatrics* in 1998, the baby born to a mother given blue cohosh to stimulate her uterine contractions suffered a heart attack, congestive heart failure, and shock, all of which were attributed to the glycosides and alkaloids in the cohosh preparation. Such products are not subject to governmental controls regulating their manufacture or purity. Chemical analysis of commercial preparations of blue cohosh showed a hundredfold difference in the strength of active ingredients among products from different manufacturers.

Because of its toxicity, few herbivores are reported to eat *Caulophyllum*. In an investigation of forest herbs eaten by white-tailed deer, one researcher in Minnesota found that deer will browse blue cohosh in late summer, when the plant's toxicity levels are likely to be lower. And in one region of Japan, *C. robustum*, an Asian species of blue cohosh, is eaten by a species of ladybird beetle. Of interest is that the beetle (*Epilachna pustulosa*) feeds primarily on a species of thistle (*Cirsium* sp.), but in the Sapporo region of Japan it feeds on *either* thistle or blue cohosh. Those feeding on blue cohosh mature faster, grow larger, and have a higher rate of survival than those that feed on the thistle. Documentation of small genetic variations between the beetles of the two feeding-preference groups has established a genetic basis correlated to their host-plant preference. It was only 40 years ago that the beetles were first noted to feed on blue cohosh. It will be interesting to see if the *Caulophyllum*-eating beetles, with their higher survival rate, will, over time, prove to

Fig. 37. A close-up of a flower of blue cohosh showing petal-like sepals, fan-shaped, nectar-secreting petals, and mostly still-unopened anthers; only one anther sac has its small flap lifted to expose the pollen.

Fig. 38. (Top) A fly, one of the most common visitors to the dull-colored flowers of blue cohosh. **Fig. 39.** (Above) A hover fly investigating a flower of blue cohosh. Hover flies (also called flower flies) visit many types of flowers and are often mistaken for bees.

be more reproductively successful and eventually out-number the thistle-eating members of their species.

The American botanist Asa Gray, in his 1859 paper on the similarities between the East Asian flora and that of other North Temperate regions, declared *C. robustum* to be identical to *C. thalictroides*. Later botanists determined that Asian blue cohosh was a distinct species differing from the American species in having three stem leaves, longer panicles of flowers with narrow petaloid sepals, and long, slender staminal filaments. Eastern North America and eastern Asia share many genera (and those genera are infrequently found in other parts of the world), but it would be unusual to find identical species in these two geographic areas that have been separated for so many millennia. The two species demonstrate a disjunct distribution pattern that is seen in several other taxa treated in this book (for some examples, see the chapters on baneberry, Jack-in-the-pulpit, Mayapple, and twinleaf).

Until 1981 the only recognized species of *Caulophyllum* were *C. thalictroides*, the blue cohosh of eastern North America, and *C. robustum*, from East Asia. However, in 1981, a new species, giant blue cohosh (*C. giganteum*), was segregated from *C. thalictroides* by H. Loconte and W. H. Blackwell. The differences between the two taxa had been noted earlier but had been viewed as merely variation within the species or perhaps as representing two varieties of *C. thalictroides*. Loconte and Blackwell elevated giant blue cohosh

to the rank of species, based on its larger overall size and fewer-flowered inflorescences with their consistently purple flowers (as compared with *C. thalictroides*' many-flowered inflorescences, which have flowers that may be yellow [fig. 33], green, or purple [fig. 34] and flower earlier in the season).

Blue cohosh has several unusual aspects: as the plant emerges from the soil, the color of the stem and folded leaves is a deep blue-purple (fig. 36); and the plant flowers early in spring before its leaves are fully expanded (this is especially true of giant blue cohosh, whose flowers open even before its leaves have begun to unfurl). The structure of its flowers is a subject of controversy among botanists—some (including H. Loconte, the author of the generic description of

Barberry Family

Caulophyllum in *Flora of North America*) consider the small, fan-shaped, nectar-producing structures between the sepals and the stamens (fig. 34) to be reduced petals, whereas others view them as nectaries that have been derived from stamens. The latter view is based on observations of the fusion of the stamens and the nectaries at an early stage of development. The floral parts are in multiples of three, as typically found in monocots but rarely in dicots; and the anthers have an amusing way of opening—by two small flaps that open upward like tiny window awnings (fig. 37). There is additional disagreement over whether there are two whorls of three sepals with bracts beneath them or if, in fact, the bracts represent a third whorl of sepals, as claimed by J. F. Brett and U. Posluszny in their 1982 paper published in the *Canadian Journal of Botany*.

Observations of blue cohosh have revealed that its few insect visitors are chiefly flies (figs. 38, 39), along with a lesser number of small bees and wasps. Since flies usually feed at only a single flower until satiated and then leave, they are not very effective pollinators, and most fertilization in *C. thalictroides* is the result of self-pollination. Although blue cohosh is self-fertile, giant blue cohosh rarely is and sets comparatively few fruits and seeds.

One of the most fascinating features of blue cohosh is its seed. Notice that I used quotation marks around the words "fruits" and "berries" above, since what appear to be blueberry-colored fruits developing from the flowers of *Caulophyllum* are actually

Fig. 41. Two "fruits" (actually seeds) of blue cohosh with the one on the right fully mature whereas the one on the left is at an earlier stage of development, a strategy that permits the plant to remain in fruit and attractive to birds for a longer period.

Fig. 40. The blueberry-colored mature "fruit" of blue cohosh is actually a seed with a thin, blue seed coat. The seed coat has been partially peeled from the seed on the right.

the seeds of the plant covered only by a thin, fleshy, blue seed coat (fig. 40). The ovaries of blue cohosh begin to develop into fruits after fertilization, but the ovules contained within expand so rapidly that they quickly rupture the ovary wall, which dries and withers away, leaving the naked seeds. This unusual situation prompted John Hutchinson, an early twentieth-century botanist from Kew, to describe *C. thalictroides* as a "gymnospermous dicotyledon," since generally only gymnosperms (such as pines and spruces) bear naked seeds. (The term "gymnosperm" is from the Greek *gymnos*, "naked," meaning, in this instance, not enclosed in an ovary, and *sperma*, "seed"). Linnaeus had originally placed blue cohosh into the genus *Leontice* (as *L. thalictroides*), a genus that shares many features with blue cohosh but has capsular fruits. Based on the difference in fruits, in

Fig. 42. The startlingly aqua-colored seeds of blue cohosh that are at an intermediate stage of maturity. The seeds will turn dark blue as they mature, perhaps at different times.

Fig. 43. Mature seeds of blue cohosh in late August as the leaves are beginning to senesce.

1803, André Michaux described a new genus, *Caulophyllum*, which included blue cohosh. However, at that time he believed, mistakenly, that the fruits of his new genus were drupes perched at the ends of stalk-like stipes. The "stalks" of the seeds of blue cohosh are, in fact, sturdy funicles that once attached the seeds to the placenta of the ovary, much as the umbilical cord attaches the young of a mammal to the placenta of its mother. Perhaps the seeds "fool" the birds that feed on them as well, for what appears to be a succulent berry has little edible flesh surrounding the seed.

In most species having bird-dispersed fruits, the fruits do not ripen until autumn, the time when the greatest numbers of fruit-eating birds are migrating southward. However, the seeds of blue cohosh ripen over a period of a month or more during the summer, from late July into early September. In August, the seeds present a striking display with green, pink, aqua, and blue seeds, sometimes all on the same infructescence (figs. 41, 42). The irregular pattern of ripening may provide just enough seeds over a long period of time to satisfy the resident frugivorous birds. However, few seeds are actually removed until the first wave of fruit-eating birds migrates through in early September, by which time the majority of seeds will have ripened (fig. 43). The seeds are buoyant in water and, thus, have the potential for an alternate method of dispersal.

Plantain Family

Fig. 44. The upper part of a blue-eyed Mary plant showing the whorled leaves below and a whorl of flowers and small bracts at the top of the plant.

Fig. 45. A dense concentration of blue-eyed Mary plants. Photographed in Missouri.

Blue-eyed Mary

Collinsia verna
Plantain Family (Plantaginaceae)

This small flower is one of my favorites because of its deep blue color and its evocative name. Blue-eyed Mary makes an impressive display when growing in masses (fig. 45) and is equally beautiful when viewed close-up as a single flower.

Habitat: Rich, moist woods and streambanks.

Range: New York to Michigan and southern Wisconsin, south to western Virginia, Kentucky, and Arkansas.

Blue-eyed Mary had eluded me until just a few years ago, when I had the opportunity to visit Missouri in early spring. Although the species grows in my home state of New York, it is uncommon and is found in only a few counties in the northern and western parts of the state. I am always intrigued by some of the more charming common names of plants (enchanter's nightshade, ladies'-tresses, dragon's mouth, and pussytoes come to mind), and I am always eager to see these plants "in the flesh," so that I can ascertain for myself the basis for such imaginative names. Thus, I was delighted to happen across a large patch of blue-eyed Mary while botanizing not far from St. Louis. The flowers did not disappoint; they were, at least in part, a bright true blue—a color uncommon in our native wildflowers and perhaps bluer than any person's eyes that I have ever seen (fig. 44). The name "blue-eyed Mary" is applied to several species in the genus *Collinsia,* as is its other common name, "innocence." Two other species of *Collinsia* inhabit the northeastern quarter of the United States. One, found mainly in the Midwest, has flowers with purple corolla lobes (*C. violacea*); the other, *C. parviflora,* is generally more western (but is recorded within the range of this book in Michigan, Vermont, and Ontario), and it has smaller flowers with corolla lobes that are less intensely blue than those of *C. verna. Collinsia* is endemic to North America. The genus has 20–25

Plantain Family

species, and it is at its most diverse in the West, especially in California. *Collinsia* may be divided into two groups: one, with sessile flowers, is found only in California and Baja California; the other with pedicelled flowers (including *C. verna*), ranges east to west across North America. Some of the western species, particularly *C. heterophylla*, are known as "Chinese houses," a reference to the form of their inflorescences, which, like the successive layers of roofs of a Chinese pagoda, have whorls of flowers that decrease in size toward the top. Blue-eyed Mary shares its common name with a European wildflower in the unrelated borage family: *Omphalodes verna*, which has smaller and lighter blue flowers similar to those of forget-me-not.

The scientific name of blue-eyed Mary may be a source of confusion, because *Collinsia* is sometimes mistaken for *Collinsonia*, a genus of the mint family. The former was named in 1817 by Thomas Nuttall to honor Zacchaeus Collins, an American botanist, naturalist, and mineralogist who was vice president of the Academy of Natural Sciences of Philadelphia, an institution he helped to found in 1812. *Collinsia verna* is the type species of the genus, that is, the first species to be designated in the genus *Collinsia*. When Nuttall discovered the plant in Ohio, it was at the end of its life cycle; he collected seeds from which he grew the plants that became the type specimen. The species epithet, *verna*, refers to spring, the season in which the plant flowers. Other species have been named to honor Collins as well, among them, a sedge (*Carex collinsii*), a gentian (*Gentiana collinsiana*), and a species of hawthorn (*Crataegus collinsiana*). On the other hand, the mint genus *Collinsonia* is a Linnaean name commemorating Peter Collinson. Collinson, an English cloth merchant, was a passionate plantsman who financed the plant collecting expeditions of John Bartram, "America's first botanist." In return, Collinson received seeds of North American plants to plant in his own renowned garden of exotic plants and to distribute to wealthy British gardeners and others interested in plants from the New World. He was thus responsible for the introduction of many American plant species into British gardens.

It is still difficult for me to think of pretty little blue-eyed Mary as a member of the plantain family. The family is better known for its inconspicuously flowered lawn weeds, such as broadleaf and English

Fig. 46. An inflorescence of English plantain (*Plantago lanceolata*). Note how different the flowers are from those of *Collinsia verna*, which is now also a member of the plantain family.

plantain (*Plantago major* and *Plantago lanceolata*) (fig. 46). However, based on molecular evidence, species of *Collinsia* (along with many other colorfully flowered species, such as beardtongue [*Penstemon*], speedwell [*Veronica*], and butter-and-eggs [*Linaria*]) were recently transferred, according to the APG, from the Scrophulariaceae to the Plantaginaceae. The movement of so many genera of "scrophs" into either the Plantaginaceae or the Orobanchaceae (see the chapters on one-flowered cancer-root and squawroot) has left the Scrophulariaceae much poorer in species. Plantaginaceae has become further expanded and morphologically diverse by the addition of species

Blue-eyed Mary

Fig. 47. An oblique view of two flowers of blue-eyed Mary. Note the glandular hairs on the narrow lobes of the calyx.

from previously recognized monogeneric families—for instance, *Hippurus*, mare's tail, (formerly in the Hippuridaceae) and *Callitriche*, water-starwort, (formerly in the Callitrichaceae)—and by the inclusion of the genus *Globularia* (but other genera of the former Globulariaceae are now placed in the Scrophulariaceae). Such taxonomic changes, especially those resulting when a large family such as Scrophulariaceae is split into several other families, cause consternation for botanists and amateurs alike, but the ultimate goal of a more scientifically based classification system is worth the initial frustration of relearning new family assignments.

Blue-eyed Mary is a lax plant with the stems attaining heights of 5 to 10 inches, topped by a whorl of four to six flowers and small leafy bracts. Lower on the stem, leaf whorls may have one to a few pedicelled flowers. The zygomorphic flowers are unlike any others in its former family, Scrophulariaceae. Superficially, they look much like the flowers of a typical legume, such as a pea or bean, but for other reasons they are completely unrelated to legumes. The calyx has five narrow pointed lobes, often with glandular hairs (fig. 47). The corollas, fused at the base into a tube, are two lipped, with the upper lip having two lobes and the lower lip three. The third lobe of the lower lip is hidden between, and under, the

other two, so that it is not evident when viewing the flower. The upper lip, usually white in this species, is analogous to the banner, or standard, petal of a pea flower; the two side lobes of the deep blue (ranging to pink or lavender) lower lip resemble the wings of a legume flower; and the third, folded, lobe is similar to a legume's keel petal (fig. 48). Hidden within the third lobe are the reproductive structures: four stamens (the lower two longer than the upper two) and a single style. As in a pea flower, the reproductive parts are exposed only when an insect of suitable size lands on the lower lip to probe the flower for nectar. The insect's weight depresses the lower lip, exposing the third lobe and causing it to open to reveal the enclosed stamens and pistil (fig. 49). Several species of early-flying native bees, including bumblebees (fig. 50), are capable of effecting pollination. Nectar is secreted from a gland at the base of the corolla tube, where it collects. To reach the nectar, a bee (bees are the most common visitors) must insert its proboscis into the small opening at the base of the petal lobes and reach into the tubular part of the corolla. Just above the narrow opening is a brown-spotted yellowish structure, referred to as the palate, which probably directs the bee to the place where it must probe beneath the palate to reach the opening of the nectar spur. Only bees with sufficiently long tongues can

Plantain Family

Fig. 48. A close-up view of an upper whorl of the inflorescence of blue-eyed Mary. Note the brown-spotted yellow "palate" at the base of the upper lobe of the corolla.

reach the nectar. In the process of collecting nectar, the bees' undersides are dusted with pollen from the exposed anthers; thus bees with hairy abdomens (e.g., *Bombus* and *Osmia)* are the most effective pollinators. Some multitasking bees simultaneously collect pollen with their hind legs while imbibing nectar. When the bee flies off, the keel returns to its original closed position, thereby protecting the reproductive parts from flies and other insects that might take the pollen without effecting pollination.

Ants are reported to visit extrafloral nectaries on the leaves of *C. parviflora*, the most widespread species of blue-eyed Mary. Extrafloral nectaries are those that occur on parts of the plant other than within the flowers. They often play a role in the defense of the plant by attracting ants that then defend this sweet resource (and thus the plant) from other herbivorous insects that might harm the plant (e.g., caterpillars that eat the leaves). Both flowers and seed capsules are fed upon by the larva of a small blue butterfly, the spring/summer azure (*Celastrina argiolus*); the caterpillar can cause significant damage to the flower buds. Such extrafloral nectaries do not occur on the leaves of *C. verna*.

Fig. 49. A close-up of a *Collinsia verna* flower with the lower lip held open as would occur when an insect lands on it. Note the three exposed stamens that normally would be hidden within the third lobe of the lower lip (the style and a fourth stamen are not visible; a fifth stamen is vestigial).

Fig. 50. A bumblebee visiting the flowers of blue-eyed Mary. (© 2004 April Randle)

Blue-eyed Mary flowers remain open for about five days, during which time the stamens elongate and dehisce sequentially as they reach the tip of the "keel" petal. Loose pollen that has not been collected by insects falls into the keel but remains viable throughout the life of the flower. The style does not elongate until later in the flowering period, about when the third anther dehisces. It is at that time that the stigma becomes receptive and comes in contact with the anthers, often resulting in self-pollination. Cross-pollination can still occur in *C. verna* because bees carrying pollen from other flowers may contact

the stigma at this late stage as well. Pollination success in plants from which insects have been excluded is 75% that of plants that are cross-pollinated by insect pollinators.

Fertilized ovaries develop into globular capsules with four seeds that are dispersed by falling near the base of the plant toward the end of May; the plant then senesces. Blue-eyed Mary is a winter annual with germination taking place in the fall. Over 35% of seeds germinate in the first autumn after they are produced, with the young seedlings overwintering and resuming growth in spring. Seeds that have not germinated can remain viable in the soil for at least three years, with about 6% germinating in the second autumn and another 3% in the following year. In this manner, under optimal conditions, increasingly larger patches of blue-eyed Mary develop by self-seeding. Generally annual plants like blue-eyed Mary are not as well suited for the spring ephemeral lifestyle as are perennials. Perennials have underground storage organs that maintain food resources capable of sustaining the plant throughout a year in which conditions are not optimal for pollinators. In such a year, they might fail to reproduce. Annuals have no such storage capacity and *must* produce viable seeds each year in order for the population to survive. Since *C. verna* is self-compatible, it is not totally dependent on insect visitation for reproduction, and because its seeds remain dormant throughout the summer, a difficult time for seed germination due to high temperatures and limited water, blue-eyed Mary has a better rate of germination success than most spring annuals, whose seeds germinate soon after maturing. Fall weather conditions are often more conducive to seedling survival, and seedlings that overwinter have a head start on the growing season once spring arrives.

Poppy Family

Fig. 51. Celandine-poppy with flowers and buds. Note the hairiness of the sepals enclosing the flower buds.

Fig. 52. An inflorescence of celandine. The four-petaled flowers have numerous stamens and linear ovaries that are beginning to elongate in fruit.

Celandine and Celandine-poppy

Chelidonium majus and *Stylophorum diphyllum*
Poppy Family (Papaveraceae)

Two members of the poppy family share (at least in part) the same name—celandine; the first is an introduced plant from Eurasia; the second is native.

Habitat: Celandine—moist woods or dry open areas; celandine-poppy—rich, moist woods.

Range: Celandine—introduced from Eurasia, naturalized from Quebec and Ontario to Iowa, south to Georgia and Missouri. Celandine-poppy—native from Michigan, south to Tennessee and Arkansas and east to West Virginia and western Virginia; naturalized in much of the remaining Northeast; rare in southwestern Ontario, where it is endangered.

What's in a name? Confusion—if the name is celandine! A rose may be a rose may be a rose (with apologies to Ms. Stein), but celandine, when applied to a flower, may refer to any of three different species, in three different genera, belonging to two different families! Such is the problem with common names. True, the most widely used common names for these species are slightly different, but they are close enough to engender confusion when the plants are discussed.

Two of the "celandine" species (those in the poppy family) are treated in this chapter and have in common yellow flowers that bloom in spring, the probable reason for the similarity in their names (the third "celandine," a member of the buttercup family, is treated in another chapter as lesser celandine). The flowering period of the celandine-poppy occurs only in early spring, whereas celandine begins to bloom in late spring and continues into summer. The flowers of both species have four petals (as is common in many members of the poppy family), numerous stamens, and a single pistil. The flowers of celandine-poppy are larger, showier, and more yellow-orange than those of celandine and have a prominent style (unusual in the poppy family), which underlies the origin of the generic name *Stylophorum*, from the Greek *stylos*, "style," and *phoros*, "bearing" (fig. 53).

Poppy Family

Fig. 53. Close-up of a four-petaled flower of celandine-poppy and an opening bud. The two sepals will fall as the bud continues to open. Note the relatively long style.

Celandine is the only member of the genus *Chelidonium*, a genus closely related to *Stylophorum* (the genus of celandine-poppy, which has just two additional species in eastern Asia). Celandine is a biennial with basal rosettes of leaves that remain green throughout the winter of its first year (fig. 54). Celandine-poppy, on the other hand, is perennial, appearing annually from underground rhizomes. The leaves of both species are matte green, but the deeply lobed leaves of celandine are larger and have more rounded tips than those of celandine-poppy (fig. 55). In *Stylophorum diphyllum* there are two leaves almost opposite each other on the stem just beneath the flower; in *Chelidonium majus* there is only one. Both plants are hairy to some degree and have a yellow-orange sap (figs. 56, 57).

The fruits of celandine are smooth, upright, and at maturity split into two valves that open upward from the base (fig. 57); fruits of celandine-poppy are bristly, hang downward at maturity (fig. 58) and have four valves that open from the apex of the fruit toward the

base (fig. 59). Seeds of both species have elaiosomes (figs. 60, 61) and are dispersed by ants (see the chapter on bloodroot for a discussion of elaiosomes). *Chelidonium* and *Stylophorum* also share many of the same chemical compounds in their roots, among them the alkaloids berberine, sanguinarine, and chelidonine. As further evidence of their close relationship, both of these genera contain chelidonic acid, the only genera of the poppy family to do so (chelidonic acid is also found in other plant families, for example, the Liliaceae). Let us look at each of the celandine-named species separately.

Celandine (also known as greater celandine)
(*Chelidonium majus*)

The generic name of celandine (*Chelidonium*) has its origins in the Greek *chelidon*, meaning "swallow" (the bird). The name was given to the plant because of an ancient belief that swallows bathed the eyes of their blind nestlings with the plant's yellowish sap to enable them to see. *Chelidon* is also the basis for the species' common name, celandine, which in twelfth-century Middle English became *celidoine*. The epithet *majus* means "major" or "large." *Chelidonium majus* is often called greater celandine to differentiate it from lesser celandine (*Ranunculus ficaria*; discussed in its own chapter). Celandine's four-petaled yellow flowers and linear ovaries (see figs. 52, 57, and 60), which develop into long, narrow dehiscent capsules, might be mistaken for those of a plant in the mustard family (Brassicaceae)—a family characterized by four-petaled flowers and (frequently) long, narrow fruits called siliques. However, careful examination will reveal the characteristics of the poppy family: numerous stamens rather than the typical six (four long and two short) of the mustard family; seeds not attached to a thin membrane separating the fruit compartments; and a colored sap (yellow-orange, in this case) that exudes from all vegetative parts of the plant when damaged.

As might be expected in plants of a family known to have medicinal compounds (e.g., opium from poppies), the numerous alkaloids of *Stylophorum* and *Chelidonium* have been investigated for potential medicinal use. They have shown activity against fungi, bacteria, and trypanosomes (protozoans) and have a

Fig. 55. Stem leaves of celandine (left) and celandine-poppy (right)—note the difference in size and lobing. Celandine-poppy has two stem leaves almost opposite each other on the stem, whereas those of celandine are alternate.

Fig. 54. The basal leaves of celandine—still green under the snow.

variety of other pharmaceutical effects including the inhibition of cell growth in various cancers. Celandine, known as verruca herb, has been used topically in European folk medicine for the treatment of warts (verrucae) and other skin conditions and systemically for the treatment of liver disorders. However, in Germany, within a two-year period in the late 1990s, ten cases of acute hepatitis were documented as having been caused by celandine preparations used to treat liver problems. Research on the effectiveness of *C. majus* against potentially dangerous diseases caused by *Fusarium* fungi shows promise that the active compounds in the roots may one day provide remedies for these difficult-to-treat conditions in both humans (e.g., infections of the cornea or nails) and plants (e.g., Fusarium wilt in tomatoes and potatoes).

The rich storehouse of chemicals in celandine has been utilized for other scientific purposes as well. Since the 1940s, fluorescent extracts from the roots of celandine have been used as a stain in the microscopic examination of plant tissues, making it easier to see specific structures. However, the fluorescence was often so strong that it imparted a "washed out" appearance to some of the tissues being viewed. In an attempt to eliminate this negative aspect of the procedure, a group of chemists tested each of the several alkaloids from celandine roots separately and determined that the principal active ingredient is berberine. Berberine, when used with an aniline blue counterstain, provides much better definition of plant tissues, particularly lignin and suberin, making it possible to detect other previously hard-to-distinguish structures. These same chemical compounds serve the plant as a defense mechanism against pathogens and herbivores. Because they are toxic to insects and vertebrates alike, they severely curtail herbivory.

Celandine is one of 100 species of plants that have been monitored over a period of 30 years in the Washington, DC area for their dates of first flowering (the date that the first flower to open is noted by one of the monitors). Eighty-nine of the 100 species have been shown to have earlier bloom dates over the study period in accordance with a 1.2°C increase in average minimum temperature. The average advance in bloom date was 2.4 days, but in some species, the advance was far greater—14.6 days in the case of celandine (*C. majus*). Such changes could negatively affect a plant's

Poppy Family

Fig. 56. An inflorescence of celandine. Note the four-petaled flowers and the hairy sepals enclosing the buds. Yellow-orange sap may be seen exuding from a broken leaf stalk at the lower right.

Fig. 57. The upright, narrow, linear fruits of celandine. Note the orange sap exuding from the stalks of the two fruits that were broken off.

chances for pollination. Unless the activity timetable of the plant's pollinators is affected to the same degree as that of the plant, the pollinator's period of activity may no longer coincide with the flower's blooming time.

Fig. 58. The pendant, bristly fruits of celandine-poppy.

Celandine-poppy (also known as wood-poppy) (*Stylophorum diphyllum*)

The derivation of *Stylophorum* was given earlier. The epithet *diphyllum* is from the Greek (*di*, "two," and *phyllos*, "leaf") and refers to the two stem leaves beneath the flower.

The flowers of celandine-poppy are quite striking, one to two inches across (fig. 51), as compared with the three-quarter-inch flowers of celandine (fig. 52). The hairy ovary quickly matures into a bristly fruit that drops its seeds to the ground in late May and early June. The seeds are the sole means of reproduction and can be produced by self-fertilization if

the flowers are not cross-pollinated by insects. Ants eagerly scavenge for the seeds, which have large, fleshy elaiosomes that are rich in nutrients (fig. 61). Morphologically, these elaiosomes are classified as strophioles, because they are located at the seed's hilum, that is, the point of attachment of the seed to its stalk (the funicle). The seeds are immature and must undergo a cold period (stratification) over the winter before they can germinate the following spring.

Since *Stylophorum* and *Chelidonium* share many of the same chemical constituents—primarily alkaloids—much of what has been discussed above under the celandine section applies to the celandine-poppy as well. Because of its rich source of potentially useful alkaloids (among them: berberine, also found in barberry, and sanguinarine, found in bloodroot), celandine-poppy (along with Mayapple) is among our native species under consideration for development as a crop plant. The alkaloid berberine in the roots of celandine-poppy was put to another use by Native Americans: it provided them with a yellow dye. Investigation of the chemistry of *Stylophorum* by J. O. Schlotterbeck at the beginning of the twentieth century resulted in the discovery of an interesting property of the alkaloid sanguinarine—when crystals of the compound were shaken or broken, they emitted light while simultaneously making a crackling sound!

Fig. 60. Fruits of celandine—one about to dehisce, others that have already dehisced and shed their tiny seeds, and seeds with elaiosomes that have fallen onto a celandine leaf.

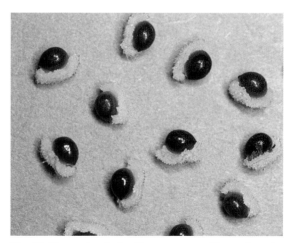

Fig. 61. The seeds of celandine-poppy are shiny and speckled and have a prominent white elaiosome that is attractive to ants. They remind me of tiny gastropods—cowries crawling about with their smooth shells.

Fig. 59. A recently dehisced fruit of celandine-poppy. The pointed edges will soon curl upward.

Buttercup Family

Fig. 62. A flower and bud of columbine. Note the red spurs of the petals and the yellow petal tips. The styles have already elongated, but the stamens are not yet opened and the stigmas are not yet receptive.

Fig. 63. Columbine growing on a rocky hillside with other spring wildflowers in a wildflower preserve.

Columbine (also known as wild columbine and American columbine)

Aquilegia canadensis
Buttercup Family (Ranunculaceae)

Flowers of the buttercup family have a remarkable diversity in floral shape. Those of columbine, monkshood, and delphinium, for example, differ markedly from the standard open bowl shape of a typical buttercup or anemone. Some genera have radially symmetric (actinomorphic) flowers, like a buttercup, whereas others, including columbine, are bilaterally symmetric (zygomorphic). American columbine is one of the few species in the East with red flowers, although white-flowered plants are occasionally found (figs. 64, 65).

Habitat: Dry, rocky woodland margins (fig. 63), rocky cliffs and ledges; rarely in swamps.

Range: Nova Scotia to Saskatchewan, south to Florida and Texas. Columbine is hardy to zone 2 (−50°F).

If the popularity of a wildflower can be judged by the number of common names applied to it, columbine is clearly a favorite. Throughout its range columbine is variously known as rock bells, dancing fairies, Jack-in-trousers, meeting houses, Granny's bonnets, wild honeysuckle, and rock lily—among others.

There are competing explanations for the derivation of the generic name, *Aquilegia*, which was given by Linnaeus. It is either from the Latin *aquilinum*, meaning "eaglelike," a reference to the resemblance of the floral spurs to the talons of an eagle, or from the Latin *aquarius*, meaning "water carrier," for the nectar that collects in the spurs. The range of the species includes Canada (among other places in eastern North America), hence the epithet *canadensis*. The common name, columbine, is said to have been given to the plant because of the fancied resemblance of the spurs to a circle of doves (*columba* in Latin). Doves symbolized the Holy Spirit, and because of this religious significance, the European *A. vulgaris* appears in the medieval Unicorn Tapestries.

Buttercup Family

Fig. 64. Two plants of columbine, one with normal red-and-yellow flowers, the other smaller plant in front with rare white flowers.

Fig. 65. A plant of columbine with white flowers. Many species have occasional white-flowered plants.

Columbine is one of our special spring wildflowers; it resembles no other species in the northeastern flora. Blooming in May throughout much of its range, it is often found in association with rue-anemone, miterwort, foamflower, and other spring ephemerals (figs. 66, 67). Columbine is especially striking when growing on rocky cliffs, its delicate flowers adding a startling burst of color to the gray rocky substrate (fig. 68). In his poem, "Columbine," John Burroughs wrote:

> Above a lichened niche it clung,
> Or did it leap from out a seam? —
> Some hidden fire had found a tongue
> And burst to light with vivid gleam.
> It thrilled the eye, it cheered the place,
> And gave the ledge a living grace.

With its dangling flowers delicately dancing on slender stalks, columbine cannot avoid catching the eye—not only ours, but also those of the ruby-throated hummingbird (*Archilochus colubris*), the only species of hummingbird native to the eastern United States.

Although hummingbirds will visit flowers of many shapes and colors, the flowers of columbine are ideally structured to attract their attention, and their time of bloom coincides with the arrival of the first ruby-throated hummingbirds to return to the eastern United States from their wintering localities in Mexico and Central America. The flowers provide an early source of nectar for the returning birds (fig. 69).

Fig. 66. Columbine growing among other spring wildflowers, including rue-anemone and violets.

Fig. 67. Columbine growing on a mossy cliff with other spring wildflowers, miterwort on the left and foamflower on the right.

Fig. 68. (Left) Columbine growing from a crevice in a cliff face. Such a sight inspired a poem by John Burroughs—"Columbine." **Fig. 69.** (Right) A spur of a columbine petal cut open to show the glistening nectar inside.

Buttercup Family

Fig. 70. (Left) A hummingbird's-eye view of the entrance to the nectar spurs of columbine.

Fig. 71. (Above) An apical view of a columbine flower showing the knoblike tips of the petal spurs where nectar is stored.

Indeed, the ranges of columbine and ruby-throated hummingbirds are almost congruent in the eastern United States. The color red is known to be especially appealing to birds, and the length of columbine spurs (13–25 millimeters; 0.5–1 inch) excludes access to the nectar to all visitors other than hummingbirds (and some species of long-tongued bees). This combination of characters makes columbine perfectly suited for hummingbird pollination. With only one species of hummingbird in the Northeast, few plant species have evolved to have red flowers, a color that is not generally attractive to most other pollinators. Most birds have a poorly developed sense of smell, and, indeed, the flowers of our eastern columbine are not noticeably fragrant. However, they do produce aromatic compounds in their anthers, principally octanol, a compound that is found in all species of *Aquilegia* regardless of the nature of the pollinator. As might be expected in a flower that is pollinated by birds (or self-pollinated), *A. canadensis* has fewer of these aromatic compounds than other species of *Aguilegia*.

Hummingbirds are unique among nectar-drinking birds in that they are capable of hovering in flight while imbibing nectar; other nectar-drinking birds must perch either on or adjacent to the flowers from which they take nectar. The ruby-throated hummingbird hovers beneath the bell-like flowers of columbine, inserts its long bill into the opening of one of the five petal spurs (fig. 70), and with its 15- to 20-millimeter (0.6- to 0.8-inch) brush-tipped tongue laps nectar that

Fig. 72. A columbine flower with some petals and stamens removed to reveal the shiny inner scalelike staminodes that surround the ovary.

Fig. 73. (Left) A bumblebee collecting pollen from the anthers of columbine. Note the pollen in the corbiculae (pollen baskets) on the bee's hind legs

Fig. 74. (Right) A columbine flower with a hole torn into one of the nectar spurs by a bumblebee that took a short cut to the nectar stored in the tip.

has accumulated in the knoblike tips of the spurs (fig. 71). The nectar is dilute (a 20–23% sugar solution is typical of hummingbird flowers), making it more easily absorbed by the capillary action of the hummingbird's tongue. Since the nectar from a single floral visit does not provide much caloric value, the hummingbirds must continue to visit additional flowers to obtain their necessary caloric resources (they also supplement their diet with insects, a source of protein). In the process, the hummingbird's head and bill are dusted with pollen, which the bird transports to another columbine flower, where it is brushed off on the long styles. Although the hummingbird is the most efficient pollinator of columbine, its visits are infrequent, and columbine is primarily self-pollinated.

As mentioned in the chapter on baneberry, some botanists consider the petals of all members of the Ranunculaceae to be staminodes; however, in the description of the family in *Flora of North America*, the author states that true staminodes occur in only two genera of the family: *Clematis* and *Aquilegia*. The staminodes in these genera are unusual. Most staminodes are merely sterile stamens located between the whorl of petals and the whorl of stamens and are referred to as "outer" staminodes. However, in *Aquilegia* and *Clematis*, the staminodes are scalelike and occur between the staminal whorl and the carpels that make up the ovary. They surround the ovary tightly

and remain attached to the receptacle after the other floral parts have fallen (fig. 72). These "inner" staminodes are thought to be derived from stamens representing the last stamen in each of the 10 vertical groupings of normal stamens; occasionally, they have anthers at their tips.

Long-tongued bumblebees are able to share in the nectar resource provided by columbine (fig. 73), but because bees are not drawn to red or orange flowers, their attraction to columbine flowers is most likely explained by the contrasting bright yellow margins of the petals. A short-tongued bumblebee species, *Bombus affinis*, has its own method of obtaining the columbine's nectar—it either punctures or tears open the spur with its mandibles (fig. 74), thereby only needing to insert its proboscis a short distance to reach the nectar at the tip of the spur. As documented in movie sequences taken in a Wisconsin population of columbine, 90% of the spurs were perforated by this species. Once a spur is perforated, smaller bees, such as introduced honeybees and small native bees, are able to utilize the opening to obtain nectar. Any of the bees may collect pollen as well, but it is particularly sought after by queen bumblebees, which must provision their nests for the young of the year. Since the queen bees visit several flowers in one flight, they are very successful cross-pollinators. Bees "prefer" nectar with a higher sugar content than birds (about 36%

Buttercup Family

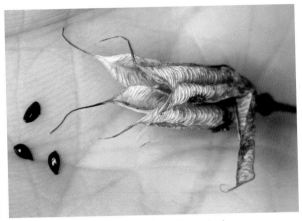

Fig. 75. (Left) Two immature fruits of columbine showing the five fused follicles with the styles still attached.
Fig. 76. (Right) An open follicle of columbine from which some seeds have been shaken out.

average), but they will take the less-sugar-rich columbine nectar during pollen-gathering visits.

Although the styles of columbine elongate before the anthers release their pollen (thereby minimizing the possibility of self-pollination), the stigmas are not receptive until the flower's anthers open. Thus any pollen that was brought from another plant and deposited on the stigmas before they were receptive could only effect cross-pollination if it were to remain viable until the anthers of that flower opened, often four days later. In any event, very little pollen is deposited on the stigmas prior to the opening of the anthers. Hummingbirds may visit to obtain nectar when the flower is first open, but most bees visit columbine primarily to forage for pollen (or sometimes pollen and nectar) and so do not visit columbine until after the anthers have dehisced. Since in manipulating the flower pollen-foraging bees (and sometimes even spur-perforating bees) contact the reproductive organs, fertilization may still occur. As mentioned earlier, *A. canadensis* is self-fertile.

The fruits of columbine are aggregates of five follicles (fig. 75). When ripe, each follicle dries and splits open along an inner seam to expose small, shiny, black seeds (fig. 76). The seeds are shaken out of the opened follicles by the wind. Columbine is a perennial that reproduces only by seed, and, unlike the seeds of many of our other spring flora, they have no attached food bodies (elaiosomes) that might attract ants to serve as dispersal agents. By the mid-seventeenth century, seeds of columbine had been collected

Fig. 77. Rocky Mountain columbine (*Aquilegia coerulea*) growing in Colorado, where it is the state flower. The red flowers are Indian paintbrush (*Castilleja* sp.)

Fig. 78. (Left) A flower and immature fruits of a short-spurred European species of columbine, *Aquilegia vulgaris*, growing in the French Alps. The flowers are bee pollinated. This species is widely grown in gardens and serves as the parent of many hybrids. **Fig. 79.** (Right) Rocky Mountain columbine in Colorado showing the long spurs, from which hawk moths take nectar.

by colonists and brought back to Europe, where the flowers were highly admired for their unique beauty. Because there are no hummingbirds in Europe, few red flowers are found there, and those of the American columbine were considered particularly desirable.

While *A. canadensis* is the only species of columbine in the eastern United States, more than 20 other species are found throughout the United States and Canada. Perhaps the best known is Rocky Mountain columbine (*A. coerulea*), the state flower of Colorado (fig. 77). The beautiful flowers of this species prompted Edwin Payson, an early twentieth-century botanist to state, "*Aquilegia caerulea* [*sic*] is without doubt the most showy and splendid American species of this genus . . . it is not uncommon to see a hillside meadow so completely covered with *Aquilegia caerulea* [*sic*] as to hide all other vegetation and to make it seem a fairyland of huge, dancing blue and white stars" (p. 151). While the original spelling of the epithet of Rocky Mountain columbine is *coerulea*, most

authors prefer to use *caerulea*, the standard spelling for the Latin word for "blue," and this is the spelling used by the state of Colorado for its floral emblem.

Aquilegia is a circumboreal genus with a total of 70–80 species in North America, Europe, and Asia—the species number varies according to which authority you consult. While discrepancy in species number may be puzzling to the layman, one must realize that species are designated by man, not by some innate attribute, and opinions as to what qualifies a plant for recognition as a species (or sometimes even a genus) can be quite subjective. Asa Gray, a noted nineteenth-century Harvard botanist, once stated, "Species are but judgments—judgments of variable value, and often very fallible judgments" (Payson, p. 133). The genus *Aquilegia* is thought to have originated in Europe and to have radiated outward to the North American continent and to Asia. The Eurasian species, in general, have shorter spurs, many of them strongly hooked as in *A. vulgaris* (fig. 78). Speciation (the evolution

Buttercup Family

Fig. 80. Golden columbine (*Aquilegia chrysantha*) is a long-spurred, western species of columbine pollinated by hawk moths. Photographed in Utah.

of new species) appears to have occurred rapidly in response to changes in pollinators. The most observable adaption to new pollinators is the range of spur lengths, which vary from as little as 7.5 millimeters (0.3 inches) to an impressive 180 millimeters (7.1 inches). It appears that ancestral Eurasian *Aquilegia* species with short spurs were pollinated by bees, but when *Aquilegia* entered the western hemisphere, the presence of a novel potential pollinator, the hummingbird, was a factor in the evolution of longer spurs in some species. Subsequently, from those species, additional new species with even longer nectar spurs evolved to accommodate hawk moths with tongues that exceed in length that of the hummingbird. Rocky Mountain columbine (*A. coerulea*; fig. 79) and golden columbine (*A. chrysantha*; fig. 80) are two western species of columbine pollinated primarily by hawk moths. *Aquilegia coerulea* flowers, with spurs 28–72 millimeters (1.1–2.8 inches) long, are visited by the white-lined hawk moth (*Hyles lineata*), a species with a short tongue (by hawk moth standards), but in columbine populations where longer-tongued hawk moths (*Sphinx vashti*) are present, the spurs of the same species are longer. The yellow-flowered

A. chrysantha, with slightly longer spurs on average (42–65 millimeters; 1.7–2.6 inches) than Rocky Mountain columbine, is visited by the longer-tongued species of sphinx moth. Columbine species may hybridize in nature where they co-occur and share pollinators. As might be expected, the flowers of species visited primarily by crepuscular or nocturnal pollinators are light in color and, rather than pendent, are oriented upward or outward to better accommodate the moths' method of obtaining nectar. Almost all shifts to different pollinators have resulted in longer spurs. In these instances of coevolution between flower and pollinator, the columbine flowers benefit from the potentially increased pollination that results from additional visitors, while the hummingbirds and moths benefit from having flowers adapted to their needs. Bees can also effect pollination in western species of columbine when gathering pollen from the long-spurred flowers.

Although there are long-tongued hawk moth species in Eurasia, no columbine species there have developed long nectar spurs as an adaptation to hawk moth pollination. The jump from bee pollination to hawk moth pollination was apparently too great a

Fig. 81. Leaves of columbine with evidence of the feeding of the columbine leafminer (*Phytomyza aquilegivora*), the larva of a small fly.

leap without an intermediary "stepping stone" such as that provided by hummingbirds in the New World (although diurnal clear-winged "hummingbird hawk moths" [*Hemaris thysbe*] have been observed drinking nectar from the relatively short-spurred, purple-flowered *A. alpina*).

Other insects associated with columbine are the columbine duskywing butterfly (*Erynnis lucilius*, whose larvae construct leaf nests on the plant and feed on the leaves), a borer moth larva, and a sawfly (wasp) larva. In addition, like many other members of the buttercup family, columbine species are host to several species of leafminers (*Phytomyza*), including the columbine leafminer (*Phytomyza aquilegivora*).

Phytomyza leafminers are the larvae of small flies. They feed on the leaf tissue between the upper and lower surfaces of the leaf, leaving a telltale meandering "mine" visible on the leaf (fig. 81).

In the era before modern medicine, people commonly utilized local plants to treat various maladies; some had good effect, most did not. Almost all plants found use in folk medicine, columbine included. Native Americans are reported to have used the plant to treat kidney and bladder problems, fever, mouth irritation, and poison ivy rash, among other aliments. However, like many members of the buttercup family, columbine contains toxic compounds and should never be used as a home remedy.

Poppy Family

Fig. 82. The inflorescences of Dutchman's breeches (seen from above) resemble pink clotheslines with tiny pairs of pantaloons hung out to dry.

Fig. 83. A bumblebee (*Bombus* sp.) hanging from the flowers of Dutchman's breeches and inserting its proboscis into a flower to obtain nectar. Note the flared yellow tips of the outer petals.

Dutchman's Breeches

Dicentra cucullaria

Poppy Family (Papaveraceae)—Fumitory
Subfamily (Fumarioideae)

Dutchman's breeches is known for its curiously shaped flowers resembling the wide trousers once worn by men in Holland. It is one of our earliest-flowering spring wildflowers.

Habitat: Rich loamy soils in woodlands or clearings, often in rocky areas.

Range: Canadian Maritimes, Quebec, Maine to Minnesota, south to Georgia, Arkansas, and Kansas; also in Washington, Oregon, eastern South Dakota, and western Idaho.

Looking like pantaloons hung on a line to dry (fig. 82), Dutchman's breeches never fails to charm the beholder. The odd-looking flowers have four petals—two white, conical spurs (the pantaloons) tipped in bright yellow, and two hinged, yellow inner petals adorned with a white, ruffled crest. Occasionally pink-tinged flowers are found (fig. 84). The name of the genus, *Dicentra*, is derived from the Greek *dis*, meaning "two," and *kentron*, "spurred." The species name, *cucullaria*, is Latin for "hooded," a reference to the fact that the two inner petals form a closed hood over the stamens and pistil. The stamens are in two groups of three, fused together and in contact with the stigma and, therefore, easily able to deposit pollen onto it—although the species cannot be self-fertilized. Nectar is secreted from glands on the two middle stamens that project into the spurs, and the nectar accumulates in their tips. There are also two small, deciduous sepals that are rarely noticed since they are the same color as the petals and are usually shed shortly after the flowers open. Two tiny bracts are located beneath the flower on the slender pedicel (flower stalk).

Dutchman's breeches was first described in 1753 by Linnaeus. He named it *Fumaria cucullaria*, based on a plant that had been cultivated in a garden at Uppsala, Sweden. The plant had been introduced into Europe

Poppy Family

Fig. 84. Dutchman's breeches flowers with a pinkish tint and more-rounded spurs than usual.

to treat them as a separate family (Fumariaceae) or as a subfamily of the poppy family (Papaveraceae). Many American botanists currently working on this group of plants place the four above-mentioned genera into a separate fumitory family, the Fumariaceae. The division between this group and the strict poppy family group is based primarily on the symmetry of the flowers, with bilaterally symmetric flowers placed in the Fumariaceae and radially symmetric flowers in the Papaveraceae. Bilaterally symmetric flowers generally can be divided into two mirror images along only one plane, but those of *D. cucullaria* and its close relative, *D. canadensis* (squirrel corn), are unusual in that they can be bisected through *two* perpendicular planes. Radially symmetrical flowers, such as poppies and bloodroot, can be bisected through an infinite number of planes. In addition, members of the fumitory subgroup have clear sap whereas those of the poppy subgroup have white or other-colored sap. Using both morphological and molecular data, recent studies of the poppy family and its close relatives strongly support the classification of these two groups as a single family, Papaveraceae, which includes two subfamilies, Fumarioideae and Papaveroideae. I have chosen to follow this classification as put forth by the

almost a century earlier at the Chelsea Physic Garden, a London garden begun in 1673 as an apothecaries' garden for the purpose of teaching their apprentices how to grow medicinal plants. Not until 1833 was the genus *Dicentra* created by the German botanist Johann Bernhardi, who recognized that the unique characteristics of Dutchman's breeches flowers justified their segregation from the genus *Fumaria*. At one time 20 species of *Dicentra* were listed as occurring in North America and Eurasia. Now over half that number (all of them Eurasian species) have been transferred to other genera within the poppy subfamily Fumarioideae. Just one species of *Dicentra* is found in Japan and in both Siberia and the Kamchatka Peninsula in Russia. *Flora of North America*, a multivolume technical flora, recognizes nine species of *Dicentra* as occurring in North America.

There is continuing disagreement among taxonomists regarding the proper family placement for the northeastern genera *Dicentra*, *Corydalis*, *Fumaria* (fumitory), and *Adlumia* (Allegheny vine)—whether

Fig. 85. Flowers of squirrel corn, a close relative of Dutchman's breeches, have rounded spurs and paler flared tips of the outer petals as compared with those of Dutchman's breeches.

Dutchman's Breeches

Fig. 86. The small, yellow storage bulblets of squirrel corn are just below the surface of the ground. Their resemblance to corn kernels is the basis for the common name of the plant.

APG, the current internationally recognized authority for plant-family classification.

Members of the fumitory subfamily are rich in alkaloids that have bioactive properties. Richard Manske, a British chemist working in the mid-twentieth century, reported that he found novel compounds in each of the 30 Fumarioideae species that he investigated. Both Dutchman's breeches and squirrel corn have several compounds classified as isoquinoline alkaloids. Bicuculline was the first to be isolated from Dutchman's breeches. Cattle allowed to graze in open woodlands where these plants are present suffer from convulsions and even death as a result of eating the leaves or particularly the cucullarine-rich bulblets of the plants. Heavy rains can cause the bulblets to become exposed and thus easily pulled up and eaten with the leaves as the cattle graze. The plants are unpalatable and generally avoided by cattle if enough of their preferred forage is available, but if fodder is scarce in early spring, they may resort to consuming *Dicentra*. Squirrel corn appears to be less toxic than Dutchman's breeches. Both Dutchman's breeches and squirrel corn have been referred to as staggerweed (or blue staggers) because their ingestion causes cattle to have a staggering gait. Horses are less frequently affected, and sheep seem not to suffer any ill effects. Thus, heavy grazing by sheep could be used to rid an area of *Dicentra*, rendering it safe for cattle to graze. Like other toxic alkaloids (e.g., opium from poppies), those from *Dicentra* have beneficial medicinal uses as well. Bulbocapnine, derived from squirrel corn, has been used to

Fig. 87. Unlike those of squirrel corn, the smaller underground bulblets of Dutchman's breeches are white and are found a few inches below the ground surface. In both species, food resources are stored in the bulblets for the following year's growth.

Poppy Family

Fig. 88. The leaves of Dutchman's breeches are on the left and those of squirrel corn on the right. Note that the leaves of squirrel corn are more finely dissected and slightly more blue-green in color.

treat Ménière's disease and muscular tremors, and the botanical drug complex, corydalis, which is found in the bulblets of both Dutchman's breeches and squirrel corn, has been shown to be useful in treating chronic skin lesions and was once used to treat syphilis. Handling Dutchman's breeches is said to cause contact dermatitis, though I have never experienced this.

The shape of the floral spurs of Dutchman's breeches is variable—in some flowers the spurs are less pointed (fig. 84), or they may be closer together than usual. This sometimes leads to confusion with its sister species, *D. canadensis* (squirrel corn). The flower of squirrel corn is similar in structure to that of Dutchman's breeches, but its spurs are rounded rather than pointed (fig. 85). Squirrel corn has a crest (usually white, but sometimes pink) that ornaments the inner petals and extends noticeably beyond them. Squirrel corn's common name is derived from its underground storage bulblets that resemble edible yellow corn kernels (fig. 86), whereas the bulblets of Dutchman's breeches are white to pinkish (fig. 87). In squirrel corn, these storage organs, sometimes erroneously called tubers, occur just below the surface of the ground; however, in Dutchman's breeches, they are found a few inches deeper. If the soil is disturbed so that the bulblets are exposed to light, they may become more deeply colored. The leaves of the two closely related species are delicate, finely divided, and soft green. It is difficult to tell the plants apart by their leaves alone unless you observe them side by side

(fig. 88). Then it will be seen that the leaves of squirrel corn are more finely divided and slightly bluer green than those of Dutchman's breeches. Finally, unlike the scentless Dutchman's breeches, the flowers of squirrel corn have a sweet smell reminiscent of hyacinths. The attractive squirrel corn was brought to Europe as a garden plant in 1830.

Fig. 89. A bee's-eye view of the Dutchman's breeches flowers, emphasizing the attractive bright yellow color that surrounds the openings into the spurs.

Fig. 90. (Left) The flowers of squirrel corn being visited by a queen bumblebee (*Bombus* sp.). **Fig. 91.** (Right) Bee flies (*Bombylius* sp.) visit the flowers of Dutchman's breeches to sip nectar with their long tongues. They are probably not very effective pollinators because their long legs keep their hairy bodies far from the reproductive organs.

Fig. 92. (Above left) A small native bee (*Andrena* sp.) sipping nectar from a flower that has been torn open by a prior nectar robber. **Fig. 93.** (Above right) Three holes have been made in this flower of squirrel corn by insects attempting to obtain the nectar without entering the flower and thus not effecting pollination.

The flowers of Dutchman's breeches are amazingly well adapted for pollination by queen bumblebees that are common in early spring. Bumblebee queens overwinter in a state of diapause, emerging just when Dutchman's breeches is in flower. The bees must search for a nectar source to fill their energy

Poppy Family

Fig. 94. (Left) The fruits of Dutchman's breeches form soon after flowering, just as the trees overhead are beginning to leaf out. Dutchman breeches' leaves are still green and have almost completed their photosynthetic period for the year. **Fig. 95.** (Right) Pressure of the growing seeds within these ripe fruits will cause them to split open and spill the mature seeds.

requirements and for pollen with which to provision their underground nests for the larvae that will develop from eggs deposited by the queen. As Dutchman's breeches flowers have no fragrance, bees are attracted to them by the contrasting white and bright yellow colors (fig. 89). Once a bee has landed on a flower, it hangs from the spurred petals, inserts its long proboscis ("tongue") into one of the "pantaloon" petals to sip nectar (fig. 83), and then repeats the nectar-gathering from the second "pantaloon leg." Queen bumblebees visit the flowers of squirrel corn in the same manner (fig. 90). In the process of drinking nectar, the bee's tongue brushes against the stamens, and its body contacts the stigma. Pollen from previously visited flowers is brushed off on the stigma, and pollen previously rubbed onto the stigma from the anthers of the same flower is deposited on the bee's abdomen to be carried to yet another flower. Even though the pollen of an individual flower is commonly shed onto its own stigma, neither species is self-pollinating, that is, they cannot be fertilized by their own pollen. Few other insects have a tongue long enough to reach the nectar, so bumblebees are the most successful pollinators of Dutchman's breeches and squirrel corn. Long-legged bee flies in the genus *Bombylius* can reach the nectar with their long tongues, but because they ordinarily hold their bodies well away from the plant's reproductive parts, they are less effective as pollinators (fig. 91). Some honeybees are capable of pollinating Dutchman's breeches by hanging from the inner petals and reaching the nectar with their shorter proboscises. However, honeybees are not native to the United States and, thus, did not evolve with this species; they have simply learned to take advantage of this early source of nectar.

Other insects have devised a more direct way to obtain the nectar—they bite a hole in the spur, thereby obtaining direct access to the nectar, They have thus circumvented the flower's reproductive mechanism and have not contributed to the pollination success of the flower. Once a hole has been made in a spur, many other short-tongued insects, including small native bees (fig. 92), can take advantage of the easy access to "steal" the nectar. Even queen bumblebees of one species, *Bombus affinis*, have been observed "cheating" the system by biting through the spur. Such insects are termed nectar robbers since they do not provide a service to the plant (i.e., pollination) in return for their free lunch. Squirrel corn is also observed with holes in its spurs, indicating that its nectar is similarly pilfered (fig. 93).

Both *Dicentra* species are true ephemerals, producing leaves, flowers, and fruits in early spring. The fruits develop quickly and are mature by the time the

Fig. 96. Once the fruits and seeds are mature, the leaves of Dutchman's breeches turn yellow and die.

Like spring beauty and Mayapple, Dutchman's breeches is affected by fungal rust, in this case, *Cerotelium dicentrae*. Interestingly, the life cycle of this rust requires that it spend part of its life on an alternate host, *Laportea canadensis*, in the nettle family. The fungus appears on the leaves of Dutchman's breeches as small, orange spots after the capsules have matured.

Dicentra eximia, a third species of *Dicentra* found in the Northeast, is called wild bleeding heart because of its deep pink (or sometimes white) heart-shaped flowers, with their pendent "drop of blood" (figs. 99, 100). The white-flowered plants may be mistaken for those of squirrel corn at quick glance, but the flowers are longer and slenderer, and the leaves thicker in texture and not as delicately cut. Wild bleeding heart grows in mountainous areas throughout the

overarching trees are beginning to leaf out (figs. 94, 95). Only the underground bulblets overwinter to produce new growth in the following year. After the fruits have split open to release their seeds, the leaves turn yellow and die (fig. 96). Like many other spring-flowering woodland species, the seeds have elaiosomes that are relished by ants (fig. 97), which carry the eliaosome-bearing seeds off to their nests, thereby dispersing the seeds (fig. 98).

Dutchman's breeches and squirrel corn inhabit rich, moist soils in northeastern forests, often growing in rocky areas. Although the two species can co-occur, squirrel corn favors the wetter sites and blooms about a week or 10 days later than Dutchman's breeches. Both species range throughout the Northeast and Midwest, but Dutchman's breeches also occurs in Washington, Oregon, eastern South Dakota, and western Idaho. Plants in this western population have been separated from the more eastern population for over 1000 years and appear more robust in habit. They were once considered a separate species, *D. orientalis*, but, in fact, they appear no different from similarly robust plants growing in the Blue Ridge Mountains of Virginia and are now included in *D. cucullaria*.

Fig. 97. (Top) Ants are attracted to the small, lipid-filled, white elaiosomes (food bodies) attached to the shiny black seeds. **Fig. 98.** (Above) An ant grasping the elaiosome of a seed of Dutchman's breeches to carry it back to its nest, where the elaiosome will be consumed and the seed discarded.

Poppy Family

Fig. 99. (Left) Wild bleeding heart (*Dicentra exima*) is related to both Dutchman's breeches and squirrel corn but maintains its leaves and sometimes even its flowers throughout the growing season. Its range is restricted to the Appalachians from North Carolina and Tennessee north to Maryland and Pennsylvania. It favors rocky habitats. **Fig. 100.** (Right) Occasionally, white forms of wild bleeding heart are found. They may be distinguished from the white-flowered squirrel corn by the longer, narrower flowers and the greener, coarser leaves.

southern Appalachians, often in rocky crevices. Its fernlike leaves, and sometimes its flowers, persist into summer. The pretty flowers of wild bleeding heart made it an attractive candidate for early introduction (1811) into horticulture in England. Like Dutchman's breeches, it received its scientific name as a species of *Fumaria*, based on a plant grown in a European garden in 1815. The illustration accompanying the description of the plant serves as the type of the species (the basis for its name) since there is no herbarium specimen. Wild bleeding heart is related to the showier, garden-grown bleeding heart from Asia that has long been known as *Dicentra spectabilis*. Because

of its beautiful and interesting flowers, *Dicentra spectabilis* (fig. 101) had been cultivated in China and Japan for centuries. It was first sent to Europe in the middle of the nineteenth century by the famous plant hunter, Robert Fortune, and from Europe was subsequently introduced into the United States. The Asian bleeding heart has now been transferred to another genus, *Lamprocapnos*, much to the dismay of gardeners. It is difficult for laymen to accept a name change for a favorite plant that has been known by one name for so long. Taxonomists do not change the names of plants arbitrarily. The reason for making a change is based either on new evidence (often molecular) of a plant's

Fig. 101. The showy flowers of this Japanese species of bleeding heart make it a popular garden plant. Once considered a member of the same genus as our wild bleeding heart and known as *Dicentra spectabilis*, it has been shown to differ enough from *Dicentra* that it warranted transfer to another genus—it is now classified as *Lamprocapnos spectabilis*.

relationship to other species or on research into the history of the naming of the plant. Such research may turn up an earlier name that was given to the plant, which according to the rules of the International Code of Botanical Nomenclature must be given priority and be used as the name for that plant.

Buttercup Family

Fig. 102. A female early meadow-rue plant showing the simple flowers with four green sepals and several elongate styles.

Fig. 103. A male early meadow-rue plant with flowers composed of four sepals and many pendent stamens.

Early Meadow-rue

Thalictrum dioicum

Buttercup Family (Ranunculaceae)

Early meadow-rue is a dioecious species, that is, having male and female flowers on separate plants. The two genders of the flowers are morphologically different in appearance, with the female flowers decidedly less showy than the males. Male flowers resemble small versions of the fringed lampshades popular in Victorian times (fig. 104).

Habitat: Moist forest, especially rocky slopes.

Range: Eastern United States, except for Florida and Louisiana, and the Midwest, except for Oklahoma; also the Canadian Maritimes.

The flowers of the separate male and female plants of early meadow-rue are so different in appearance that one might think that they were two different species. The male flowers of early meadow-rue are fringed with pendent yellow-green-to-purplish stamens that are in nearly constant motion at the slightest breeze (fig. 103). Pollination is effected almost exclusively by wind, as demonstrated by Janet Steven and Donald Waller in an experiment in which insects were excluded from the female flowers of early meadow-rue. When compared with plants that were open to insect visitors, no difference in the numbers of fruits produced was found. The flowers of early meadow-rue have no petals, only sepals. They are small, but the male flowers are showy due to the many stamens dangling from each flower (fig. 105). It is, therefore, the male plants that are most often noticed. It is not too difficult to find a plant with female flowers nearby if one looks carefully. The greenish sepals of the female flowers are longer and wider than those of the male flowers. They surround a tight cluster of pistils bearing long, slender styles that extend outward, making it more likely that they will intercept pollen wafting on the breeze (figs. 102, 106). The stigma extends down the side of the style, providing more surface area on which the pollen can land. The dried style is persistent, forming a beak on the fruit, which is an achene.

Buttercup Family

Fig. 104. A close-up of male flowers showing dangling stamens that release their pollen when blown by the wind.

The leaves of both male and female plants are similar: compound, with many small, broad, lobed leaflets (fig. 107); young leaflets with scalloped margins are tightly clustered before expansion (fig. 108). The leaves and other vegetative parts of *Thalictrum dioicum* may be glandular or not; this variability can be a source of confusion in distinguishing this species from others in the genus.

Linnaeus named this species in *Species Plantarum* in 1753. He based the generic name, *Thalictrum*, on an ancient Greek name, *thaliktron*, which had been

Fig. 105. (Left) Although tiny, the many flowers of male plants, always in motion, make the plant quite conspicuous. **Fig. 106.** (Right) A close-up of a female flower showing the long white styles extending from the green ovaries at the base of the flower.

Fig. 107. (Left) A compound leaf of early meadow-rue, with leaflets that are scalloped at their apices. **Fig. 108.** (Right) Early meadow-rue's scalloped leaflets are tightly clustered before they begin to expand in early spring.

applied to a similar plant in early Greece. *Thaliktron*, in turn, is derived from the same Greek root as *thaleia*, meaning either "abundance" or "blooming," and is related to *thallos* ("green shoot"), and *thallein* ("to grow luxuriantly" or "to thrive"). The common name of early meadow-rue denotes its relationship to other meadow-rue species (*Thalictrum* spp.) and its time of bloom (early). The name "rue" is derived from the similarity in appearance of the leaves to those of true rues in the genus *Ruta*.

Thalictrum has between 120 and 330 species, mostly in temperate regions of the world. The reason for the wide range in the number of species is that classification of the species of this genus is difficult, and many names may well represent variation within a single species.

Early meadow-rue is strictly dioecious (from the Latin for "two houses," a reference to the separation of male and female flowers on different plants). Other species of *Thalictrum* utilize a variety of reproductive methods: some species are hermaphroditic (bisexual), with stamens and pistils in the same flower; such flowers may be cross-pollinated by insects (e.g., *T. thalictroides*) or by wind (*T. alpinum*), or they may be self-pollinated (e.g., *T. mirabile*). In *T. pubescens* (tall meadow-rue), the flowers appear either unisexual or bisexual, the male flowers having only stamens, whereas the female flowers have pistils as well as apparent stamens. However, the "stamens" of tall meadow-rue's "bisexual" flowers produce nonviable pollen and thus are actually staminodes (infertile stamens); the flowers, although bisexual in appearance, are functionally female. As a result, tall meadow-rue functions as a dioecious species, the stamens most likely serving simply as an attractant for insects.

Only 6% of flowering plant species are dioecious. Dioecy ensures cross-pollination, because the unisexual flowers cannot pollinate themselves. The evolution from a bisexual state to a dioecious one may be an advantage in that it allows each plant to become

Buttercup Family

Fig. 109. A Canadian owlet caterpillar (*Calyptera canadensis*), a species that feeds on early meadow-rue, observed on its host plant. (© 2009 David Wagner)

more efficient at achieving one aspect of reproduction (either pollen production or fruit and seed production) without expending the energy to produce *both* male and female organs.

By correlating flower types with chromosome numbers, researchers have developed a hypothesis proposing that the early ancestors of all *Thalictrum* species had insect-pollinated, bisexual flowers. Over time (perhaps due to infrequent visitation by insects), some *Thalictrum* species became more reliant on wind to transport pollen from one plant to another, while other species, in which insect visitation was infrequent, became autogamous (self-fertilizing) in response to infrequent insect pollination. There are conflicting opinions as to whether dioecy evolved in conjunction with wind pollination or resulted from it. The fact that wind-pollinated bisexual species still exist today (e.g.,

T. alpinum) would seem to support the latter option. Evolution to wind pollination resulted in more successful seed production, since pollen is transported even on days that would not be conducive to insect visitation. Wind-pollinated species generally have reduced perianth parts (petals or sepals) and produce great numbers of very small pollen grains. The ratio of pollen grains to ovules in early meadow-rue is reported by researchers Melampy and Hayworth to be 115,000:1! This seeming superabundance of pollen is necessary in that most of the wind-blown pollen is intercepted by, and deposited on, nearby vegetation or other obstacles and thus is not available to perform its basic function of fertilization. In areas where meadow-rue plants are few, seed set is lower, because pollen is less likely to land on the optimal destination (female flowers of the same species). Little is known about the distance that wind-dispersed pollen can travel in a forested habitat. Although meadow-rue blooms in early spring, before the trees and shrubs have leafed out, the trunks and branches of the woody plants still inhibit pollen dispersal at this time.

When early buds of most single-sex flowers are dissected, evidence of incipient organs of the opposite sex is almost always found, but these organs soon abort during the early developmental stages of the floral bud. The buds of early meadow-rue, however, show no evidence of the presence of organs of the other sex, even in their earliest stage of development. Verónica Di Stilio and colleagues found that the presence or absence of stamen or pistil development was regulated genetically. Gender is usually stabile (resistant to change) in long-lived perennial plants, but in rare instances, when environmental conditions change markedly, individual plants have been observed to undergo gender change (see the chapter on Jack-in-the-pulpit).

Di Stilio and colleagues also discovered that gene expression determines the type of cells on the epidermal (outer) layer of the sepals. In the wind-pollinated early meadow-rue, the cells making up the surface layer of the sepals are flat, whereas analogous cells in species with showy, petallike sepals (such as rue-anemone [*T. thalictroides*]) are covered with asymmetrical, conical projections. The refraction of light by these irregular surfaces is thought to produce the brightness that makes the flowers more visible and thus more attractive to insects. Such refractive surfaces are typical of petals or petallike sepals in flowers that are insect pollinated.

Members of the buttercup family are known for their toxicity, due in part to the presence of cyanogenic glycosides. In the northeastern United States, such glycosides are found in about 200 species of plants. Their presence, usually in the vegetative portions of the plants (and in the seeds), helps to defend the plants from consumption by herbivores. Early meadow-rue contains cyanogenic glycosides as well as alkaloids, which also serve as herbivore deterrents. Cyanogenic glycosides are common in many of our food plants. They are present in bitter almonds (but not the domesticated nuts); the seeds of apples, cherries, apricots, and related fruits; lima beans; and the tubers of cassava (manioc), a staple food in many tropical countries. When livestock (or humans) chew plants that contain cyanogenic glycosides, the destruction of the tissues allows the compartmentalized chemical components to mix, converting the glycosides into glucose, hydrogen cyanide (also known as prussic acid), and other molecules. Both livestock and humans may be poisoned by consuming the plants, but the degree of poisoning is dependent upon several factors: the amount consumed, the size of the individual, the amount of glycoside in the plant, how much of the glycoside has been converted to hydrogen cyanide by hydrolysis, etc. Death in children has resulted from the ingestion of only a small amount of cyanogenic glycoside (as might be present in a small number of bitter almonds).

Because many plants with toxic properties have been found to be of medicinal value when administered in a controlled dosage, the alkaloids of *Thalictrum* species are being investigated for possible medicinal use. The roots of early meadow-rue were used by Native Americans to treat diarrhea and vomiting, as well as heart palpitations.

Despite the toxicity of the plant, some insects have evolved to be able to feed on early meadow-rue without harm. The larvae of four species of moth have been documented as feeding on meadow-rue: the straight-lined looper moth (*Pseudeva purprigera*), the pink-patched looper moth (*Eosphoropteryx thyatyroides*), and the green crocus geometer (*Xanthotype sospeta*), all of which are inconspicuous inchworm caterpillars; and the rather spectacularly patterned yellow, black, and white Canadian owlet (*Calyptera canadensis*; fig. 109). The Canadian owlet is the only member of its genus in North America. Some of its tropical and subtropical Asian relatives are notorious for taking blood from mammals (including rhinos, cattle, and humans!) by piercing their flesh with their sharp-barbed mouthparts. This practice has resulted in the nickname vampire moths. The piercing mouthparts are more generally used to pierce the skins of fruits such as oranges, peaches, and plums.

Saxifrage Family

Fig. 110. Early saxifrage (*Micranthes virginiensis*) flowering in early spring with a few leaves still showing their red winter coloration.

Fig. 111. The starry white flowers of early saxifrage are closely arranged when the inflorescence first begins flowering.

Early Saxifrage

Micranthes virginiensis
(formerly *Saxifraga virginiensis*)
Saxifrage Family (Saxifragaceae)

The saxifrages differ more in their vegetative anatomy than in their flowers, which—with some exceptions—are mostly small and white with five equal petals. Because of their beautiful growth forms, many members of the genera *Micranthes* and *Saxifraga* are desirable as rock-garden plants.

Habitat: Rocky cliffs, outcrops, and hillsides; wooded slopes (often in mossy substrates), and stream banks.

Range: Eastern United States, except for Wisconsin, Iowa, and Florida; and in Ontario, Quebec, New Brunswick, Manitoba, and Nunavut in Canada.

The main subject of this essay, early saxifrage, is a widespread perennial species, ranging from far northern Canada south to Georgia and westward into the Midwest. The plants of early saxifrage grow separately or in clumps, their flattened rosettes of overwintering basal leaves turning from green to a bright red in winter but becoming green again by the time the plants flower in early spring (fig. 110). In times of dry weather, especially during the summer months, the leaves curl in from the tip and the sides, but the advent of rain allows most of them to return to their original size and shape. Early saxifrage can grow in acidic conditions, but it is more often found in calcareous soils, frequently growing in rocky habitats. In particular, early saxifrage thrives on calcareous cliffs, which, if shaded, may be covered by a thick layer of moss (fig. 112). Early saxifrage is also one of the relatively few species adapted for growth in serpentine areas. Soils in serpentine areas may be either acidic or basic but are notable for containing unusually high levels of heavy metals. Those few species that can grow in such soils must be able to tolerate the presence of heavy metals, the low calcium to magnesium ratios, and the low levels of nutrients that typify serpentine barrens.

In late fall, flower buds form in the center of the cluster of serrated leaves of early saxifrage and then slowly enlarge throughout the winter. When the day length has increased to above 12 hours in early April, the inflorescence begins to elongate, and small seedlings, produced from the previous year's scattered seeds, begin to grow. Almost all of the many seedlings will have perished by the end of their first winter,

Saxifrage Family

Fig. 112. Several early saxifrage plants growing in a thick carpet of moss (*Philonotis fontana*) that covers an almost vertical cliff face, another common habitat for this species.

Early in the season, before the flower stalk has reached its full height, the flowers are borne in dense clusters (fig. 111), sometimes opening even before the stalk has begun to lengthen (fig. 115). As the season progresses, the inflorescence stalk and its branches continue to grow and change in appearance, becoming more open and lax (fig. 116). The stalks may ultimately reach a height of 16 inches (40 centimeters). Red-tipped glandular hairs covering the upper portion of the hairy stalk (fig. 117) deter small insects, such as ants, from reaching the flowers and drinking their nectar. The true pollinators of the flowers are thought to be native bees (fig. 118) and tachinid flies, the two most frequently observed visitors. Two-peaked follicle-like fruits develop quickly after flowering and split open along their top margin when the seeds are mature (fig. 119); the fruits may turn a bright red if exposed to strong sunlight (fig. 120). Seeds are shaken out by the wind and may be dispersed further on the feet of passing animals.

Such seemingly insignificant native plants as early saxifrage may play a role in ensuring the health of important commercial crops. In a study of cultivated blueberry pollination by the Maine Agricultural Experiment Station, investigators found that the native-bee species responsible for pollinating blueberry flowers frequently have a lifespan that is longer than the four weeks that the blueberries are in bloom. Thus, if the bees are to survive, they must find other sources of pollen and nectar to sustain themselves and their young both before and after the time that the blueberries are in flower. Plants cultivated in small fields surrounded by native vegetation were shown to have higher numbers of pollinators and to produce a greater amount of fruit than those grown in large fields. The greater amount of pollen and nectar produced by the surrounding species of plants—including early saxifrage—that line the borders of the small fields is most likely a contributing factor to the greater productivity of the smaller fields. Not only is there more food available in close proximity, but the bees also do not have to expend as much energy searching for it. Healthier, longer-living bees result in better crop production. Taking such information into consideration when planning crop field size can lead to benefits for both the farmer and the environment.

succumbing to desiccation or frost heaving; they also will die if the site becomes covered with leaf litter. In addition to reproducing by seed, early saxifrage is capable of vegetative regeneration from sections of its rhizome that have become detached from the original plant.

The sepals of early saxifrage are more or less triangular and remain erect even after the fruit has formed, their tips often suffused with red. Unlike most of the western species of saxifrage, the five white petals of early saxifrage are not notched. Ten stamens surround the two carpels, which are united at their bases but diverge widely as the fruits mature (fig. 113). Many aberrant forms of early saxifrage have been noted: the variety *chlorantha* has green petals, the forma *plena* has double the number of petals (but fewer stamens), and plants found over 100 years ago on the east side of Manhattan had no petals and an excess of stamens—15 (see fig. 114 for another aberrant example with 6 petals, 13 stamens, and 3 styles).

Fig. 113. (Left) A flower of early saxifrage with two petals and sepals removed so that the two carpels, joined at the base, can be seen.

Fig. 114. (Above) An aberrant flower of early saxifrage with six petals, 13 stamens, and three styles and stigmas. Note the red tips of the triangular sepals.

Fig. 115. A tiny rosette of leaves of early saxifrage that has opened its flowers before its inflorescence has begun to elongate.

Fig. 116. A plant of early saxifrage with a stalk and branches that have begun to elongate. They will continue to spread and grow until the plant is about twice this tall and becomes more lax than erect.

The journals kept by Thoreau over 150 years ago provide a record of natural history events, including the flowering times of many of the plant species growing in Concord, Massachusetts, Thoreau's home territory northwest of Boston. In his journal entry for April 10, 1853, Thoreau wrote, "The saxifrage is beginning to be abundant, elevating its flowers somewhat, pure trustful white amid its pretty notched and reddish cup of leaves. The white saxifrage is a response from earth to the increased light of the year; the yellow crowfoot to the increased heat of the sun" (p. 107). During the past 100 years, the mean temperature in the Concord area has risen almost 2.5°C (about 3.8°F) and is likely to continue to increase. Early saxifrage is one of many species that have been affected by this change in climate. Researchers from Harvard and Boston universities have been tracking the flowering times of hundreds of the plant species in the area of Concord and Walden Pond, where Thoreau once lived and recorded his observations. They have discovered that many plant species are declining in abundance and are flowering by an average of seven days earlier than in Thoreau's time. Such changes could result in

Saxifrage Family

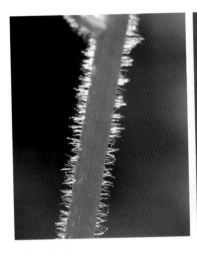

Fig. 117. (Left) A flower stalk of early saxifrage showing the glandular hairs toward the apex. It is thought that the sticky hairs deter ants from taking nectar from the flowers.

Fig. 118. (Right) A small native bee visiting the flowers of early saxifrage. Note that the bee's underside is covered with pollen.

the flowers being out of synch with their pollinators, which may not have changed their time of emergence or their activity schedule to coincide with the altered timetable of the flowers. The carefully recorded observations of Thoreau serve as a baseline against which current climate researchers can compare present data in their assessment of the effect of the warming temperatures on local flora and fauna.

The most common northeastern saxifrages (early saxifrage, swamp saxifrage, and lettuce saxifrage) have recently been segregated out of the genus *Saxifraga* and placed into the genus *Micranthes*. Another North American saxifrage species, also segregated out of *Saxifraga*, was placed into its own monotypic genus as *Cascadia nuttallii*. *Cascadia* is native to the Cascade Mountains of the Pacific Northwest. Both

Fig. 119. A small fruit of early saxifrage that has dehisced (opened) along its top junction. Some of the tiny seeds are still in the fruit.

Micranthes and *Cascadia* were generic names used for these species in the past, but all had been subsequently "lumped" into the more inclusive *Saxifraga*. With the advent of molecular technology as a tool used to define taxonomic relationships, Douglas and Pamela Soltis and others have determined that the aforementioned species should, indeed, be segregated out of *Saxifraga*. Early saxifrage, long known as *Saxifraga virginiensis*, is now *Micranthes virginiensis*. Swamp saxifrage, common in boggy areas throughout the Northeast and now known as *Micranthes pensylvanica*, is a much taller plant than early saxifrage and has small flowers with either white or reddish-orange petals (fig. 121). Lettuce saxifrage (*M. micranthidifolia*) is found along streams in the southern part of the Northeast and southward from there. Its leaves are larger than those of early saxifrage but much the same in shape (fig. 122). The name "lettuce saxifrage" was given to the plant because its leaves are considered edible (as are the leaves of most species of *Micranthes* and *Saxifraga*). The common name saxifrage is still used for members of both *Saxifraga* and *Micanthes*. As mentioned in the chapter on Dutchman's breeches, there is generally good reason for such taxonomic changes, but it *can* drive one crazy—a saxifrage that is not a *Saxifraga*! There are visible morphological differences that can be used to distinguish between the two genera: members of *Saxifraga* have leaves that are both basal and along the stem (though stem leaves are reduced in size), whereas those of *Micranthes* are almost exclusively basal; the seeds of *Saxifraga* may be either smooth or beset with small bumps (papillae),

Fig. 120. (Left) A plant of early saxifrage growing on an open, sunny cliff. Note the sepals that persist through the fruiting state, the widely spreading beaks of the fruits, and the red color of the fruits caused by exposure to strong sunlight. **Fig. 121.** (Above) Flowers of swamp saxifrage (*M. pensylvanica*) with pale, creamy-orange petals. Note that the two beaks of the ovaries in the older flowers (with yellow pollen visible on the anthers) have started to bend outward, whereas those of the less mature flowers (with orange anthers still closed) are still erect.

whereas those of *Micranthes* are ribbed (seeds of *Cascadia* are spiny). The genera are also separated by other, more technical, characteristics.

The affinity of many species of saxifrage for rocky terrain provides one explanation for the origin of the scientific name of the genus. *Saxifraga* is derived from the Latin *saxum* meaning "rock" and *frangere*, "to break." When the small seeds of saxifrage lodge (and germinate) in crevices in rock faces (fig. 123), the resultant plants give the appearance of having split the rock. An alternate explanation is based on the Doctrine of Signatures (see the discussion in the chapter on hepatica). A well-known European species (*S. granulata*—the type species of the genus) bears small, granular bulbils at the base of the plant that resemble urinary tract "stones." As per the Doctrine of Signatures, their presence purportedly signified that the plant should be efficacious in treating patients suffering from such stones. A preparation made from the plant was thought to break the stones into smaller pieces. Several other species of *Saxifraga* and *Micranthes*, including early saxifrage (*M. virginiensis*), bear these small bulbils on compressed subterranean stems. The origin of the generic name *Micranthes* is the Greek *mikros*, for "small,"

Fig. 122. Lettuce saxifrage (*M. micranthidifolia*), with sharply toothed leaves, growing along a brook—a habitat typical for this species.

Saxifrage Family

Fig. 123. (Above) Early saxifrage growing in a rocky habitat.
Fig. 124. (Right) Livelong saxifrage (*Saxifraga paniculata*) rosettes illustrating the lime-encrusted margins of the leaves.

and *anthos*, for "flower" and is descriptive of the flowers in the genus.

Two interesting northeastern American saxifrages have been retained in the genus *Saxifraga. Saxifraga paniculata* (formerly *S. aizoon*), known variously as livelong saxifrage, encrusted saxifrage, or White Mountain saxifrage, has a wide distribution in the boreal regions of the Northern Hemisphere. Livelong saxifrage is a calciphile (calcium lover), growing mostly in lime-rich soils. The plant's roots absorb water containing dissolved lime from the substrate, which is then secreted through small pores (hydathodes) along the margins of the leaves, forming a white deposit that outlines (or encrusts) the leaf margins (fig. 124).

Fig. 125. A tiny plant of alpine-brook saxifrage (*S. rivularis*) photographed growing in the alpine zone of the White Mountains of New Hampshire, well south of its normal range. Note the three-lobed leaves.

The second saxifrage, alpine-brook saxifrage (*S. rivularis*), is generally found further north, throughout much of Canada or at high elevations in the northwestern United States. However, there is an outlying population in the White Mountains of New Hampshire, where it grows above treeline. Alpine-brook saxifrage is a tiny plant with ivylike, lobed leaves and white flowers (fig. 125). The species is also native to northern Europe. Its presence in New Hampshire is interesting because the White Mountains are not high in elevation (the maximum elevation on Mt. Washington is 6,288 feet [1,917 meters]), and they lie well south of the usual range of this species. However, the White Mountains experience extreme weather conditions, with winds exceeding hurricane force on more than 150 days of the year, and the treeline is between 4,800 and 5,200 feet. The location of the White Mountains at the convergence of several storm tracks is responsible, at least in part, for the cold and windy conditions that make them habitable by species more typically found in regions further north.

Not only has the genus *Saxifraga* (the largest in the saxifrage family) been split, but, indeed, based on results from molecular research, the entire family (long a catchall for odd genera that did not quite fit into other families) has lost several genera. Such well-known former saxifragous genera as *Ribes* (currants), *Hydrangea*, *Parnassia* (grass-of-Parnassus) and *Penthorum* (ditch-stonecrop) have now either been assigned to other families or placed into their own families.

Fig. 126. The pretty-flowered, prostrate plants of purple saxifrage (*Saxifraga oppositifolia*) survive in the extreme conditions of the most northerly place where plants grow on earth (Lockwood Island on the north coast of Greenland). However, the species is also found in alpine regions at lower latitudes. This plant was photographed in the French Alps.

Most saxifrages are herbaceous perennials that grow in mountainous regions of Europe, Greenland, North America, and Asia. A few species extend southward into the Andes in South America; to Yemen, Ethiopia, and Morocco's Atlas Mountains in Africa; and to the Himalayas and the mountains of southern China in Asia. Saxifrages are remarkable for their hardiness. For the most part, they are small plants with flowers that are delicate in appearance, but a large number of saxifrage species inhabit some of the most inhospitable environments on earth. They grow right up to the borders of perpetual snow in the Arctic; in fact, several species inhabit territory as far north as any plant can survive. One circumpolar species, purple saxifrage (*Saxifraga oppositifolia*), is one of only four plant species to grow in the northernmost place on earth where plants can grow, Lockwood Island, on the north coast of Greenland, at 83°24' N. This delicate, purple-flowered beauty carpets wide stretches of Arctic barrens, blooming so early that it is rarely seen by people, other than the Inuits of far northern Canada, who eagerly eat the flowers as soon as they appear in the very early spring. Fortunately, purple saxifrage is also found in high alpine regions further south (fig. 126), thus offering non-Arctic explorers the opportunity to appreciate its beauty. Purple saxifrage's ability to survive in such extreme environments is credited to an unusual feature of its leaves: its stomates occur only on portions of the succulent, leathery leaves that

are overlapped by other leaves; thus, the stomate-bearing portions of the leaves are protected from drying winds that might otherwise desiccate them. The flowers produce nectar and are visited by flies when weather conditions permit, but fortunately, with few insects capable of flight at the cold temperatures of such a harsh environment, purple saxifrage is also capable of self-pollination. Other saxifrage species endure extreme weather conditions at high elevations, including one, *S. alpigena*, that lives above 5,000 meters (16,400 feet) in the Himalayan Mountains. A magnificent plant, known as the King of Saxifrages (*Saxifraga longifolia*), grows only in the Pyrenees and adjacent mountains of eastern Spain. A monocarp, it develops a strikingly large rosette of long leaves over a period of four to six years, during which time the plant stores energy reserves in its underground parts for the eventual production of a once-in-a-lifetime 1,000-flowered inflorescence that may reach 70 centimeters (27.5 inches) in height before the plant dies (fig. 127). Reproduction occurs only by seed.

The common saxifrages that inhabit the northeastern United States are generally not among this hardy group of extremists. For the most part, they are found in lowland areas, but sometimes they grow in sites that would be uninhabitable by most other plants, including small crevices in craggy cliffs.

Fig. 127. The "King of Saxifrages" (*S. longifolia*) is monocarpic. It spends four to six years developing a dense rosette of long leaves and storing resources in its subterranean portion until it can produce its massive flower-covered inflorescence . . . and then dies. Photographed on the French side of the Pyrenees.

Bunch-flower Family

Fig. 128. False hellebore and skunk cabbage (with broader leaves) growing along a stream with marsh marigold (yellow flowers) in the foreground. Contrast the pleated stem leaves of false hellebore with skunk cabbage's broader basal leaves with branching veins.

Fig. 129. The striking pleated leaves of false hellebore.

False Hellebore

Veratrum viride
Bunch-flower Family (Melanthiaceae)

False hellebore grows in wet habitats, often in association with skunk cabbage (*Symplocarpus foetidus*, fig. 315), a situation that has led some people to confuse the two large-leaved species, especially when false hellebore first emerges in the spring. While neither is palatable, skunk cabbage is sometimes eaten by wild-food aficionados after extensive processing; however, false hellebore is dangerously toxic. People who have mistakenly ingested false hellebore believing it to be skunk cabbage—or the even less similar wild leek (*Allium tricoccum*) or poke-weed (*Phytolacca americana*)—have become seriously ill. With appropriate medical treatment, most people recover within 24–48 hours, but lack of prompt treatment can lead to death.

Habitat: Swamps, streamsides, and wet woodlands.

Range: Quebec, Labrador, and New Brunswick, south to Georgia and Alabama (except for South Carolina) in eastern North America; and from Alaska and the Northwest Territories, south to California and inland as far as Montana and Wyoming in western North America. False hellebore is not found in the central portions of either Canada or the United States.

False hellebore is not even distantly related to the Eurasian hellebore (*Helleborus* spp.), a member of the buttercup family, nor to the European orchid known as helleborine (*Epipactis helleborine*), which has become an invasive weed throughout much of the Northeast. The name "false hellebore" might originally have been applied to species of *Veratrum* because, like *Helleborus*, they contain highly toxic compounds. *Veratrum* is derived from the Latin *vere*, meaning "true," and *ater*, meaning "black," a reference to the black rhizomes of some species. False hellebore is known by several other common names: American false hellebore, green hellebore, Indian poke, and corn lily, a name based on the superficial resemblance of the habit (overall form) of the plant to that of corn (fig. 130).

There are about 40 species of *Veratrum*, all limited to the northern hemisphere, with the greatest number of species found in China. The genus was once included in the much broader lily family, but molecular research has shown that *Veratrum*, along with many other former lily-family genera, should be segregated from Liliaceae into several smaller families. *Veratrum* is now included in the Melanthiaceae,

Bunch-flower Family

Fig. 130. A plant of false hellebore in bud. The resemblance to a corn plant, the reason for its alternate common name "corn lily," may be seen.

the same family as *Trillium* and *Paris* (see the chapter on trilliums).

The leaves of false hellebore and skunk cabbage emerge in early spring, both appearing as tightly wrapped cylinders of leaves; those of false hellebore are strongly vertically grooved (fig. 131). These species are easy to distinguish from each other by careful observation of the leaf morphology. False hellebore leaves are distinctly "pleated," like an accordion (fig. 129), such that a cross-section made through the width of the leaf would appear as a series of irregular V shapes (fig. 132). The veins run parallel to the length of the leaf, as is typical of monocots. The leaves of skunk cabbage (a member of the Jack-in-the-pulpit family) are not pleated and, unusual for monocots, have branching venation. As the plants mature, the stem of false hellebore greatly elongates with leaves whose bases sheath the stem arising along its length. In contrast, the leaves of skunk cabbage grow only at the base of the plant (fig. 128). The radiating, fleshy roots of false hellebore, like those of skunk cabbage, are contractile, helping to anchor the plants in wet soils. Based on leaf and inflorescence scars on the rhizome, one can ascertain the blooming history and the age of the existing rhizome, but since older portions of the rhizome disintegrate after several years, the total age of the plant cannot be determined. It is thought that some clones of false hellebore can live to be in excess of 100 years old.

False hellebore plants do not flower until they are 7 to 10 years old. Their flowers are arranged along a tall, branching inflorescence at the top of the plant (fig. 133). They are attractive when viewed close up but are often overlooked because their six green tepals blend in with the surrounding green vegetation. The flowers have small, bright yellow, kidney-shaped anthers that open along their curved edge to shed pollen before the stigmas are receptive. Such plants are said to be protandrous (functionally male before becoming functionally female). Stigmatic tissue covers the inner surface of the three styles (fig. 134). While most false hellebore flowers are bisexual, some, especially on the lower branches of the inflorescence, have only stamens (fig. 135). Little is known about possible pollinators, but flies have been observed visiting the flowers. Ants, unlikely pollinators, are commonly seen taking nectar from the paired glands that form a dark green V shape at the base of each tepal (fig. 136).

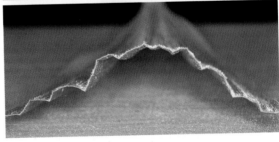

Fig. 131. (Top) Young plants of false hellebore emerging in early spring. The vertically ridged leaves are tightly wrapped around each other to form a cylinder. Fig. 132. (Above) A cross-section of a leaf of false hellebore showing the zigzag profile of the pleated leaf.

Fig. 133. The branched inflorescence of false hellebore.

Species in the genus *Veratrum* contain a wide array of toxic steroid alkaloids. Ingestion of any part of the plant, but especially the rhizome or roots, can result in illness within 30 minutes to four hours. Symptoms include low blood pressure, a reduced heart rate, and suspension of, or difficulty with, breathing. These effects were known for centuries, but in the 1930s clinical trials were conducted to test various components of *Veratrum* as a treatment for hypertension. They led to the production of blood pressure drugs that were used until the 1950s, when better treatments were developed. One study showed that, of the two-thirds of the patients who had positive results from the drug treatment, one-half had unpleasant, adverse reactions. Certain alkaloids of *Veratrum* have also been shown to be teratogenic (i.e., causes birth defects).

It was this teratogenic effect that led indirectly to the answer to an age-old question: is the initiation of the birth process determined by the mother or by the fetus? As long ago as the fifth century BC, Hippocrates suggested that the timing of the birth process was controlled by the fetus. However he had no evidence to support this hypothesis. In the 1930s, an American obstetrician, Dr. Percy Malpas, published a paper about women with prolonged pregnancy who subsequently delivered babies lacking a part of their brain.

As the ovary ripens into a three-lobed capsule, the tepals and styles remain attached (fig. 137), and mature fruits split open along the outer sutures (seams) of the three carpels (fig. 138). Seed production is erratic, since mature plants may flower only every five years, and then often en masse within a given population. The winged seeds are dispersed by the wind (fig. 139). Many germinate and form new colonies of plants, but reproduction in *Veratrum viride* is mainly vegetative, occurring from special buds that mature on the rhizome in years when the plant does not flower. The tall, bright green plants are striking in appearance and are used occasionally in wetland gardens.

Fig. 134. A close-up of a flower of false hellebore in which the white stigmatic surface is visible on the interior surface of one of the three styles.

Bunch-flower Family

Fig. 135. (Left) Unisexual male flowers on a lower branch of the inflorescence. **Fig. 136.** (Right) An ant taking nectar from the darker green, V-shaped glands at the base of the tepals of false hellebore.

Thirty years later, in Idaho, it was noted that pregnant sheep that had grazed on *Veratrum californicum* carried their lambs well past term—as much as 100 days—at which point the unborn lambs had to be surgically removed. The lambs had gross abnormalities, including a single, central eye, along with deformities of the base of the brain. Analysis determined that the condition could be attributed to the exposure of the fetus to the teratogenic alkaloids of *Veratrum* early in gestation, specifically around the fourteenth day of the ewe's pregnancy. Since the pituitary gland, which normally controls the release of a sequence of hormones late in pregnancy, was missing in the affected lambs, the normal increase in estrogen and decrease in progesterone that takes place shortly before birth did not occur. It was determined that it was the release of these hormones by the pituitary gland (and adrenal glands) of a normal fetus that initiated the birth process. This discovery led medical researchers to the conclusion that prolonged pregnancy in human mothers could be caused by an absence of pituitary hormone in the fetus that they were carrying, due to the lack or malformation of that portion of the brain that includes the pituitary gland.

Veratrum's poisonous properties also led to its use as an insecticide, particularly for flies. In 1915 a bulletin of the USDA recommended using the powdered roots and rhizomes of *Veratrum viride* to treat the piles of horse manure that accumulated in cities in the days when most transport was horse drawn. Manure, of course, was a prime breeding ground for flies, and flies were responsible for the spread of disease. Other uses of false hellebore included "corn medicine," which was used to protect seed corn from consumption by crows and other birds. Peter Kalm described this application in his *Travels in North America*, published in 1770. Settlers learned from Native Americans to boil the underground parts of *Veratrum* in water and then allow the corn kernels to soak in the cooled water overnight before planting them. Birds that ate the corn became intoxicated, and their erratic fluttering scared away other birds. Other Native Americans, when preparing for battle, dipped their arrowheads in the toxic juice squeezed from the roots of false hellebore.

Despite its high toxicity, false hellebore is a preferred food of grizzly bears upon their emergence from hibernation. Cattle have been known to eat the leaves late in the season, when most of the toxic principles have been degraded. Toxic alkaloids are produced during the time of active growth and then broken down and metabolized as the plants senesce. For this reason, Native Americans chose to harvest the rhizomes for medicinal use in winter, when the

Fig. 137. An immature, three-parted fruit that will split along the sutures (seams) when ripe. Note that the sepals persist in fruit.

Fig. 138. (Left) A mature fruit of false hellebore.

Fig. 139. (Right) An opened fruit of false hellebore with several winged seeds.

toxicity was at its lowest. False hellebore was used to treat fevers, pain, high blood pressure, and coughs.

Veratrum album (white hellebore) is a European species very similar in appearance to the North American false (or green) hellebore (fig. 140) but having somewhat rounder tepals (compare fig. 141 with fig. 142). It grows in wet meadows at altitudes greater than 800 meters (2,625 feet), where the long, cold season ensures the dormancy required by the seeds for germination. Traditionally, it has been used in homeopathic medicine for the treatment of hypertension and mental conditions. Much of the *Veratrum* marketed in the United States for insecticidal or medicinal purposes was imported from Europe. Until the 1980s, when it was banned for causing illness in children, powdered root of white hellebore was a principal ingredient in "sneezing powders," used in practical jokes to make people sneeze uncontrollably. *Veratrum*

Bunch-flower Family

Fig. 140. A plant of white hellebore (*Veratrum album*) photographed in Spain. Note the similarity to the American false (green) hellebore. At one time *Veratrum viride* was considered to be the same species. Both species have been used medicinally.

Fig. 141. A close-up of the flowers of white hellebore covered with dew. Note how the sepals are rounder than those of false hellebore. Photographed in the Picos de Europa in Spain.

album has also been known to cause illness among livestock that resort to grazing on it when little else is available. Nevertheless, white hellebore is fed upon by over two dozen insect species and numerous species of snails. It is a difficult species to control because its thick rhizomes with their large amounts of stored carbohydrate can easily regrow after mowing, and digging up the tough, contractile roots is very labor intensive. In one instance, annual mowing over a seven-year period reduced the size of the plants but not the numbers.

As with *V. viride* in the United States, the European *V. album* is sometimes mistaken for another large leafy plant that grows in the same wet alpine meadows: in this case, yellow gentian (*Gentiana lutea*; figs. 143, 144). The roots of yellow gentian contain an extremely bitter glycoside that serves as the basis of a tonic used to treat digestive disorders and debility of any cause, and as an appetite stimulant; it is a principal ingredient in Angostura Bitters and in a popular French liqueur called Suze, as well as an ingredient in the American soft drink Moxie. Although *G. lutea* is protected by conservation laws, it is still widely collected for all of the above purposes. Those mistaking *V. album* for yellow gentian have become seriously ill.

Fig. 142. A close-up of the flowers of false hellebore. Compare the more pointed sepals with those of white hellebore in figure 141.

Fig. 144. A flowering plant of yellow gentian. This species, widely used to produce a tonic and other medicinal products, grows in the same wet alpine meadow habitat as white hellebore. If white hellebore is mistakenly collected by someone thinking that it is yellow gentian, its use may result in severe illness. Photographed in Italy.

Fig. 143. (Left) Three plants of yellow gentian (*Gentiana lutea*). When not in flower, the plants may be easily confused with those of white hellebore.

Primrose Family

Fig. 145. Many plants of featherfoil crowded together at the edge of a seasonal pond.

Fig. 146. Two flowering plants of featherfoil. Note the clustered inflorescences and the whorls of featherlike leaves just beneath the water's surface.

Featherfoil

Hottonia inflata
Primrose Family (Primulaceae)

Featherfoil is an unusual aquatic plant that is one of only two species in the genus *Hottonia*; the other inhabits temperate regions of Europe and southwest Asia. A native of the eastern United States, featherfoil is found along the coastal plain in the northern part of its range and extends further inland in the middle and southern parts of its range.

Habitat: Low-elevation seasonal ponds, swamps, and quiet streams.

Range: Eastern United States from Maine to Florida and inland into the Midwest; more common in the south.

Featherfoil is an annual plant found primarily in shallow ponds that fluctuate in water level throughout the year (fig. 147). The presence or absence of the species in any year is determined by this seasonal fluctuation: it appears in years when the water levels drop in the typical fashion, that is, high water in spring and low water in late summer to early autumn; and it does not appear in years when the water is not drawn down by late summer. When conditions are optimal, the plants may grow so densely as to cover the water's surface (fig. 145). Featherfoil occasionally has a terrestrial growth form sprouting from stranded vegetation parts on the muddy margins of water bodies. *Hottonia inflata* is considered endangered, threatened, or of special concern throughout much of its range.

The common name of the plant, featherfoil, is derived from the distinctly featherlike leaves that spread out just below the surface of the water (fig. 146). Although the plant may give the appearance of being a floating aquatic (fig. 148), it is firmly rooted in the soil at the bottom of the pond. However, because its stems are brittle, they may be broken by the action of animals or water, with the result that the fragment can be temporarily free-floating. It may then take root in the wet soil at the margin of the pond. By this means, featherfoil is capable of vegetative dispersal. The long

Primrose Family

Fig. 147. (Above) A seasonal pond in Delaware with featherfoil growing in the shallower margins.
Fig. 148. (Below) Several plants of featherfoil that appear to be floating at the water's surface.

Fig. 149. Rob Naczi, a 6'5" botanist, holding a plant of *Hottonia inflata* to show how long the underwater stems are (over 1 meter).

Fig. 150. A mass of featherfoil plants with their stems sprawling across the top of the water.

underwater stem may exceed a meter in length (fig. 149) and can sometimes be seen at the water's surface among the flowering plants (fig. 150). Some sections of the stem are solid and others hollow (fig. 151), giving it the buoyancy necessary to reach, and remain at, the surface. There are adventitious roots and sparse, scattered leaves along the stem; where it reaches the water

surface, a whorl of finely dissected, comblike leaves radiates beneath the upright flowering stalks (fig. 146).

Plants may produce from one to many hollow, inflated flowering stalks in a clustered arrangement that arises from the level of the water surface. The inflated stalks (fig. 152) provide the buoyancy necessary to hold the flowers and fruits above the water. At each contracted node of the hollow stalks is a ring of small (three- to six-millimeter), white flowers (fig. 153). The bisexual flowers have a calyx fused into a tube at its base with five narrow lobes that are twice the length of the corolla. The tubular corolla flares into five slightly spreading lobes. A small bract is at the base of each flower. All vegetative parts of the plant, other than the subterranean roots and the underwater stems, are covered with minute, short-stalked glands.

I could find no published studies on the pollination of featherfoil, and the only insects that I observed crawling on and into the flowers were ants (fig. 154). Ants are infrequent pollinators because, with some exceptions, they have smooth exoskeletons to which pollen does not easily adhere. In addition, many ants secrete antibiotic compounds that can reduce germination of pollen grains. It is possible that the ants were imbibing nectar from the flowers without providing a service in return (i.e., pollination). The sticky glands on the plant might play a role in attempting to deter these nectar robbers, as they do in such species as sleepy catchfly (*Silene noctiflora*). Fruits and seeds develop quickly, and the fruit capsules release their numerous seeds (fig. 155) by late spring or early summer. The seeds drift to the bottom of the pond where they remain throughout the summer. Not until the more shallow sections of the pond have been dry for a month or so, in September and October, do the seeds of *H. inflata* germinate on the exposed mud of the pond's bottom. As the juvenile plant's cotyledons expand and water levels begin to rise again in autumn, a bubble of gas forms between the two cotyledons, enabling the tiny seedlings to float to the surface. After a short period at the pond's surface, they again sink to the bottom where they develop roots. The seedlings of featherfoil have "falling" starch grains, called statoliths, that are sensitive to gravity and serve to keep the plant properly oriented. The delicate young featherfoil plantlets overwinter at the bottom of the pond, protected from winter's freezing temperatures by

Primrose Family

Fig. 151. A stem just below the whorl of feathery leaves that has been sectioned to show its hollow core; other sections of the stem are not hollow.

Fig. 153. A close-up of the flowers of featherfoil. Note the tubular corolla and the small glandular hairs that cover the narrow calyx lobes.

the high water levels of autumn and winter, although some plants are stranded on muddy shores that do not get flooded and still may be able to survive the winter (fig. 156). In spring, the plantlets resume growth, producing a submerged stem, or stems, of sufficient length to bring the whorl of feathery young leaves up to the water's surface. As the leaves enlarge, the plant develops a series of inflated inflorescences that remain in bloom over a period of approximately two weeks

in early to mid-spring (depending on the latitude). The cycle then begins anew, but only if the water draws down sufficiently in late summer.

Hottonia is considered to be a winter annual because its seeds germinate in autumn when the weather becomes cool. But unlike most winter annuals, featherfoil seeds need high summer temperatures to break dormancy, a characteristic more typical of summer annuals. The cold temperatures of winter

Fig. 152. A peduncle (flowering stalk) of featherfoil that has been cut open to show the hollow interior; it is constricted at the nodes. Note the short flower pedicels, each subtended by a single small bract.

Fig. 154. An ant visiting the flowers of featherfoil. Ants were observed entering the corollas.

Fig. 155. A longitudinal section of a fruit (ca. 2 millimeters in diameter) with immature seeds.

Fig. 156. Young plants of featherfoil and cotyledons that were stranded near the shore of a pond and are now locked in ice. It is thought that some of these plants manage to survive the winter. (© 2010 Eric Lamont)

usually trigger the seeds of winter annuals to return to a state of dormancy, but those of featherfoil remain nondormant, as is common in many perennials. The possibility of some "terrestrial form" plants overwintering conflicts with the winter annual designation. Thus, the life history of featherfoil does not fit neatly into any well-defined category.

The European counterpart of *H. inflata* has been better studied. *Hottonia palustris* is found in temperate regions throughout Europe and the southwestern part of Asia. It differs from its American relative in that its main stem branches at the water surface, just below the inflorescence, and it produces just a single inflorescence, the stalk of which is not hollow. The flowers are arranged in whorls on long pedicels at the nodes of the peduncle. *Hottonia palustris* flowers are much larger (two centimeters) than those of *H. inflata*, more widely open, and white to pink with a yellow "eye," and so are more reminiscent of the flowers of its relative, the true primrose (*Primula*) than those of *H. inflata*. An alternate common name for this species is water-violet. The flowers have been reported to be visited by bees and flies. Water-violet is sold as an aquarium plant.

The genus *Hottonia* was named for the late seventeenth-century Dutch botanist, Petrus (Pieter) Hotton, a physician and the chair of botany at the University of Leiden. The Latin epithet of the American species, *inflata*, refers to the inflated flower stalk; that of the European species, *palustris* (Latin for "swampy" or "marshy"), refers to the aquatic habitat of the plant (fig. 157).

Fig. 157. Featherfoil plants reflected in the water.

Pink Family

Fig. 158. The flowers of fire-pink have five narrow petals, notched at their tips, with a small lateral lobe on either side. Pollen in healthy flowers, such as this one, is white. Note the crown of petal appendages surrounding the opening of the tubular portion of the corolla.

Fig. 159. The brilliant red flowers of fire-pink contrast with the surrounding green vegetation. The enlarged dark anthers indicate that these flowers have been attacked by anther smut.

Fire-pink

Silene virginica
Pink Family (Caryophyllaceae)

Fire-pink is not likely to go unnoticed; its brilliant red flowers stand out from the surrounding vegetation in southern and western parts of the Northeast. Fire-pink's color and long tubular corolla make it a prime candidate for visitation by hummingbirds.

Habitat: Dry open woods, stream banks, rocky slopes, and roadsides.

Range: Eastern United States except for New England; more prevalent in the Midwest and southward into Georgia; ranging as far west as Oklahoma; also known from southern Ontario.

The Caryophyllaceae family is found mainly in the North Temperate regions of the world, as well as in mountainous areas of Africa, but it also has the distinction of having one of its members, *Colobanthus quitensis* (Antarctic pearlwort), as the only dicot and one of only two species of flowering plants found on the continent of Antarctica (the other is a hair grass,

Deschampsia antarctica). The family has many species known for their pretty flowers that are popular as garden plants and cut flowers (e.g., carnations, baby's breath, sweet William, and corn cockles).

In members of the pink family, the leaves are opposite each other (occasionally whorled) and usually sessile on the stem. Many species of the genus *Silene*, including *S. virginica*, have sticky hairs covering the stems, leaves, and inflorescences (fig. 160). The hairs most likely deter small insects, such as ants, from crawling up the stem to take nectar. The stickiness may, in fact, be responsible for the name of the genus. *Silene* is thought to be derived from the Greek *seilenos*, which in turn is based on *Silenus*, the name of the foster father of the Greek god Bacchus. Silenus was said to be covered with foam, perhaps prompting Linnaeus to compare the sticky secretion of *Silene* to the sticky foam covering Silenus. Linnaeus named both the genus *Silene* and the species, *S. virginica*, in his 1753 publication, *Species Plantarum*. Fire-pink is common in Virginia, and Linnaeus must have examined collections from there and named the species for its collection locality. Once one has glimpsed the bright red flowers of fire-pink, no explanation of the common name is necessary; the intense red color fairly glows among other plants in the landscape.

Silene is the largest genus in the pink family, with up to 700 species (that is, if other genera, such as *Lychnis*, are subsumed into *Silene*, as proposed by John Morton, the author of the treatment of the genus *Silene* in *Flora of North America*; other taxonomists feel that the genera should remain as separate entities). The flowers are most commonly bisexual, including those of fire-pink and have sepals fused at the base to form a tube with prominent veins. The five petals are clawed (sharply narrowed at the base) and gradually widen to where they join the blades of the petals. In addition, each petal has two appendages at the junction of the claw and blade that together form a small "crown," termed the corona, around the opening of the corolla tube (fig. 158). There are usually three to five styles and 10 stamens. *Silene virginica* is one of the few red-flowered species of the genus (in the northeastern United States, there are only two others, both rare and both primarily more southern in distribution: *S. rotundfolia*, which grows on sandstone bluffs in West Virginia and in very localized areas from

Pink Family

Fig. 160. The sticky hairs on the tubular calyx and other parts of the plant probably prevent ants from taking nectar from the flowers.

southern Ohio to Alabama and Georgia; and *S. regia*, a species favoring prairies but, like *S. rotundifolia*, also found from southern Ohio into Alabama and Georgia. Most other species of *Silene* have flowers varying in color from white to pink to purplish. The narrow petals of fire-pink are notched at their tips and have one small, pointed tooth along each side of the petal (fig. 158). The fruits are capsules that are pendent at maturity and split open at the apex, forming three (to four) pointed "teeth," each of which may split into two. The seeds fall to the ground at the base of the plant.

As might be predicted, hummingbirds are the principal pollinators of fire-pink. To test this hypothesis, researchers Charles Fenster and Michele Dudash enclosed plants of fire-pink in wire mesh cages designed so that hummingbirds were excluded but potential insect pollinators could have access to the flowers; other fire-pink plants were left uncaged to serve as controls. Fewer fruits were produced on the caged plants, and those fruits had fewer seeds—an indication that hummingbirds are responsible for most of the effective pollination in this species. Fenster and Dudash observed native solitary bees and syrphid flies visiting the flowers and, in a few instances, bumblebees. Normally, hummingbirds aggressively defend their nectar resource from pilferage by bumblebees, but in years when hummingbird populations are low, bumblebees may play a greater role in fire-pink pollination since their access to the flowers may not be challenged by the hummingbirds. The bees have unchallenged access not only to the flowers but also to the nectar within the flowers, which, not having been depleted by hummingbirds, will have accumulated to

higher levels in the floral tube and thus be more easily reached by the bees.

In a subsequent study Fenster and colleagues, in experiments using artificial flowers, determined that hummingbirds preferentially visit flowers having larger petal blades and longer tubes—traits that correlated with a greater nectar reward. More frequent visitation to plants with larger flowers would result in a higher percentage of large-flowered plants being reproductively successful. A possible outcome of this preference could result in a progressive natural selection for larger flowers in *Silene virginica*. Fenster et al. also showed that fire-pink produces nectar at an increasing rate throughout the flower's four-day lifespan and that each flower of fire-pink receives an average of two visits per day from ruby-throated hummingbirds. Because the nectar is continuously replenished, fire-pink is visited by hummingbirds repeatedly throughout its flowering period. During the first two days, the stamens dehisce and release pollen. Each hummingbird visit results in a large number of pollen grains being transferred to subsequently visited flowers that may be in the female phase. On the third day, the flower transitions to the female stage, when its stigmas open and become receptive, facilitating the germination of pollen deposited on them. This situation, in which a reward (in this case, nectar) is provided to pollinators during both male and female stages of anthesis (time that the flower is open), enhances the likelihood that hummingbirds will visit during each phase, helping to promote successful pollination.

The flowers of fire-pink, like those of many other species of *Silene*, are subject to attack by a type of basidiomycete fungus that causes the disease anther smut. Smuts cause major problems in many crop plants, resulting in great financial loss for farmers. However, in Mexico a type of smut that effectively replaces the kernels of maize with large, dark, tumor-like galls has been utilized since Aztec times as a favored food by the local inhabitants. Known as *huit-lacoche*, it is caused by the pathogenic fungus, *Ustilago maydis*. The smut afflicting the anthers of *Silene* is thought by some researchers to be caused by a species in the same genus: *Ustilago violacea*. This species of smut has been reported to cause disease in more than 100 species of the pink family throughout Europe and North America. Taxonomists differ on the identification of the fungal species responsible, with some claiming that the fungus responsible for causing anther smut in *Silene* species is properly classified as *Microbotryim violaceum*, a species in an entirely different order of fungi.

Whichever taxonomic camp is correct, the relationship of anther smut and *Silene* is intriguing. The fungus effectively replaces the pollen in the flower's anthers, resulting in dissemination of the fungal spores by the plant's pollinators. Thus, in fire-pink, the ruby-throated hummingbird not only provides the beneficial service of pollination but also plays a negative role by spreading the fungal pathogen from an infected flower to other flowers. Rarely, the infection is only partial, with some of the anthers showing evidence of disease and others continuing to produce pollen. The fungus appears not to harm the plant other than to prevent it from reproducing. Not only do the spores replace the pollen in the anthers, but the fungus causes the ovary to become reduced, rendering the plant sterile. Fire-pink is a short-lived perennial. Although smut-infected plants do not suffer greater mortality than healthy plants, recovery from the disease is rare, and the plants will remain sterile for the remainder of their lives. The only visible sign of fungal infection is that the anthers appear larger and darker (fig. 159), something that is more obvious in lighter-colored species of *Silene*, such as the white-flowered European *S. latifolia* (formerly known as *S. alba*). Known as white campion in New England, where this species was originally introduced to North America by European colonists, this species has spread slowly southward. However, based on examination of early herbarium collections, it appears that anther smut did not affect this species in the New World until relatively recently, after it had spread as far south as Virginia, where it came into contact with fire-pink and its fungal pathogen.

Because the corolla of *S. virginica* is deep red and the anthers are naturally a dark purplish color before they open, anther smut is less readily apparent in the flowers of fire-pink. In fact, it was not noted by botanists until 1988, when Janis Antonovics and collaborators discovered it while studying anther smut disease in white campion in Virginia. Subsequent examination of herbarium specimens of *S. virginica* confirmed that anther smut had been present

on fire pink for more than 100 years but had gone undetected by those botanists who had collected the plants. Some mycologists had noted the smutted anthers earlier than 1988, but they had not reported its presence, either in the scientific literature or in databases of fungal pathogens and their plant hosts. Antonovics demonstrated that the anther smut on fire-pink and the one that affects white campion are not the same but most likely represent two slightly different variations of a species that infects only their target hosts.

Since the reproductive stage of the fungal smut occurs only when the plant is in flower, dispersal of the spores can happen only during that short period of time—perhaps three weeks a year—when the plant flowers in spring. As mentioned above, the principal dispersal agent of the fungus is the ruby-throated hummingbird, which transports the spores on its head and bill just as it would pollen grains. Although hummingbirds generally visit flowers in close proximity to each other and will follow the shortest route between flowers on neighboring plants, they do, over time, visit flowers throughout a fairly large territory. The fungal spores, therefore, are afforded a means of long-range dispersal. A secondary means of spore dispersal is aerial, by which spores are dislodged from the anthers of an infected plant and drop onto surrounding juvenile plants below. If the spores germinate and then conjugate successfully, they can infect the juvenile fire-pink plants by developing a mycelium that grows up through the stem until it reaches a flower bud, where it is able to transform the anthers into spore-making "factories." Based on the number of juveniles that are infected before the time of their first flowering (as determined by monitoring juveniles and observing the presence of smut in the anthers of the first flowers produced by the plant), it appears that in *S. virginica*, aerial transmission may play a greater role in spore dispersal than transport by hummingbirds.

The spread of the disease is slow, occurring mostly in clumps within a population, but examination of historical herbarium specimens indicates that there has been, over time, a gradual increase in the rate of transmission. However, some adult plants are resistant to the fungus, and their seeds that have fallen to the ground do not become infected by spores that may rain down upon them.

Milkwort Family

Fig. 161. Fringed polygala growing in association with the rare dwarf lake iris (*Iris lacustris*) near the shores of Lake Michigan in Wisconsin.

Fig. 162. A dense patch of fringed polygala blooming in a coniferous woodland in Ontario.

Fringed Polygala

Polygala paucifolia
Milkwort Family (Polygalaceae)

Fringed polygala is one of our most beautiful spring wildflowers. Its bilaterally symmetric flowers are often mistaken for those of an orchid or a legume. Two of its common names are gaywings and bird-on-the-wing, both references to the spreading, winglike sepals.

Habitat: Moist rich woods.

Range: Quebec and New Brunswick to Saskatchewan, south to Connecticut, New York, and Wisconsin, and south in the mountains to Georgia.

Although the plants and flowers of fringed polygala (*Polygala paucifolia*) are quite small, one cannot help but notice them on the forest floor. The flowers are a bright magenta-pink, and the plants usually grow in colonies, making quite an impressive display (fig. 162). Their curious form inspires questions:

First, what family might this lovely plant belong to? And second, why is the flower shaped as it is (fig. 163)? One's first impression is that the flower could be an orchid because of its peculiar zygomorphic form, but upon closer inspection, one sees that the diagnostic features of an orchid flower are lacking—there is no column of male and female reproductive parts nor an enlarged petal (the labellum, or lip). The two "wings" and the keel-like petal that encloses the reproductive parts are typical of pea-family flowers,

Fig. 163. The odd, airplane-shaped flowers of fringed polygala. Note the paler fringe of appendages on these flowers.

Milkwort Family

Fig. 164. A frontal view of fringed polygala. The fringe of bifurcated appendages serves as a landing platform for insects.

Fig. 166. An albino form of fringed polygala photographed in Virginia.

leading one to guess that the flower might be that of a legume (pea family); but unlike pea flowers, there is no standard (banner) petal. Rather, fringed polygala belongs to a large genus that comprises over a third of the species in the Polygalaceae, a plant family found nearly all around the world. Until recently, the polygala family was placed in the order Polygalales, but molecular research has shown that the Polygalaceae is related more closely to the legume family (Fabaceae) than thought and must be moved from its own order, Polygalales, into the Fabales, the order that includes the legumes.

The flowers of fringed polygala resemble miniature pink airplanes without tails (fig. 163). The fuselage of the "plane" consists of the three pink petals, two of which enwrap the third (the keel), which, in turn, encloses the reproductive parts. The keel bears the "propeller" at its apex, a fringe of pink or white bifurcated appendages (fig. 164) that serves as a landing platform for visiting insects. Bumblebees are the principal pollinators; the weight of the bee's heavy body on the fringe of the keel causes a slit on the top of the keel to open, revealing the style and stamens (fig. 165). Pollen from the stamens is rubbed onto the

Fig. 165. A fringed polygala flower with its keel artificially depressed to show how the style and stamens are exposed through a slit on the upper side of the keel that opens when a bee alights on the fringe.

Fig. 167. Spiny milkwort (*Polygala subspinosa*) is common in rocky, semidesert areas of Utah and Arizona and is uncommon or rare in New Mexico and Colorado.

Fig. 168. Two fringed polygala flowers just above the plant's wintergreen-like leaves.

bee's hairy body as it probes deeply into the base of the flower for nectar. At the same time, pollen from a previously visited flower may be scraped off onto the bilobed stigma. Thus, the unusual arrangement of the floral parts may be seen as an adaptation to pollination by bumblebees. Of course, a plane needs wings, which in this case are represented by two of the five sepals of the plant. The spreading, winglike sepals are large and, having the same pink color as

Fig. 169. A plant of wintergreen (*Gaultheria procumbens*) in flower. Note the similarity of the leaves to those of fringed polygala. Although fringed polygala is sometimes called flowering wintergreen, the small, white flowers of wintergreen are very different from those of fringed polygala. Wintergreen is in the blueberry family (Ericaceae).

the petals, are easily mistaken for petals. The other three sepals are smaller and inconspicuous. Rarely, as in many other species of plants, white-flowered forms of fringed polygala are encountered (fig. 166).

Species of *Polygala* are found on almost every continent and in a variety of habitats. The United States has over 60 species, most of them in the Southeast, but in the western part of our country, *P. subspinosa* grows in near desertlike conditions (fig. 167). In the northeastern United States, all *Polygala* species are herbaceous, but some species grow as trees or shrubs in other parts of the world. There are no other

Fig. 170. Fringed polygala growing in a thick bed of moss, a favorite habitat.

Milkwort Family

Fig. 171. (Above) Two inflorescences of orange milkwort (*Polygala lutea*), another northeastern species of milkwort. Note the small appendages at the end of the keel rather than the longer fringe seen in *P. paucifolia*. **Fig. 172.** (Right) A southern hairstreak (*Fixenia favonius*) nectaring at an inflorescence of orange milkwort.

genera of this family in our region. Fringed polygala is the showiest of the polygala species in the Northeast. Its 13- to 19-millimeter flowers are large by comparison with those of other local polygalas, and they are borne either singly or as only a few flowers clustered at the apex of the plant, just above the three to six dark green leaves. The visible leaves are up to four inches in length, but beneath them are tiny scalelike leaves arranged alternately along the stem. The upper leaves resemble those of wintergreen (*Gaultheria procumbens*), which can be the cause of mistaken identity

when the plants are not in flower. This similarity is the basis for another common name for fringed polygala—flowering wintergreen. This, of course, is misleading, as it implies that the true wintergreen is nonflowering. The small, white, bell-like flowers of wintergreen are less conspicuous than and bear no resemblance to the colorful flowers of gaywings, but they are definitely true flowers (figs. 168, 169). While the leaves of wintergreen are evergreen, those of fringed polygala last for

Fig. 173. (Left) Orange milkwort (*Polygala lutea*) growing side by side with short-leaved milkwort (*Polygala brevifolia*) in an acidic bog habitat in the New Jersey Pine Barrens.

Fig. 174. (Right) Cross-leaved milkwort (*Polygala cruciata*) is named for the pairs of opposite leaves that form a cross; it is also an inhabitant of sandy bogs in the Pine Barrens.

Fig. 177. Alpine milkwort (*Polygala alpestris*), with its delicate, white-fringed blue flowers, dots the alpine meadows of Vercours, France.

Fig. 175. Blood milkwort, or field milkwort (*Polygala sanguinea*), grows in fields and meadows.

only one season. It is easy to differentiate between the leaves of the two species: crush a leaf and smell it—the leaf of wintergreen has a familiar and pleasant wintergreen aroma.

Also hidden near the base of *P. paucifolia*, or even below the ground level, are a few cleistogamous flowers that set seed without the aid of a pollinator. The term "cleistogamous" is from the Greek *kleistos* for "hidden" and *gamous* for "marriage," referring to the hidden sexual reproduction that occurs in these

Fig. 176. *Polygala venulosa* is found in association with dry dwarf scrub vegetation in Greece and elsewhere in the Balkans.

flowers. Cleistogamous flowers have the appearance of small flower buds that never open. They contain reduced pistils and stamens and produce seed through self-pollination.

Polygala fruits are two-valved capsules, with those of one species, orange milkwort (*P. lutea*), differing from those of the other local species in that the two larger sepals remain attached to the capsule even after it ripens. Seeds of our native polygalas have an elaiosome, which attracts ants to gather, and then disperse, the seeds. Fringed polygala can reproduce vegetatively as well, by producing rhizomes from its small tubers. The species is very sensitive to disturbance and does not reestablish after destructive events such as clear-cutting of the forest.

Fringed polygala is a plant of semishaded sites in forests without a closed canopy; it is often found under conifers or sometimes in lush beds of moss (fig. 170). It may grow in association with other woodland plants such as starflower or twinflower, and in the Great Lakes region, with the rare dwarf lake iris (*Iris lacustris*; fig. 161). At the northern extent of its range, fringed polygala sometimes inhabits more open areas. Some other northeastern species of *Polygala* grow in quite different habitats.

Perhaps rivaling fringed polygala for showiest of the northeastern species is orange milkwort (fig. 171), a native of acidic, sandy soils such as are found in the Pine Barrens of New Jersey. What the flowers lack in size, they more than compensate for with their bright orange color. The flowers grow in tightly clustered

Milkwort Family

Fig. 178. The colorful flowers of box-leaved milkwort (*Polygala chamaebuxus*) are bicolored, either pink and yellow or creamy white and yellow, making it a favorite low shrub for ornamental use. The flowers do not have the fringe that characterizes many other species of *Polygala*. Photographed in the French Alps.

Fig. 179. (Left) *Securidaca longifolia*, a relative of *Polygala*, is a woody vine (liana) that grows along the Rio Negro and Amazon rivers in Brazil.

Fig. 180. (Right) Although the flowers of *Securidaca* are similar in appearance to those of *Polygala*, their fruits are samaras that are dispersed by wind and water.

Fig. 181. The roots of Seneca snakeroot (*Polygala senega*) were once gathered on a large scale as an ingredient in patent medicines used to treat respiratory maladies such as bronchitis. As its common name suggests, the Seneca Indians also employed snakeroot in the treatment of rattlesnake bite.

Thirty-three species of *Polygala* are found in Europe. They are adapted to conditions ranging from the arid soils of Greece (fig. 176) to the lush, calcareous mountain meadows of Italy and France (figs. 177, 178). As mentioned earlier, polygala species native to other parts of the world may be woody plants. *Securidaca*, another genus in the family, has flowers that could easily be mistaken for those of *Polygala*, but it is a genus composed of tropical trees and lianas (woody vines), with most of its species native to South America (fig. 179). It differs from *Polygala* in that, instead of a capsule, its fruit is a one-sided, winged samara, which is adapted for dispersal by wind or water (fig. 180).

The genus name, *Polygala*, is from the Greek *poly*, meaning "much" or "many," and *gala*, "milk"—not because the plants have a milky sap, but because it was once believed that animals that grazed on polygala plants would yield more milk. The specific epithet, *paucifolia*, means "few leaves"; aside from the few "normal" green leaves just beneath the flowers, the other leaves are tiny and scalelike and rarely noticed.

Polygala paucifolia has no current economic uses, but it was once used by the Iroquois Indians to treat skin maladies. Members of the genus from different parts of the world provide fiber, alcoholic beverages, herbal medicine, and ornamental shrubs, including *P. myrtifolia* from South Africa, which is now grown worldwide in Mediterranean climates. Only *P. senega*, among our local species, is reported to have an ethnobotanical use (fig. 181). The Seneca Indians used the chewed roots to make a poultice for treating rattlesnake bites. Chemical compounds in the roots, including spinasterol, have been shown to counteract the lethal effect of snake venom by blocking the action of enzymes in the venom. The Senecas also made a tea from the root, which was used in treating coughs. Foam-forming saponin glycosides contained in the root have the ability to increase the production of mucous, leading to the use of products made from the root as expectorants. Until the 1950s, Seneca snakeroot was widely used in patent medicines, and collection of wild-growing plants was an important income-producing activity for the native people of Saskatchewan and Manitoba. The roots were dried and shipped to processors for use in herbal remedies. Use of the natural product declined after synthetic expectorants were introduced in the 1960s.

heads that elongate throughout the blooming period. Rather than a fringe of appendages at the tip of the lowest petal, there are just a few tiny lobes, and unlike the bee-pollinated fringed polygala, orange milkwort is pollinated by butterflies (fig. 172). Orange milkwort is considered endangered in New York and extirpated in Pennsylvania. It is not uncommon to see polygala species growing in association with other members of the genus, as occurs with *P. lutea* and short-leaved milkwort (*P. brevifoli*a) in the Pine Barrens of New Jersey (fig. 173). Cross-leaved milkwort (*P. cruciata*; fig. 174) also grows in the sandy bogs of the Pine Barrens, but the colorful blood, or field, milkwort (*P. sanguinea*; fig. 175) prefers the less acid and more fertile soil of fields and meadows. Most northeastern species of milkwort have small flowers arranged in a long raceme, sometimes with many densely congested flowers so as to appear headlike.

Buttercup Family

Fig. 182. Round-lobed hepatica with lavender flowers blooming in the leaf litter in early April.

Fig. 183. Round-lobed hepatica with pink flowers. Flower color in hepatica varies from white through pink and lavender to deep purple.

Hepaticas
Round-lobed Hepatica and Sharp-lobed Hepatica

Anemone americana and Anemone acutiloba
Buttercup Family (Ranunculaceae)

The many colors of the early-blooming hepatica never fail to delight the hiker who ventures into the woods in early April.

Habitat: Both species—either dry or moist upland woods.

Range: Quebec and Nova Scotia to Minnesota and Manitoba, south to Georgia, Tennessee, and Missouri.

Although the first native wildflower species to bloom each year in the Northeast is skunk cabbage, for many people skunk cabbage just does not conform to their concept of what a spring wildflower should be—it is not small, delicate, or pastel colored. Generally in the northeastern United States, the first flower that does correspond to the more typical image of a spring wildflower is hepatica, usually found in flower by early April in the middle of its latitudinal range. Like many of our native woodland wildflowers, hepatica blooms before the trees leaf out. This timing allows the plants to utilize the sun's energy to photosynthesize and thus make carbohydrate during the season that the sun's rays are able to reach the forest floor. In some species, for example, trout-lily and Dutchman's breeches, the plants are truly ephemeral. That is, they complete the production of leaves, flowers, and fruits within a very short time and then disappear from sight until the following spring. The carbohydrate made by the leaves is stored in their underground tubers, rhizomes, or corms.

In contrast, the leaves of hepatica plants, which also grow from an underground rhizome that stores "food" for the following year's growth, are evergreen, at least through a complete year. Leaves produced in the spring remain on the plant for a full year, through the next spring's blooming period (fig. 184). The leaves, which are able to photosynthesize to a minor extent on warm winter days, are ready to begin

Buttercup Family

Fig. 184. (Left) Round-lobed hepatica in flower with a leaf from the previous year still retained (lower right). **Fig. 185.** (Right) Old red leaves of sharp-lobed hepatica withering as the new leaves open and fruits begin to develop.

Fig. 186. Newly flushed leaves of *Anemone americana*.

full-scale photosynthesis before the leaves of other plants have even appeared. Thus, hepatica is able to produce its flowers earlier than most other spring wildflowers. The old leaves, often tattered and worn, wither completely only after the flowers have begun to form fruits and the new leaves have appeared (fig. 185). By May, fresh green leaves unfurl (fig. 186) and begin to capture whatever sunlight can penetrate

Fig. 188. (Top left) A typical leaf of *Anemone americana*. **Fig. 189.** (Bottom left) A typical leaf of *Anemone acutiloba*. **Fig. 190.** (Right) Variegated leaves of *Anemone americana*.

Fig. 187. A stamp from Finland depicting the European species of hepatica now called *Anemone hepatica*.

Fig. 191. Three hairy bracts subtending the flower of hepatica.

Fig. 192. Dark-burgundy-colored, leathery leaves from the previous year.

Fig. 193. *Anemone americana* growing on a steep, wooded slope along the Housatonic River in Connecticut.

through the canopy above to continue manufacturing carbohydrates for the following year's growth.

The simple beauty of hepatica, so welcome after a long, bleak winter, prompted the famous naturalist and writer John Burroughs to say, "There are many things left for May, but nothing fairer, if as fair, as the first flower, the hepatica. I find I have never admired this little firstling half enough. When at the maturity of its charms, it is certainly the gem of the woods" (p. 188). The flower has inspired several poetic tributes by Burroughs and others, among them William Cullen Bryant (1794–1878):

> Blue as the heaven it gazes at,
> Startling the loiterer in the naked groves
> With unexpected beauty; for the time
> Of blossoms and green leaves is yet afar.

Still others have chosen to portray the flowers of hepatica on the postage stamps of several countries, including those of the United States and Canada. The lovely example shown here is from Finland (fig. 187).

When I first learned to identify local wildflowers, it was thought that there were two species of hepatica in the Northeast: *Hepatica americana* had leaves with rounded lobes (fig. 188) and grew in local woodlands, where it was tolerant of somewhat acidic soils, and *Hepatica acutiloba* had pointed-lobed leaves (fig. 189) and was more frequently found in mountainous regions on limy soils and not commonly seen along the Eastern Seaboard. Both types of leaves may be

beautifully variegated (fig. 190). Hepatica was originally described as *Anemone hepatica* by Linnaeus in 1753, and since then it has been transferred back and forth between *Anemone* and *Hepatica* numerous times. Those who still consider *Hepatica* to be separate from *Anemone* (including those who maintain the USDA database) claim that the two formerly separate hepatica species are actually varieties of *Hepatica nobilis*, a species that occurs in Europe (what was Linnaeus's original *Anemone hepatica* and is now called that again by those who would include *Hepatica* in *Anemone*). Taxonomists in favor of maintaining hepatica in the genus *Hepatica* designate the round-lobed hepatica as *H. nobilis* var. *obtusa* and the one with sharp-lobed leaves as *H. nobilis* var. *acuta*. Their basis for keeping *Hepatica* in its own genus, separate

Buttercup Family

Fig. 194. *Anemone americana* growing among oyster shells on an old Indian midden along the Hudson River in New York.

from *Anemone*, is the presence of bracts immediately below the flower (fig. 191) and the persistent, leathery, lobed leaves; neither feature is found in any species of *Anemone*. Most botanists currently working on this group (among them the authors of the multivolume, ongoing *Flora of North America*) include *Hepatica* in the genus *Anemone* based on recent phylogenetic analysis, but they recognize that the taxonomy of *Anemone* is problematic and still in need of further study. Because I have chosen to follow the taxonomic designations of the APG (which lists *Anemone*, but not *Hepatica*, in the genera included in the Ranunculaceae) in this book, I have chosen to use *Anemone*. Thus, the round-lobed species is called *Anemone americana* and the pointed-lobed one is *Anemone acutiloba*.

It is from the leaves that the plant's scientific name, *Hepatica* (from the Greek *hepar*, "liver"), originated, and that name is perpetuated in the most-used common name, hepatica. *Anemone* is also of Greek origin and refers to the wind, perhaps a more suitable name for many of the more delicate species of *Anemone* that are commonly called windflowers. Two of hepatica's other common names are also derived from an association with liver: liverleaf and liverwort. The leaves of hepatica are lobed and typically take on a deep burgundy color as they age (fig. 192), especially those of the round-lobed variety. Early herbalists

often looked to a plant to give some clue to a possible therapeutic use of the plant, a belief called the Doctrine of Signatures. In the case of hepatica, the resemblance of its lobed, dark burgundy leaves to a human liver indicated that it should be efficacious in treating diseases of the liver. In the late 1800s, hundreds of tons of the leaves were gathered for use in patent medicines. Most herbal-plant gatherers were from the mountainous regions in the southern states

Fig. 195. (Left) The flower stalks of hepatica are covered by soft hairs that help to conserve warmth and protect the plant from extreme changes in temperature that occur in early spring. **Fig. 196.** (Right) Young leaves are also protected from cold winds by downy hairs.

Fig. 197. (Left) *Anemone americana* with deep purple flowers.

Fig. 198. (Right) The colorful flowers are easy to spot among dried leaves.

where the sharp-lobed hepatica was more common. Demand became so great that additional quantities of the dried leaves had to be imported from Germany. An estimated 425,000–450,000 pounds were either collected or imported to the United States in 1883 alone. Hepatica was a principal ingredient in such "medicines" as Dr. Roder's Liverwort and Tar Sirup (*sic*) and Beache's Vegetable Syrup. It seems amazing that hepatica was able to survive this period of overharvesting. Eventually, the demand dwindled, most likely due to the ineffectiveness of the snake-oil remedies, and today the plant is only of minor use

in a few herbal preparations. Analysis of the chemical constituents of the leaves found no components with documented medicinal value. As in many other members of the buttercup family, the fresh leaves are said to be toxic.

Both varieties of hepatica grow well in soils that are somewhat alkaline, although the round-lobed hepatica is more tolerant of a range of soil types. The plants frequently grow on slopes in rich woods (fig. 193). Hepatica is most commonly found in places underlain by limestone or marble—or among old Indian shell middens, as can be found along the Hudson

Fig. 199. Pink- and white-flowered plants growing side by side.

Buttercup Family

Fig. 200. White-flowered *Anemone americana* in leaf litter. White-flowered plants are more common in the Northeast than in the Midwest.

River in New York (fig. 194). The shells add calcium carbonate to the soil, making it more alkaline.

Hepatica flower stalks emerge clothed in a protective "fur coat" (fig. 195), which helps to insulate them from the cool temperatures that prevail in early April and to protect them from widely fluctuating temperatures and chill winds that occur in early spring. The delicate new leaves arising at their base are also covered in downy hairs (fig. 196). The flowers are usually produced before the new leaves expand. However Charles H. Peck, the New York State botanist in the late 1800s to early 1900s, noted that the new leaves of the sharp-lobed hepatica were further developed at the time of flowering than those of the round-lobed variety. To find hepatica in flower, you must walk in the woods in early spring and be on the alert for any little difference in form or color on the forest floor. The deep, burgundy color of the leaves of hepatica blends easily into the surrounding brown leaf litter, but the three-lobed shape is distinctive, so once one has a search image in mind, the leaves are easy to spot. The colorful parts of hepatica flowers (generally 6 in number, but ranging from 5 to 12) are not petals, but rather sepals. Just beneath them are three sepal-like bracts (actually modified leaves). Both hepatica varieties may be found in a range of colors from white through pink (fig. 183) and lavender (fig. 182) to my favorite—a deep lavender-blue (fig. 197). Typical of the buttercup family, the flowers have many stamens and pistils. When in flower, the deeper-colored flowers contrast particularly well with the forest litter

(fig. 198). I have observed all of these colors on plants growing side by side, so soil chemistry does not seem to be a factor in sepal color (fig. 199).

In 1936, Edgar Anderson, a botanist at the Missouri Botanical Garden, carried out a study of the color of hepatica flowers across their range. Censuses were done in Missouri, New York, and Vermont. Those flowers in the western part of the range (Missouri) were more strongly colored than those in Vermont, which were frequently white. For example, in Missouri there were no white flowers, in New York one-sixth of the flowers were white, and in Vermont one-third of the flowers were white (fig. 200). This gradation of color, becoming lighter from west to east, is found in other species as well, among them

Fig. 201. A round-lobed hepatica plant with flowers having many more sepals than the usual six.

Fig. 202. (Left) The open, bowl-shaped flowers of hepatica are accessible to many kinds of pollinators. Note the numerous stamens and pistils characteristic of flowers in the buttercup family.

Fig. 203. (Right) A solitary bee, the principal pollinator of hepatica, visiting a flower.

Dutchman's breeches (*Dicentra cucullaria*), which is often tinged with pink in the Ozarks and usually creamy white in the East, and bird's-foot violet (*Viola pedata*), which is generally bicolored purple and lavender in the Ozarks and plain lavender in New England. One hypothesis for this color variation is that lighter-colored flowers are more conspicuous in the dense, darker forests of New England and are, thus, easier for pollinators to find; they are, therefore, more likely to be reproductively successful. The eastern plants also had a slightly higher average number of sepals (fig. 201), again increasing the likelihood of their being found by pollinators. In the bright, more open habitats of the Midwest, deeper-colored flowers are more noticeable and therefore more attractive to potential pollinators.

The bowl-shaped flowers of hepatica (fig. 202) are accessible to many different kinds of insects. Peter Bernhardt, now a professor at St. Louis University, studied the pollination ecology of hepatica in upstate New York in the 1970s. He found a total of 40 different insect species visiting the flowers of *Anemone acutiloba*. The underparts of the insects were dusted with hepatica pollen, indicating that they were capable of transferring pollen from one flower to another. The earliest spring visitors in Bernhardt's study were flies, followed by solitary bees and then honeybees. However, in a study conducted in the 1990s, a beetle, *Asclera ruficolis* (see fig. 413), was found to be the most frequent visitor to hepatica flowers, accounting for over 95% of visits. But since *Asclera ruficolis* stays

within a small range, it is not a very efficient pollinator. Bernhardt found the most important insects for effecting pollination were solitary bees (fig. 203), native species that have evolved with hepatica. The paucity of potential pollinators in the chilly April temperatures is offset by hepatica's capability for self-pollination. Self-pollinated flowers produce multiple hairy achenes (a type of fruit), but far fewer than if the flower had been cross-pollinated.

In common with many spring woodland bloomers, hepatica produces seeds that are provisioned with a food body (an elaiosome), which is attractive to ants. In exchange for carrying the seeds away from the mother plant and "sowing" them in other parts of the forest, the ants are rewarded with the lipid-rich, edible elaiosome. Research has shown that ants preferentially select the "seeds" (actually fruits called achenes) having the largest, freshest elaiosomes and will not carry seeds from which the elaiosomes have been experimentally removed. After eating the elaiosomes, the ants discard the seeds, generally in or near their nests, a site rich in nutrients to promote seed germination and growth. This mutualistic relationship provides the ants with a nutritional resource while resulting in longer-range dispersal for the seeds of the plant. Germination of the seeds is slow, with the radicals (precursors to roots) not appearing until fall, and the cotyledons (the first, or "seed," leaves) delayed until late winter or early spring. The seeds must go through a cold period to break the dormancy of the epicotyl (the above-ground portion of the plant).

Jack-in-the-pulpit Family

Fig. 204. A Jack-in-the-pulpit inflorescence (*Arisaema triphyllum* subsp. *triphyllum*) in spring, blooming among violets.

Fig. 205. An infructescence of Jack-in-the-pulpit fallen to the ground in autumn.

Jack-in-the-pulpit

Arisaema triphyllum

Jack-in-the-pulpit (or Aroid) Family (Araceae)

Jack-in-the-pulpit is found as a dioecious plant having male flowers on one plant and female flowers on another. Occasionally flowers of both types are found on the same inflorescence. An individual plant may reverse from male to female and back again in successive years depending on environmental conditions.

Habitat: Rich moist or wet woods and swampy places.

Range: Nova Scotia to North Dakota, south to Florida and Texas.

Most aroids inhabit the tropical regions of the world, particularly those of Asia and South America; only 10 of the more than 100 genera are found in North Temperate areas, with 5 of those native to the northeastern United States. Members of the family are easy to distinguish worldwide by their characteristic inflorescence. Virtually all species, from the aquatic water lettuce (*Pistia stratioites*; fig. 206) of

the tropics, with a one-quarter-inch white inflorescence, to the dragon arum (*Dracunculus vulgaris*; fig. 207) from Mediterranean Europe, with a two-foot tall, deep reddish-black inflorescence, have the same basic structures: a flower-bearing spadix subtended and often surrounded by a bract (the spathe).

Almost everybody knows Jack-in-the-pulpit, even if only by name. It does not take a great deal of imag-

Fig. 206. The one-quarter-inch inflorescence of water lettuce (*Pistia stratiotes*), a floating, aquatic plant from the tropics. Photographed in Amazonas, Brazil.

Jack-in-the-pulpit Family

Fig. 207. The two-foot, fetid-smelling inflorescence of dragon arum (*Dracunculus vulgaris*). Photographed in Crete, Greece.

bisexual flowers on the ball-shaped spadix of skunk cabbage, those of Jack-in-the-pulpit are unisexual.

The etymology of the scientific name of the genus, *Arisaema*, comes from the Greek *aris* or *aron*, referring to *Arum*, a similar plant in Europe, and *haima* or *haimatos*, meaning "blood," for the red-spotted leaves of some species. The specific epithet, *triphyllum*, denotes the three-part leaves.

Variation in form is found in *A. triphyllum* throughout its range. Although most taxonomists currently recognize these differences at the level of subspecies, others think that the differences are significant enough to warrant reclassification of the current subspecies as distinct species. Three subspecies of *Arisaema* are currently recognized in the Northeast. *Arisaema triphyllum* subsp. *triphyllum*, which has a spathe that is either green-and-white or purple-and-white striped, is, by far, the most common of the three and the one that is most likely to be encountered throughout the range of the species (figs. 204, 208). The subspecies *stewardsonii* is characterized by a strongly ribbed spathe, which is usually green-and-white striped (purple within at the base), with a narrow, inrolled flange at the tube apex (fig. 209). It is found in swamps, marshes, and other wet habitats in the more northern areas of the range and extends further south in the mountains. The spathe of the more southern subspecies, subsp.

ination to see why it was so named. The spadix is columnar in shape with a long extension called the appendage ("Jack"), which is enclosed and overhung by the spathe (Jack's "pulpit"; fig. 208). Unlike the

Fig. 208. (Left) Two inflorescences of *Arisaema* subsp. *triphyllum*. Fig. 209. (Middle) The strongly ribbed spathe of *Arisaema triphyllum* subsp. *stewardsonii*. Fig. 210. (Right) An inflorescence of *Arisaema triphyllum* subsp. *pusillum*, with a solid purple hood interior.

Fig. 213. An aberrant four-leaved Jack-in-the-pulpit.

Fig. 211. (Top) A storage corm of Jack-in-the-pulpit with deciduous roots. **Fig. 212.** (Above) A leaflet of Jack-in-the-pulpit showing the parallel secondary veins that branch from the midrib and join an arching vein that runs along the leaflet margin.

Fig. 214. The three-part leaves of Jack-in-the-pulpit (left) and poison ivy (right). Note the lobing of the poison ivy leaflets and the stalked terminal (central) leaflet.

pusillum, is nearly always entirely green or purple (rarely striped) within (fig. 210), and the appendage arising from its spadix is slenderer than that of the other two subspecies. Overlap in all of these characteristics makes it difficult to determine whether the differences are important enough to merit recognition of the subspecies at the species level. Some taxonomists recognize a fourth subspecies, *quinatum*, which is native to the southeastern states. It has five-parted leaves and a bent spadix appendage; other botanists include it in the subspecies *pusillum*. Unusual forms of *Arisaema triphyllum* have led to the development of several cultivars with attractive characteristics, such as white-veined leaves or particularly strongly veined spathes.

Jack-in-the-pulpit grows from an underground food storage organ called a corm. In addition to reproducing by seed, Jack-in-the-pulpit reproduces vegetatively from smaller corms (cormlets), which develop around the margin of the main corm. Clusters of plants that arise as offshoots of the parent plant are clonal, having the same genetic makeup as the parent; they cannot reproduce sexually with one another. Deciduous roots grow from the corm to absorb water and nutrients; they are contractile, pulling the corm deeper into the soil (fig. 211). At the time that the fruits form, the deciduous roots separate from the corm and wither; new ones will grow the following year. Rhizomes may also grow from the corms and can give rise to new plants. Older parts of the corm are sloughed off as new tissue is added at the top, so even if a plant is 20 years old, no part of it is actually more than 4 years old. Thus, the plants do not experience senescence and may live for many years.

Another common name for Jack-in-the-pulpit is Indian turnip. Indian turnip was eaten after being

Jack-in-the-pulpit Family

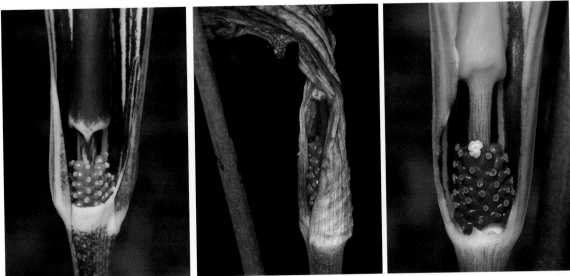

Fig. 215. (Left) The young green ovaries are topped by fuzzy white stigmas on the spadix of a female inflorescence. **Fig. 216.** (Middle) As the fruits of Jack-in-the-pulpit begin to develop, the spathe withers. **Fig. 217.** (Right) The spadix of a female plant with a nonfunctional staminode above the ovaries.

Fig. 218. A flowering plant of *Arum concinnatum*, a close European relative of Jack-in-the-pulpit. Photographed in Crete, Greece.

boiled and dried, but since it is in the same family as skunk cabbage and known to contain calcium oxalate crystals, it should be avoided. Native Americans also used the corms medicinally: internally to treat bronchitis and rheumatism, and externally to treat snakebite. The calcium oxalate crystals are present in all parts of the plant, even the red pulp of the attractive berries (fig. 205).

Young Jacks produce just a single three-part leaf and no inflorescence. Although *Arisaema* is a monocot, the netlike venation of the leaves, as in those of skunk cabbage, is more characteristic of a dicot (fig. 212). Rarely, an aberrant plant with more than three leaflets is found (fig. 213). When examining the leaves of Jack-in-the-pulpit, take care to ascertain that you are looking at the correct species. The three-part leaves are sometimes mistaken for the three leaves of *Trillium*, but they have a vein that runs parallel to the margins of the leaflets that *Trillium* leaves do not have. They may even be confused with the leaves of poison ivy, but the leaflets of poison ivy generally have some lobing and the terminal (middle) leaflet is stalked (fig. 214).

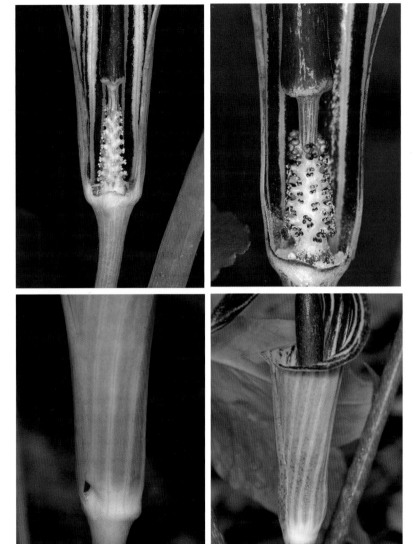

Fig. 219. (Left) The base of the spadix of a male Jack-in-the-pulpit inflorescence; the spathe has been partially cut away to show the spadix with its tiny male flowers.

Fig. 220. (Right) Pink pollen, fallen from the anthers of this male inflorescence, has accumulated in the base of the spathe. The rounded structures at the top of the spadix are unopened stamens.

Fig. 221. (Left) The overlapping base of the spathe on the male inflorescence often has a small gap (the dark opening) through which insects may escape.

Fig. 222. (Right) The spathes of female inflorescences generally do not have a gap; insects may become trapped inside.

As the corm increases in size, the greater food stores allow the plant to put energy into reproduction, and plants with one leaf and an inflorescence are produced. Jack-in-the-pulpit is genetically bisexual, but in nature it almost always appears as dioecious (male flowers on one plant and female flowers on another). Small, one-leaved plants most commonly produce a male inflorescence, whereas larger plants will generally bear two leaves and an inflorescence with female flowers. The genus *Arisaema* is unique in the Araceae for being able to reverse the sex of its flowers from year to year in response to the amount of carbohydrate that the plant has been able to manufacture and store in its corm. If environmental conditions have been unfavorable (e.g., low rainfall, little sunlight for adequate photosynthesis, or damage to the leaves), a mature plant will produce a male inflorescence. Only if the plant has been able to produce and store enough food reserves will it have the energy required to produce a female inflorescence and the resultant fruits

Jack-in-the-pulpit Family

Fig. 223. A Jack-in-the-pulpit infructescence from which most of the red fruits have fallen. This receptacle is almost black; some are pinkish.

and seeds. A female plant that has depleted its food stores one year may revert to male in the subsequent year. In general, those plants that receive more light and that are growing in less crowded stands are more likely to be reproductive. Flower number and size for the following year is determined in the late summer of the current year. Thus, by some means, the plant "determines" whether or not it has enough food reserves to produce an inflorescence and, if so, whether it will be male or female.

The simple flowers of a female inflorescence are crowded together on the spadix. They comprise only the reproductive parts—large green ovaries topped by fuzzy white stigmas (fig. 215). Once the flowers have been pollinated, the spathe withers (fig. 216). Occasionally monoecious plants are found that are either basically female with a few male flowers above the female flowers on the spadix or basically male with a few female flowers at the base. There seems to be a narrow transitional range in plant size when this monoecious state occurs. Although bisexual inflorescences generally comprise only 1–5% of the plants in any population (and I have never encountered such a plant), in a Canadian study 13% of the plants had bisexual inflorescences. "Male bisexual" plants produce only pollen and never form fruit from their few female flowers, and "female bisexual" plants only produce fruit and no pollen. Since each bisexual plant functions reproductively only as a single sex, Jack-in-the-pulpit may be considered as a truly dioecious species. It is easy to determine the sex of the plant, first by looking at its size, and, second by exercising one's voyeuristic streak and peering down into the spathe to examine the flowers. Perhaps the female plants might be more appropriately called "Jill-in-the-pulpit." In some female plants, amorphous, fleshy structures that are nonfunctional staminodes are present (fig. 217), and, conversely, some male inflorescences will have similar nonfunctional pistillodes. Unopened stamens have the same appearance (fig. 220).

In some European species of Araceae (e.g., *Arum* spp., which looks similar to Jack-in-the-pulpit; fig. 218), small flies are the principal pollinators, but studies on the pollination of *A. triphyllum* have shown conflicting results. The inflorescences of Jack-in-the-pulpit receive few insect visitors. In a survey of 437 Jack-in-the-pulpit plants over a period of two years (comprising over 12,000 inflorescence observations), only 355 insects were collected. More than 60% of the inflorescences were never visited by insects. A study by Richard Rust showed thrips (*Heterothrips arisaemae*) to be the most prevalent and likely pollinators. The tiny thrips were completely covered with pollen when captured within a spathe with a male inflorescence and were capable of moving that pollen to another plant within a meter of the plant in which they were found. However, Jack-in-the-pulpit

Fig. 224. Four seeds of Jack-in-the-pulpit removed from three fruits with the remains of one of the fruits.

106

Fig. 225. Two blister beetles (*Meloe* sp.) on the ripe fruits of Jack-in-the-pulpit. The larger female is avidly consuming the fruits while the male attempts to court her. The kinked antennae of the male are used for grasping the antennae of the female during courtship.

flowers must be pollinated with pollen from a plant that is not part of the same clone, so some botanists, including Treiber Miklos (who wrote his Ph.D. dissertation on *Arisaema triphyllum*), think that fungus gnats are more likely to be the most effective pollinators. The gnats are capable of longer flight distances than the thrips and are thus more likely to move the pollen to plants of a different clone. Some observers have detected a faint odor emanating from the spadix that is described as either funguslike or ozonelike, which may make the inflorescences more attractive to fungus gnats. Fungus gnats carry significantly more *Arisaema* pollen than the thrips. Further studies are needed to determine the relative importance of the two proposed pollinators.

The inflorescence of *Arisaema* is present for two to five weeks. Individual flowers are simple, consisting of only the reproductive structures; there are no sepals or petals. Male flowers have two to five stamens that are either fully fused or at least partially fused at the base. The anthers open at the tip by a transverse slit. Pollen grains are tiny, with barbed spines that can easily adhere to the bodies of visiting insects. The male flowers, which are loosely arranged on the spadix (fig. 219), begin flowering at the center of the spadix and open progressively in both directions. Their pinkish pollen collects at the base of the spathe (fig. 220), where crawling insects may become covered with it. Insects usually land on the spadix and crawl down to

the flowers; the walls of the spathe are too slippery to allow insects to crawl back out, but certain kinds of insects are able to fly out of the top opening of the spathe. The spathe of most male inflorescences differs slightly from that of female plants at flowering time in that it has a tiny opening at the base of the spathe, where one side overlaps the other (fig. 221). Pollen-covered insects can escape from the spathe through this opening and go on to visit other flowers, where, if the inflorescence is female, the pollen they carry may be rubbed off on receptive stigmas, leading to cross-pollination. In female plants such a gap either does not exist (fig. 222), or it is effectively blocked by the developing ovaries, resulting in insects being trapped inside the spathe, where they usually perish.

Adult thrips seem to feed on the pollen collected in the spathe, where they deposit their eggs on the inner wall. The ensuing thrips larvae play a negative role in the relationship with *Arisaema* in that they feed on the underside of the leaves, causing significant damage, particularly in male plants. The larval feeding patterns can be seen by looking at the under surface of the leaves in late spring, and by summer one can see light-colored spots on the affected leaves' top surface as well.

Bright red-orange berries develop in late summer to early fall. They are attached to a receptacle that may be pale creamy-pink or dark purple-black (fig. 223). Each berry has from one to three (rarely up to five) seeds (fig. 224), but some, especially toward the top of the fruiting spike, have no seeds. As with the seeds of Mayapple, those of Jack-in-the-pulpit have a higher

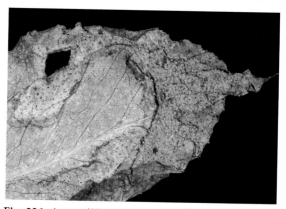

Fig. 226. A rust (*Uromyces ari-triphylli*) has attacked this leaflet of Jack-in-the-pulpit (now dried).

Jack-in-the-pulpit Family

Fig. 227. (Left) An inflorescence of green dragon (*Arisaema dracontium*), the only other species of *Arisaema* in the Northeast. Note the small spathe and the long appendage that extends from the spadix.

Fig. 228. (Right) A plant of Jack-in-the-pulpit from which deer have eaten the leaves. Because the plant will be nutritionally deprived without its leaves, it may not be able to produce the resources needed to maintain its female status in the following year.

germination rate after having passed through the gut of a box turtle (see fig. 287). The turtles also benefit the plant by dispersing the seeds into new habitats. Birds and rodents might play a similar role in seed dispersal. In October 2010, I happened upon several plants of Jack-in-the-pulpit in fruit. They were some distance off the trail, but I noticed that some of the fruits had exposed seeds, and others were scattered on the ground. I walked over to investigate and was surprised to see a pair of blister beetles (*Meloe* sp.) on the inflorescence. Adult blister beetles are herbivores, but more commonly feed only on leaves and flowers. They are sometimes considered pests because they strip the leaves from crop plants and sicken livestock that feed on hay in which the beetles have inadvertently been included. The female beetle was actively consuming the flesh of the berries and paying no heed to her suitor (fig. 225).

Like spring beauty and Mayapple, Jack-in-the-pulpit is affected by a fungal pathogen—a rust called *Uromyces ari-triphylli*, which attacks only *A. triphyllum* and its sister species in the Northeast, *A. dracontium*. It invades the entire plant, causing bright yellow-orange, spore-bearing pustules to appear on the leaves and spathe of the plant (fig. 226). The fungus has a negative effect on the plant, reducing the leaf area and longevity. Young plants that develop vegetatively from cormlets of the affected plant are infected inherently, but their seeds are not and so remain viable even when the parent plant is diseased. Larger (and therefore female) plants are more frequently and more adversely affected, with most of them reverting to male status the following year. Once infected, the plant carries the fungus for life.

As with other species discussed in this book (see the chapters on skunk cabbage, Mayapple, and twinleaf), the relatives of *A. triphyllum* are found in Asia. Only one species of *Arisaema*, other than *A. triphyllum*, is native to the northeastern United States, *A. dracontium* (green dragon). Green dragon has been shown by molecular evidence not to be closely related to Jack-in-the-pulpit. Its ancestors, therefore, must have crossed the Bering land bridge at a different time in history. Fossils of Jack-in-the-pulpit-like fruiting structures found in the Pacific Northwest have been dated to 18 million years ago. Interpolation of the fossil and molecular data by Suzanne Renner, a botanist working on Araceae, suggests that *A. triphyllum* and *A. dracontium* diverged many millions of years *before* crossing the land bridge from Asia. Fossils of three extinct species of *Arisaema* have been found across North America, indicating that, at one time, the genus was more widespread on this continent. Green dragon is taller than Jack-in-the-pulpit (up to one meter tall) and has a single leaf divided into 7 to 12 (or more) leaflets. Its small, green spathe only partially encloses the spadix and a long (up to seven inches) spadix appendage (fig. 227), which probably plays a roll in

Fig. 229. One of several species of alien earthworms that are responsible for changes in the soils of our northeastern forests, a factor in the decline of many of our woodland wildflowers. Jack-in-the-pulpit does not seem to be adversely affected by the presence of alien worms, perhaps because the noxious compounds in its tubers deter the worms from feeding in the vicinity.

attracting pollinators; in many other Araceae the spadix or its appendage generates heat, which volatilizes aromatic compounds that attract insects. The appendage extends well beyond the spathe in both male and monoecious plants, which include virtually all green dragons; purely female plants are almost never observed. As the plants increase in size, they produce a greater number of female flowers. One explanation offered for the lack of purely female plants is that a large monoecious plant that has depleted its energy reserves in the production of numerous female flowers and fruits one year may revert to the male phase the following year as it rebuilds its food stores. Unlike Jack-in-the-pulpit, almost all female flowers set fruit with viable seeds. The fruits are red-orange berries.

Understory cover in forests is decreasing in both abundance and diversity throughout most parts of the Northeast. Among the factors responsible is the overabundance of white-tailed deer, whose indiscriminate diet includes most herbaceous plants and woody seedlings. A study of the effects of browsing by white-tailed deer on spring wildflowers in Illinois showed that deer markedly reduced populations of several species of wildflowers but had little effect on the numbers of Jack-in-the-pulpit. Deer generally avoid eating *Arisaema* most likely because of the irritating calcium oxalate crystals found in the plant. However, when the deer population exceeds the supply of desirable plants, they will consume almost anything, including toxic and irritating plants (fig. 228). Yet another study of the effects of deer browsing on Jack-in-the-pulpit plants in New Jersey showed that although the numbers of plants did not significantly decrease, the individual plants were smaller, and their ability to reproduce sexually was markedly diminished. Removal of the aboveground portion of the plants results in smaller corms that then give rise to smaller (usually infertile) plants. In Wisconsin, it has been documented that during the month of June, black bears include Jack-in-the-pulpit as one of the preferred foods in their diet, thus adding a further threat to this native wildflower.

Most people are aware of the negative effects of deer on our native forests, but less known is the devastating effect of European earthworms on our flora. These worms have been introduced to the Northeast primarily by fishermen who discard their surplus bait worms near the lakes where they fish. The forests in the northern part of the country evolved without native earthworms; bacteria and other soil microbes were responsible for the recycling of nutrients. Now, several different species of alien worms have begun to colonize our northern forests (fig. 229), slowly spreading outward from their points of origin. The worms consume leaf litter, organic matter, and microbes in the soil at a rapid rate, causing a reduction in humus depth and a redistribution of soil components. Not only are seedlings often uprooted as a result of their activity, but the seeds themselves are buried at levels so deep as to inhibit successful germination. Thus, the composition of our forests is changing. A study in Minnesota documented that both plant diversity and abundance decreased as earthworms increased. One alien worm species in particular, *Lumbricus rubellus*, is especially destructive, either obliterating the ground flora completely or leaving only a few species, one of which is *A. triphyllum*. Since these relatively small worms feed in the soil zone at the level of the roots of the ground flora, it is thought that toxic compounds in the corms and roots of Jack-in-the-pulpit may repel the worms in their vicinity. While it is reassuring that Jack-in-the-pulpit appears to be at least somewhat resistant to predation by both worms and deer, it is sad that we are losing so many of our other lovely native plants due to man's interference in the natural ecosystem.

Orchid Family

Fig. 230. A group of yellow lady-slipper plants in flower. Note the leaves along the stem.

Fig. 231. Several plants of pink lady-slipper showing the broad, longitudinally ribbed basal leaves and the leafless flower stalks.

Lady-slippers
Pink Lady-slipper and Yellow Lady-slipper

Cypripedium acaule and Cypripedium parviflorum
Orchid Family (Orchidaceae)

Lady-slipper orchids, especially the pink lady-slipper, are favorites of many wildflower lovers. The unusual form and blatant showiness of many lady-slipper species make them easily identifiable and hard to miss in our shady forests.

Habitat: Pink lady-slipper—acidic soils in dry (sometimes sandy) or wet deciduous or coniferous forests, especially under pines and hemlocks. Yellow lady-slipper—calcareous soils in deciduous and coniferous woods, in light to deep shade. May be common along roadsides in certain parts of its range (e.g., the Bruce Peninsula in Ontario).

Range: Pink lady-slipper—Newfoundland and Nova Scotia west to Alberta, south through the Great Lakes to Alabama and along the east coast to Georgia. Yellow lady-slipper—at least one of the three varieties of yellow lady-slipper is found throughout the continental United States (with the exception of Florida, Louisiana, and Nevada) and in all of Canada excluding the territory of Nunavut (based on the USDA Plants Database map).

As in other species of orchids, one of the three petals of lady-slipper orchids is greatly modified into a structure called the labellum. In lady-slippers the labellum takes the form of a large inflated pouch; this is particularly true of the two species discussed here. Since ancient times, observers have fancied the lady-slipper pouch to be a lady's shoe or slipper (fig. 232), and both the scientific and common names reflect this notion. *Cypripedium* is derived from the Greek *cypris* (the island of Cyprus) and *pedilon*, meaning "shoe." The lady-slipper is named for Aphrodite, the Greek goddess of love (Venus, in Roman mythology), who was said to have arisen fully grown from sea foam (*aphros* in Greek) off the island of Cyprus—thus, "the shoe of a Cyprian." The common names in English (lady-slipper), French (*sabot de Vénus*), German (*frauenschuh*), and Russian (*Marlin bashnachock*) all refer to the flower's resemblance to a shoe. The Russian name reflects the sixteenth-century belief that the shoe was that of Mary, mother of Jesus, and is a translation of the original common name, "slipper of *our* Lady." In the United States, lady-slippers are sometimes called "moccasin flowers," particularly the pink-flowered species. An Ojibway legend tells how

Orchid Family

Fig. 232. A pair of yellow lady-slipper "shoes."

lady-slipper orchids came to be—in short, they arose from the ground where droplets of blood fell from the feet of an Ojibway Indian maiden; her moccasins had worn to shreds as she ran a great distance to obtain a medicine that saved the lives of the members of her village. The flowers took the shape of her moccasins (fig. 233).

Two additional petals arise from behind the slipper pouch; they are usually long and sometimes twisted. The three sepals are arranged so that one is uppermost above the pouch, and the other two are fused beneath it (fig. 234). While the unusual form of lady-slipper flowers is thought to be beautiful by most observers, others may view this strange modification of the "normal" floral morphology as somewhat grotesque. In any case, as discussed below, the floral structure of lady-slippers is closely linked to its pollination.

The orchid family, with over 22,000 species in 880 genera, has the greatest number of species of any plant family other than the aster family. Orchids date back an estimated 100 million years or more and have had a long period during which to evolve, with most modifications having to do with floral morphology in response to various pollinators. Few orchids are hosts to caterpillars, nor are they fed upon by other insect life. This relative immunity to insect attack might be the result of the chemical warfare waged

with their predators during their long coexistence. In general, over time, plants produce compounds to deter herbivory, which is followed by development in the herbivores of methods to either detoxify the plant compounds or to sequester them without harm to themselves. In the case of orchids, it appears for now that they have succeeded in "outwitting" the herbivorous insects.

Worldwide there are about 50 species of *Cypripedium*, which are found throughout the Northern Hemisphere from north of the Arctic Circle to as far south as Central America in the New World and to the Himalayas in the Old World. In North America we are favored with 12 species of lady-slippers, 5 of them found in the northeastern United States and adjacent Canada (*C. acaule*, *C. parviflorum*, *C. reginae*, *C. arientinum*, and *C. candidum*) and another (*C. ken-*

Fig. 233. Pink lady-slippers are sometimes called moccasin flowers because of the resemblance of their modified lips to the shape of moccasins.

Fig. 234. Two pink lady-slipper flowers showing the strong venation in the inflated pink labellum (lip). The two brownish lateral petals are angled downward. The brown upper sepal arches forward over the lip, and the two brown lower sepals are fused behind the labellum.

produce flowers at the top of leaf-bearing stems. The scientific name of pink lady-slipper, *C. acaule* (Latin for "stemless"), signifies that there is not a true stem, but rather only a flower stalk. The leaves arise from the ground as tightly coiled cylinders (fig. 235). The labellum of pink lady-slipper differs from others of its genus as well; rather than having an oval opening on the top of the "slipper," into which Venus (or Mary) might insert her foot, pink lady-slipper pouches appear closed, with their inrolled edges concealing a vertical slit running the length of the pouch (fig. 236). The pouch is often strongly veined, and in some instances, rather than pink, it is white. This is especially true in New England, where (most notably in the White Mountains) almost 25% of the population may have white flowers (fig. 237). A further difference between pink lady-slippers and others is their ability to grow in dry, as well as wet, habitats. As John Burroughs wrote in *Riverby*, "Most of the floral ladies leave their slippers in swampy places in the woods; only the stemless one (*Cypripedium acaule*) leaves hers on dry ground before she reaches the swamp, commonly under evergreen trees, where the carpet of pine-needles will not hurt her feet" (p. 6).

Pink lady-slippers produce no nectar to reward visiting insects but instead lure them with color and scent—a form of deceptive advertising. Only insects large enough and strong enough to push their way through the slit in the labellum (in this case, bumblebees) can enter into the flower. *Bombus vagans*

tuckiense) that just makes it into parts of Virginia and Kentucky, the southernmost fringe of the Northeast as defined in this book. For the discussion here, I have chosen the two species most commonly encountered throughout much of the Northeast: *C. acaule* (pink lady-slipper) and *C. parviflorum* (yellow lady-slipper), species that are easily recognized even by those without a keen interest in wildflowers.

Pink Lady-slipper

Pink lady-slipper differs from others of its genus in that its two (rarely three) broad leaves arise directly from the rhizome, appearing at ground level along with a leafless flower stalk that bears just a single flower (fig. 231). All other *Cypripedium* species

Fig. 235. The tightly wrapped leaves of two plants of pink lady-slipper emerging in spring.

Orchid Family

Fig. 236. A vertical slit on the front of the pouch serves as the opening into the flowers of pink lady-slipper. Only a strong insect, such as a large bumblebee, can push its way into the opening.

(and perhaps also *B. borealis*) is the main species of bumblebee that has been documented as pollinating *C. acaule*. Once inside, the bee finds no nectar (some writers claim that the bees feed on the glandular hairs within the pouch, though this has not been documented) and then tries to exit. The inrolled, hairy margins of the labellum prevent the bee from exiting via the same place where it had entered. The trapped bee then crawls upward toward the light coming through two small openings at the top of the slipper (fig. 238). As the bee squeezes out of the pouch through one of these openings, it must push past the reproductive structures of the orchid. In orchids, both male and female parts are fused into a structure called the column (fig. 239). The back of the bee brushes

against the stiff projections on the sticky stigma at the apex of the column, and any pollen from another lady-slipper visited previously is scraped off. The bee then continues to push upward past one of the two masses of pollen, and its back is again covered with granular pollen. Bees are infrequent visitors to lady-slippers, so this scenario is not played out very often. In fact, only about 5% of pink lady-slipper flowers are pollinated in any particular year. Interestingly, lady-slippers growing in close proximity to cultivated blueberries (also an acid-loving plant) were found to be more successful in producing fruit, most likely due to increased bee traffic drawn by the nectar-producing flowers of the blueberries.

Experiments with hand pollination have resulted in a great increase in fruit and seed production as compared with controls, that is, plants growing in the wild that are reliant on natural means of pollination. In studies over a period of several years, fruit production ranged between 44 and 100% in the hand-pollinated flowers. However, it was found that plants that produced fruits and seeds over a period of two to three consecutive years became smaller in size and ceased flowering until they were able to build up enough stored reserves to flower again. The maximum number of consecutive years of fruiting was found to be four. The inability to flower may be a result of the smaller leaf area (and thus photosynthetic capability) as the plants decline in size. On the other hand, flowering in consecutive years but without the production of fruits does not seem to decrease the plant's ability to continue to flower in subsequent years. A pink lady-slipper may remain fresh in appearance for up to three weeks before senescing. However, if pollinated, the flowers wilt within five days.

The fruits are capsules that may remain on the plants throughout the winter and even into the next flowering season. They release their thousands of dustlike seeds through longitudinal slits in the fruits (fig. 240) when they are shaken by wind or by other external disturbances. The dustlike seeds can be carried long distances by the wind (the waterproof seeds may also float), but only a few are likely to land in a place suitable for a new plant to grow. The tiny seeds carry no food reserves, thus, shortly after landing, the seed must be invaded by a mycorrhizal fungus in order to survive. Although other genera of orchids

Fig. 237. The white form of pink lady-slipper, most often found in the northern part of its range. Photographed in the White Mountains of New Hampshire.

seedlings would perish without their fungal partners, which colonize the rhizomes of developing orchid plants. Although most orchid plants can photosynthesize when they are mature, they have the added nutritional insurance of the fungal colony (now colonizing its roots rather than its rhizome). Even after the lady-slipper is mature the fungus still benefits its host during periods of dormancy by serving as a source of carbon. Because of this mycorrhizal relationship, it is extremely difficult to transplant orchids from the wild. If the fungus is not present in the new setting, the orchid will not be able to obtain the necessary nutrients. Soil fungi may play an important role in determining the distribution of various orchid species because it has been shown that seeds of some orchid species germinate only near adults of the same species. Sadly, I have frequently found holes dug in the ground where lady-slippers once grew. The vandals who poach these lovely plants from our forests may enjoy at most a year or two of orchid beauty in their gardens before the plants begin to decline, and eventually die, due to "starvation."

may have several fungal partners, for the most part it appears that the genus *Cypripedium* develops mycorrhizal relationships only with a narrow range of species within the Tulasnellaceae fungal family. The fungus absorbs water and provides nutrients (sugars and nitrogen) for the developing plant; the orchid

The fortunate pink-lady-slipper seed that lands in a place suitable to grow (acidic soil of between 3.5 and 4.5 pH) and is rapidly invaded by the proper fungus will take an average of three years to produce leaves that appear above ground. It will be another three to five years before it has stored enough energy

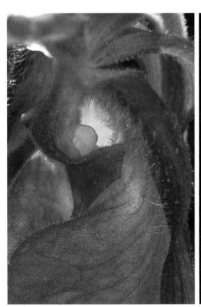

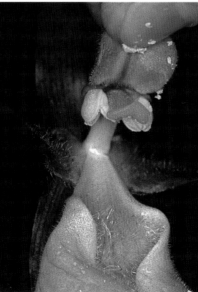

Fig. 238. (Left) The illuminated exit hole by which a trapped bee must leave. Note the hairiness of the interior of the flower and the large pollen mass.

Fig. 239. (Right) A pink lady-slipper with its upper sepal held up to reveal the reproductive structures: the column with its triangular stigmatic surface and the two masses of pollen. An exiting bee must first brush past the sticky stigma and then push its way out past one of the pollen masses.

Orchid Family

Fig. 240. A pink lady-slipper fruit showing the slits through which the dust-like seeds are dispersed.

to produce a flower, larger plants being more likely to flower. Barring disaster—poaching, herbivory, or other misfortune—pink lady-slippers are long-lived and may achieve an age in excess of 20 to 30 years if they survive the more vulnerable early years. Most orchids, lady-slippers included, do not flower every year and, as noted above, may not even appear above ground for a year or more. If a plant has decreased in size by 40%, it may begin a period of dormancy. During that period the plant may be totally dependent on the symbiotic relationship with its fungus. Once the orchid is capable of producing much of its own nutritional needs through photosynthesis, the fungus also benefits from the relationship by extracting nutrients from the orchid's roots. Recent studies have shown that the mycorrhizal fungi are often associated with nearby woody plants as well, thus enabling them to transfer nutrients from those plants to the dormant orchid's roots. The plants generally are dormant for only a year but sometimes may remain in a subterranean state for a year or two longer.

Pink lady-slipper was once considered an important medicinal plant by Native Americans and colonists alike. Peter Kalm reported in *Travels in North America*: "The moccasin flower (*Cypripedium*) which is found quite generally in the woods here, is said to

Fig. 241. A white-tailed deer browsing at a nature reserve. The overpopulation of deer in the Northeast has had a major negative impact on lady-slipper orchids.

Fig. 242. The open labellum of a yellow lady-slipper (*Cypripedium parviflorum* var. *pubescens*) is more accessible to bees than that of pink lady-slipper.

be rather good for women in the throes of childbirth. I refer to the decoction made of the root" (p. 611). Even today, some herbal remedies using sedative potions for treating nervous disorders call for the use of lady-slipper rhizomes. Little harvesting is currently being done for this purpose; most is to supply the illegal horticultural trade. It is perhaps poetic justice that those who pluck these orchids from the wild may suffer an irritating skin rash. The rash is caused by chemicals in the glandular hairs that cover the plants. One such chemical, a rare type of quinone named cypripedin, has been isolated from the European *Cypripedium* species and identified as the cause of this allergic reaction. The quinones are thought to protect the underground corms from fungal attacks by harmful parasitic fungi. Modern technology now allows orchids to be raised from seed and by cloning, resulting in the production of "legal" lady-slippers, grown by responsible growers. Since so much time must be invested in raising a lady-slipper to flowering stage, the price per plant

is relatively high—$35 and up. Plants being sold for less are likely to have been poached from the wild.

Another factor that has led to the decline of lady-slippers is their apparent tastiness to deer. In the past couple of decades, white-tailed deer have proliferated well beyond the carrying capacity of the remaining forested land in parts of the Northeast (fig. 241). The ultimate blame for this lies with human beings who have both overdeveloped the land and eliminated the predators that once kept the deer population in check. Beautiful though they are, deer are in large part responsible for the decline of our forest wildflowers and other native vegetation that once covered the forest floor. The nearly complete loss of our forest understory and the creatures that depend on it for food and cover are highly visible consequences of the browsing of too many deer.

Most states have long had an official state flower. More recently, a relatively small number of states have also declared an official state *wild*flower. New Hampshire adopted the pink lady-slipper as its state

Orchid Family

Fig. 243. Yellow lady-slipper plants showing the leafy stems.

wildflower in 1991, but its official state flower remains the lilac, a Eurasian plant introduced to the United States in the 1750s!

Yellow Lady-slipper

The yellow lady-slipper is rarely found in the acidic soils of New England, but it can be very common in the alkaline soils of upstate New York and the Midwest, particularly in the Great Lakes region. Unlike the slit pouch of pink lady-slipper, yellow lady-slipper has an oval opening atop its pouch, as is typical of most species of *Cypripedium* (fig. 242). It usually also has long, twisted lateral petals (fig. 230). Like most lady-slippers, its stem is leafy from its base to just below the flowers (fig. 243). The leaves are longitudinally pleated.

The scientific name of yellow lady-slipper has undergone several changes over the years as taxonomists worked to define its proper placement within the genus. At one time, our native yellow lady-slipper was thought to be a subspecies of the European yellow lady-slipper, *C. calceolus* (fig. 244). Based on technical distinctions, the current thinking is that the North American yellow lady-slipper is a separate species,

C. parviflorum, which occurs in three varieties. The most common of these is *C. parviflorum* var. *pubescens*, which is known as the large-flowered lady-slipper and is common throughout most of the range of the species. Its flowers are larger than those of the other two varieties discussed below and have longer lateral petals, which are colored yellow-green with red-purple speckling. It grows in rich mesic (not very wet or dry) forests, and the flowers have a somewhat rose-like or musty scent.

The other two varieties are small flowered: the first is a northern plant that, uncharacteristically, grows in acidic wetlands, such as white cedar swamps and riverine seeps. Termed var. *makasin*, its lateral petals are nearly entirely red-purple except near the base, and the flower has a very strong, sweet aroma. The other small-flowered variety, var. *parviflorum*, is a more southerly plant growing in mesic to dry-mesic deciduous forests. The red-purple lateral petals are not evenly suffused with color as in var. *makasin*; rather, the color is caused by very closely spaced dots and streaks. Like var. *pubescens*, the aroma of var. *parviflorum* is described as rose-like or musty. Other

Fig. 244. The European species of yellow lady-slipper, *Cypripedium calceolus*. Photographed in the Dolomites, Italy.

Europe has only one species of lady-slipper, the aforementioned yellow-flowered *C. calceolus* (fig. 244). This much-loved species is becoming less common in many parts of Europe, due in part to overcollecting. Although lady-slipper orchids are notoriously difficult to grow in the garden, they have been cultivated since at least 1731, when a record exists showing the European yellow lady-slipper being grown in the Chelsea Physic Garden. Both Americans and Europeans tend to love their lady-slippers to death! Indeed, in England, where *C. calceolus* was once widespread but never common, it was already noted to be declining in numbers by 1888. In the early 1900s, the plant was thought to be extirpated as a result of years of overcollecting (mainly by nurserymen) and habitat destruction. When a single flowering plant was rediscovered in 1930, a group of conservation-minded individuals (the Cypripedium Committee) took it upon themselves to guard this lone surviving English lady-slipper and to develop a conservation plan for the species. The location was kept secret and guarded. Ultimately, Sir Robert and Lady Sainsbury funded a project at Kew Gardens to develop new techniques that would allow the orchid to be reproduced in vitro and reintroduced into the wild. So far, several thousand plants have been propagated successfully and reintroduced into suitable habitats in the wild. However, the long-term rate of survival has been low due to a variety of factors: limited pollination in the wild, low fertilization success, changing habitat conditions, etc. Studies to learn more about ensuring long-lasting establishment in the wild are ongoing. A similar program exists in Switzerland.

Alexander von Humboldt, the noted German naturalist and explorer of the late eighteenth and early nineteenth centuries, wrote of seeing entire meadows full of *C. calceolus* in the Ural Mountains of Russia. We shall probably never see such a sight again, but with continued research and persistence, lady-slipper orchids may once again become, if not common, at least more numerous.

minor differences help to distinguish the two small-flowered varieties.

Yellow lady-slippers are slow to reach maturity. Like pink lady-slipper, the first leaves do not appear until the third year, and it may be another 7–13 years before the plant is mature enough to flower. Plants may become dormant, but rarely for more than a year. The flowers attract small carpenter bees (*Ceratina calcarata*) that serve as the pollinators. While visitation by bees is infrequent, it is not the only cause of low fruit and seed production. Unlike most other plants, for many orchids (including *Cypripedium*) there is a lag in time between the deposition of pollen on the stigma and the fertilization of the ovules, due to the fact that the ovules are not mature at the time that the flower is open for pollination. In *C. parviflorum* var. *pubescens* the pollen tube takes seven days to reach and penetrate an ovule.

Buttercup Family

Fig. 245. The subterranean tubers of lesser celandine. The tubers remain dormant over the summer, but their stored starch provides the nutrition needed to begin growth in late winter.

Fig. 246. A wetland forest floor carpeted with lesser celandine.

Lesser Celandine

Ranunculus ficaria
Buttercup Family (Ranunculaceae)

Lesser celandine is one of a confusing trio of plants found in the Northeast that bear the common name "celandine." (See the chapter on celandines to learn about the others.) These species serve as examples of the how the unregulated use of common names results in confusion about which species is being discussed. Not only are similar common names applied to unrelated species, but the common names for a single species often vary regionally as well.

Habitat: Wet soils, most commonly open forests and sometimes wet fields.

Range: Introduced from Europe and naturalized throughout most of the Northeast and also in the Pacific Northwest and British Columbia.

The adjective "lesser" is applied to this species of the buttercup family to differentiate it from another plant called celandine (sometimes also called greater celandine), a member of the poppy family. Both species are yellow-flowered, spring-blooming plants introduced from Europe, and both are in families that are included in the order Ranunculales. However, the similarity ends there.

Lesser celandine is in the same genus as the buttercups, *Ranunculus*, a name derived from the Latin *rana*, meaning "frog." It refers to the fact that many species of *Ranunculus* share with frogs a preference for wet habitats. The specific epithet, *ficaria*, is derived from *ficus* (the Latin word for "fig"), and another common name for this plant is "fig buttercup," reportedly from the resemblance of its tubers to a cluster of figs (fig. 245)—a stretch of the imagination to my eye.

Lesser celandine is a highly visible species in northeastern woodlands in early spring. The plants carpet wetlands with their lush vegetation and bright

Buttercup Family

Fig. 247. A flowering plant of marsh marigold (*Caltha palustris*), a member of the buttercup family that resembles lesser celandine but does not grow in masses and has colorful (yellow) sepals but no petals.

yellow flowers (fig. 246), commonly eliciting admiring comments from passersby. However, any such appreciation of lesser celandine's beauty must be tempered by the fact that this species is a serious pest, a highly invasive European alien that is replacing native spring ephemerals throughout wide swathes of wetland in the Northeast.

Lesser celandine may be mistaken for the native marsh marigold (*Caltha palustris*; fig. 247), another yellow-flowered member of the buttercup family that inhabits wetlands, but the two species differ in several ways. Marsh marigold never forms vast carpets of plants but instead grows scattered as individual (often robust) plants. The shiny leaves of lesser celandine are smaller than those of marsh marigold, and its

flowers have both sepals *and* petals (usually eight; fig. 248) compared with the (usually) six petallike sepals found in marsh marigold. The fruits differ as well: those of marsh marigold are follicles that open along one seam, while those of lesser celandine are indehiscent achenes.

Lesser celandine exists in two variants: the "normal" diploid form, known as subsp. *ficaria*, which reproduces sexually by seed; and a tetraploid subspecies (with double the number of chromosomes of subsp. *ficaria*) known as subsp. *bulbifer*, which reproduces almost entirely by tubercules (see below).

Fig. 248. The underside of a flower of lesser celandine showing the three greenish sepals and the eight green-tinged yellow petals.

Fig. 249. A close-up of tubercules in the leaf axils. The tubercules will remain on the ground after the plant has completely withered away and will begin to develop into new plantlets in late fall.

Fig. 250. (Above) A small plantlet of lesser celandine (the plantlet has been pulled from the ground and placed on a leaf for photography). Fig. 251. (Right) A plant of *Lilium bulbiferum* with bulbils visible in the axils of the upper leaves. Photographed in the Dolomites, Italy.

Relatively few species are capable of producing new plants from a part that detaches from the parent plant. However, such is the case with lesser celandine, which, in the tetraploid plants, produces in the axils of its leaves small, fleshy structures, called tubercules (fig. 249), which have the ability to grow into new plants (fig. 250). Although some authors refer to these structures as bulbils, their morphology differs from that of similarly named structures found in other plants (e.g., the bulbils of the European *Lilium bulbiferum*; fig. 251). Rather than consisting of modified leaves like the bulbils found in the leaf axils of *Lilium bulbiferum*, the tubercules of lesser celandine are storage organs, functioning in a manner similar to the plant's underground storage organs—to store starch. Anatomical studies have determined that the structures that develop from an axillary bud in the leaf axils of lesser celandine are, indeed, structurally the same as the large underground tubers. From one side of such an axillary bud a normal leaf develops, but from the other side a swelling is produced that becomes a tubercule bearing additional minute buds. To differentiate the axillary structures of lesser celandine from ordinary lilylike bulbils, I will refer to them as tubercules. (Please note that a similar term, "tubercle," is used to describe small projections that arise from an organ of a plant or animal).

Fig. 252. The tubercules of lesser celandine lie scattered on the ground in summer after the adult plants have senesced. The origin of these structures mystified European farmers of the past leading them to call them "potato rain."

Buttercup Family

Fig. 253. The leaves of lesser celandine turn yellow as the plants senesce in early summer.

When lesser celandine senesces in late spring, the tubercules lie scattered on the ground, sometimes in such great numbers that they have been termed "potato rain" for their resemblance to Lilliputian potatoes (fig. 252). The tiny tubercules remain dormant throughout the summer, but in autumn or early winter, a bud (or buds) on the tubercule begins to elongate and to develop adventitious roots that function for absorption. The bud then grows more rapidly and develops two or three scale leaves, followed by a foliage leaf (or two). In the following spring a different type of root is produced; it is thicker and becomes a new subterranean tuberous storage root. During its first year of growth, the young plantlet remains small, and its leaves senesce at the same time as those of the nearby mature plants (fig. 253). The new tuberous root of the young plant remains dormant during the summer. Plants that develop from tubercules rather than from seed mature more quickly and may even flower in the following spring. Apart from the lack of tubercules, ordinary diploid plants may be distinguished from the tubercule-producing tetraploids in that they have a more upright habit, produce more achenes, and show a greater tolerance for sunny habitats. Tubercule-bearing plants almost always grow in shaded conditions and rarely produce mature achenes. When they do, the tubercules outcompete the developing seeds for nutritional resources, and the seeds deteriorate without reaching maturity.

Lesser celandine's "potato rain" method of reproduction is responsible for its prolific spread. Research by E. M. Marsden-Jones on the reproductive capacity of lesser celandine showed that the tubercules had an 81% success rate of developing into new plants; thus, from 10 plants with an average of 24 tubercules each, 194 plants could result. The few viable seeds produced on tetraploid plants have a very low rate of germination—only 2%. In "normal" diploid plants, seeds have about a 70% germination rate.

The seedlings of lesser celandine are remarkable in the family (and highly unusual in dicots in general) in that they have only a single cotyledon, the characteristic that is both defining of monocots and the source of that term. The young "seed leaf" is much like the subsequent foliage leaves, but it has an indentation at its apex, so that it appears bilobed or heart shaped. The development of this unusual structure had long been debated by botanists—some arguing that the single cotyledon is the result of the fusion

Fig. 254. The glossy petals of lesser celandine and some other species of *Ranunculus* are said to be the shiniest in the plant world. The sheen comes from oil cells at the upper surface of the petal underlain by cells containing starch granules. Note the darker, matte surface of the pattern formed in the center of the flower by the bases of the petals; insects drink nectar from small depressions at the base of the petals.

Fig. 255. Leaves of lesser celandine marked with a reddish-brown splotch at the center.

of two normal cotyledons, others suggesting that the first true foliage leaf is, in fact, the second cotyledon, and still others claiming that there are no cotyledons, only foliage leaves. Anatomical studies completed by C. R. Metcalfe in 1936, in which he examined different stages of embryological development, showed clearly that the second cotyledon was aborted in the early stages of its development, leaving only a single cotyledon. A few other dicotyledonous plants share this unusual feature, among them *Cyclamen*, some species of butterwort (*Pinguicula*), and members of several genera of the carrot family (Apiaceae).

Also setting lesser celandine apart from most plants (other than certain species of buttercup) is the glossiness of its petals, which are said to be the shiniest in the plant kingdom (fig. 254). Not all species of *Ranunculus* share this feature, but studies of those that do have found an oily solution containing yellow pigment in the cells at the upper surface of the petal. Just below that surface layer are cells containing starch, an unusual feature in petals that is found only in some species of Ranunculaceae and that is probably responsible for providing the depth of color to the oil in the cells above. It is virtually certain that the color and sheen are important features in attracting insects—mostly bees and beetles—that sip nectar from scale-covered depressions at the base of the petals. In looking at the petals, it will be noted that the inner portion of each petal is not as shiny or as brightly colored as the outer portion. Testing for starch with iodine indicates that the duller, inner portion does not contain starch. Because this section of

the petal is partially covered by the stamens, it need not be as attractive as the more visible portion.

The leaves of this species are interesting as well. Many of them are marked to some degree with a dark reddish blotch in the middle of the upper surface (fig. 255); this may occur in either of the subspecies, subsp. *ficaria* or subsp. *bulbifer*. Livestock rarely browse the leaves of lesser celandine due to their acrid taste and the presence of a compound called protoanemonin, which causes blistering of the grazer's mouth. It can also cause a skin rash on the hands of people who come in contact with the plant. A few caterpillars are known to feed on lesser celandine in its native range, and it is subject to attack by different species of fungi, principally rusts.

A search of the Internet for *Ranunculus ficaria* yields several results, with most of the "top" several falling into the categories of medicinal or cosmetic use. Claims are made for the effectiveness of products containing extracts of the "roots" of ficaria in the treatment of hemorrhoids, sun-damaged skin, and redness of the skin, including rosacea. Analysis of root decoctions have shown that the saponins contained therein have vasoconstrictive properties, which could account for the benefits claimed from their use to reduce redness. Some "beauty" creams that contain ficaria extract sell for as much as $92 an ounce. To some, perhaps the beauty of lesser celandine flowers (fig. 256) is surpassed by the promise of a remedy found within its tubers.

Fig. 256. A beautiful display of lesser celandine, an invasive alien species that is responsible for eliminating many of our native wildflowers in wetland habitats.

Broomrape Family

Fig. 257. A young inflorescence of lousewort with its lower flowers freshly opened. Early in the season, some plants have leaves with red-purple coloration as seen in this photo.

Fig. 258. A queen bumblebee entering a flower of lousewort. The flower's stigma (the tiny white structure seen here) will pass along the crevice between the bee's head and thorax and pick up any pollen that has accumulated there.

Lousewort

Pedicularis canadensis
Broomrape Family (Orobanchaceae;
formerly Scrophulariaceae; see discussion in the
chapter on blue-eyed Mary)

Unlike the two other species of the broomrape family included in this book (one-flowered cancer-root and squawroot), lousewort's green leaves contain chlorophyll, and the plants are capable of producing their own carbohydrates through the process of photosynthesis. However, lousewort plants must still parasitize the roots of other plants in order to secure necessary water and minerals because they do not have adequate root hairs to perform this function. Such partially parasitic plants are called hemiparasites.

Habitat: Semiopen woodland areas on sandy or loamy soil, often on slopes.

Range: All of the eastern United States, extending as far west as New Mexico, and much of eastern Canada (New Brunswick, Quebec, Ontario, and Manitoba).

"Lousewort"—what an odd name for such an attractive flower! Its origin dates back to the centuries-old belief that sheep and other livestock that grazed on lousewort plants became infested with lice. Linnaeus based his naming of the genus on this bit of ancient folklore, calling it *Pedicularis* (from the Latin *pediculus*, meaning "louse"). Rather than *causing* infestations of blood-sucking parasites, lousewort is *itself* a parasite, or at least partially so. Although green-leaved and photosynthetic, lousewort (sometimes called Canadian lousewort or forest lousewort) forms subterranean attachments to the roots of other species, from which it derives water and essential nutrients. Far from being specific to one host, lousewort has been documented as parasitizing at least 80 different species distributed across nearly three dozen families of monocots and dicots. In fact, lousewort is so catholic in its tastes that it has even been found parasitizing other parasites (e.g., *Melampyrum*, or cow-wheat).

Pedicularis is a large genus, numbering about 600 species, the great majority of which are found in mountainous regions of south and eastern Asia; China alone harbors some 350 species. Only one lousewort species extends the range of the genus into the Southern Hemisphere: *P. incurva*, an Andean native of Ecuador and Colombia. Most North American species are found in the western part of the United States and Canada, with only three indigenous to the Northeast. The most common and widespread is *P. canadensis*, found in all of the eastern United States and as far

Broomrape Family

Fig. 259. Typical habitat for many species of *Pedicularis*—a sunny, wet meadow. This species is *Pedicularis verticillata*. Photographed in Italy.

west as the Dakotas, Colorado, and New Mexico, as well as in the Canadian provinces of New Brunswick, Quebec, Ontario, and Manitoba. Forest lousewort is less well known by the more attractive name wood-betony, but that name is more properly applied to the genus *Stachys* in the mint family. It is the most shade-tolerant member of the genus, growing in poor, often sandy, soil in semiopen forest. Its rhizomes persist in the soil even in the more dense shade that results when the canopy closes.

Lousewort blooms in early spring (late April to early May in southern New York and Connecticut), at a time when its pollinators (bumblebee queens) are actively establishing their annual colonies. The overwintering queens emerge from their winter tor-por having already been fertilized during the previous summer. The flowers of *P. canadensis* produce copious amounts of nectar throughout their bloom-ing period, enticing queen bees to visit the flowers frequently to gather nectar to provision honey pots in their new colonies. The queens also consume louse-wort pollen in preparation for egg laying and subsequently gather it to provide a protein-rich food for their larvae. Thus, bees noted to be carrying pollen

in the "baskets" (corbiculae) on their hind legs may be presumed to have already deposited their eggs in underground brood cells.

Lousewort is such an important source of nectar for queen bees that it has been documented as inadvertently affecting the reproductive success of an unrelated, co-blooming species: Mayapple. Mayapple flowers produce no nectar and attract few insect visitors. It is a self-compatible species capable of producing fruit without the services of a pollinator. However, those flowers that *are* visited by insects (bumblebees in particular) achieve greater success in fruit production. Mayapple colonies located within 25 meters of a population of lousewort receive many more visits from bumblebees than colonies located more distant from lousewort populations. The higher visitation rate to Mayapple may be attributed to the larger number of bumblebees attracted to the nectar-rich flowers of the nearby lousewort. Invariably, some bees investigate the flowers of the Mayapple and, in so doing, effect pollination.

Another northeastern species, swamp lousewort (*P. lanceolata*), also has a broad range, but one that is not as extensive as that of *P. canadensis*. In addition, its habitat requirements are much more restrictive. It requires a sunny exposure and, as its common name suggests, grows in wet (preferably calcareous) areas. Such damp, open habitat is required by many western North American and European species of *Pedicularis* (fig. 259); *P. canadensis* is considered unusual in the genus for its forest habitat preference. Swamp lousewort differs from lousewort in that its stems are

Fig. 260. The sparsely flowered inflorescence of *P. lanceolata* (swamp lousewort). In contrast *to P. canadensis*, the creamy yellow flowers lack two small projections at the tip of the upper lip, the leaves are opposite, and the stem is less villous (hairs are longer and not as dense as those of *P. canadensis*).

Fig. 261. (Left) A close-up of the flowers of *P. canadensis*. Note the two projections on the upper lip and the enclosed stamens visible through the translucent upper lip of the middle flower.

Fig. 262. (Right) An inflorescence of *P. canadensis* with flowers that lack any red-purple coloration in the upper lip. Note how the lower flowers are wilted while the upper ones are still fresh on the elongating inflorescence. Also note the alternate leaves in contrast to the opposite ones of swamp lousewort in figure 260 (the uppermost leaves may be subopposite).

hairless or only slightly hairy (compared with the densely villous stems of lousewort), and its leaves are opposite rather than alternate on the stem (fig. 260). The flowers of swamp lousewort are borne on a less dense inflorescence and are a pale creamy yellow; they also lack the two small projections found on the tip of the upper lip of lousewort (fig. 261). Lastly, swamp lousewort blooms later in the year, from late summer into fall, and is pollinated mostly by worker bumblebees foraging for pollen. The species is considered endangered in several northeastern states and is of special concern in Connecticut.

Pedicularis furbishiae may be the best known of the three northeastern species, despite its extremely limited distribution. Known as Furbish lousewort, this rare, small, and unremarkable yellow-flowered plant played a central role during the mid-1970s in a well-publicized test of the newly enacted Endangered

Species Act, ultimately preventing the construction of a $1.2-billion-dollar dam that would almost certainly have resulted in the extinction of this species. Furbish lousewort was discovered in 1880 by Miss Kate Furbish, who, while on a botanical outing along the St. John River in Maine, recognized it as something unique. Two years later, the species was described as new and was named in her honor. It then languished in obscurity for several decades, during which time it was rarely seen or collected. In 1976, almost 30 years after its last documented collection, Furbish lousewort was rediscovered in the St. John region during an environmental impact survey in conjunction with a proposal put forth by the U.S. Army Corps of Engineers to build a major hydroelectric dam that would change the St. John River forever. The St. John is unusual for North American rivers in that it flows north. Thus, its headwaters, being further south, melt

Fig. 263. (Left) A lousewort inflorescence photographed from above to show the whorled arrangement of the flowers with their asymmetrically oriented galeas. Note the leafy bracts in the still expanding inflorescence.

Fig. 264. (Right) An apical view of an inflorescence of the European *Pedicularis verticillata*, a prime example of the spiral arrangement of the flowers on the inflorescence. Photographed in Spain.

Broomrape Family

Fig. 265. (Left) A lousewort flower that has had a portion of the galea (upper lip) removed to show the arrangement of the style and stamens within the upper lip. Note the hairiness of the bracts and the hairs on the filaments of the stamens. **Fig. 266.** (Right) A frontal view of a lousewort flower showing the small opening through which the style is exserted from the twisted galea; pollen also falls through this opening when a bee visits the flower. The galea is fused beneath this opening but is open along the majority of the lower edge. The side lobes of the lower lip of this flower are not yet fully spread.

earlier than the downstream portions of the river. As the meltwater encounters ice dams downstream (i.e., further north), the impounded water may reach levels as much as 20 feet higher than normal. When the ice dams give way, the water rushes downstream, picks up chunks of ice, and scours vegetation from the steep riverbanks. Species that are not able to recolonize the shoreline each year are unable to survive. Furbish lousewort is a species adapted to these harsh environmental conditions and lives no place other than in a 10-foot-wide swath along the banks of the St. John on the border between Maine and New Brunswick, Canada. The species is thought to have survived the last glacial period in this geographically limited region.

Pedicularis canadensis is a clonal species, an obligate parasite that is capable of causing a decrease in size of some (but not all) of its hosts. Growing among plants of shorter stature results in the lousewort being exposed to more light, a condition that benefits the parasite by enabling increased transpiration. This, in turn, allows the parasite to draw greater amounts of water and nutrients from the host. Further augmenting the transpiration rate, the stomates of members of the Orobanchaceae remain open continuously, rather than having the more usual pattern of opening during the day and closing at night. Movement of substances between parasite and host is not exclusively unidirectional. Alkaloids and glucosides move from parasite to host, and chemical compounds known to originate

in the host are found in the parasite. This feature, as we shall see later, is important when ethnobotanical uses of the plant are contemplated.

Pedicularis canadensis flowers are interspersed with leafy bracts arranged spirally on a dense, hairy inflorescence. Flowering begins at the bottom of the inflorescence and works its way up the elongating inflorescence (fig. 262). The upper lip of each flower is offset from center, a pattern that may be best appreciated when looking down on the inflorescence (fig. 263). This striking, whorled arrangement of *Pedicularis* species is particularly pronounced in a European species, aptly named *P. verticillata* (fig. 264).

The flowers of lousewort are basically yellow, but in many cases the upper lip, called the galea, is reddish or purplish in color (fig. 257). Bees are known to be attracted to yellow but are "blind" to red. Lousewort flowers with red coloration occasionally attract ruby-throated hummingbirds to sip hidden nectar from their tubular corollas; other species of *Pedicularis* (e.g., the pink-flowered western species, *P. densiflora*) are pollinated primarily by hummingbirds. The structure of lousewort flowers facilitates pollination by bumblebees. The lower lip provides a landing platform, while the narrow upper lip contains the reproductive structures tightly compressed within its tip (figs. 261, 265). When a bee lands on the lower lip and pushes its head into the flower, the two lips are forced open, and the bee's back contacts the stigma, which protrudes through a small opening in the tip of the galea (fig. 266). The action of the bee causes pollen to sprinkle down onto its back through the same opening. Bees use their legs to groom excess pollen from their bodies, but the pollen that falls into the groove separating the bee's head from its back cannot be reached by the bee's grooming efforts. This is precisely the area that is contacted by the protruding stigma as the bee enters a subsequent flower (fig. 258), thus effecting pollination. The fruits mature in six to eight weeks. The ripe capsules split open, and when the long, horizontally oriented lower lip is struck by a raindrop (fig. 267), the tiny seeds (1,000 seeds weigh only 0.45 grams) are catapulted out—a method of raindrop dispersal that is slightly different from that of miterwort. Lousewort inflorescences have an average of 10–25 flowers and up to 50–60 seeds per capsule; thus, each stalk could potentially produce over 1,500 seeds! Lousewort also reproduces vegetatively from underground rhizomes, but reproduction by seed is important in that it promotes genetic diversity in the population.

An interesting western member of the genus, *P. groenlandica*, also has a very specific relationship with its pollinators: bumblebees of the worker caste. Like other louseworts, the upper lip of *P. groenlandica* is derived from two fused petal lobes, but in this case the lobes have united in a unique way, forming a narrow, curved shape, reminiscent of an elephant's trunk (albeit a small—and pink!—one). The broad, flaring lobes of the lower lip enhance this effect by mimicking the elephant's ears, inspiring the common name of the plant: elephant head (fig. 268). When a worker bee lands on

the flower, the "trunk" wraps around the bee's abdomen ensuring that the stigma will contact precisely the spot on the bee where pollen accumulates. Pollen is released from the anthers when they are subjected to a special type of high-frequency vibration of the bees' wings, a process called buzz pollination. The bee gleans the pollen that falls onto the lower lip of the flower and puts it into its corbiculae (pollen baskets). The lower surface of the bee becomes dusted with pollen during this process on precisely the area that will be contacted by the stigma of a subsequently visited flower. Elephant head is found in most of our western states, throughout most of Canada, and, as its epithet indicates, in Greenland. It was one of the plants collected by Meriwether Lewis on the Lewis and Clark expedition.

Surely a contender for "cutest" flower on the continent, elephant head is also well known in the field of alternative medicine for its psychoactive and medicinal properties. Claims are made that all species of *Pedicularis* possess such properties and have been utilized as tranquilizers, sedatives, and muscle relaxants. Some Native Americans make a tea of *Pedicularis* to treat coughs, and others smoke the flowers for their narcotic effect. As mentioned earlier, the chemical compounds in parasitic plants can vary according to the species of host parasitized. For example, *Pedicularis* growing on *Senecio* (ragwort) will contain senecio alkaloids from the host and thus be toxic. This is an import aspect to consider for those who might risk experimentation with botanical medicinals. Host-produced toxins taken up by the parasite may render the parasite deadly!

Fig. 267. (Left) A fruiting stalk of lousewort. The seeds are catapulted away from the plant when raindrops hit the protruding lower lip of the fruit.

Fig. 268. (Right) Part of an inflorescence of elephant head (*Pedicularis groenlandica*), a species native to the western United States, much of Canada, and Greenland. Note the strong resemblance of the flowers to the heads of small, pink elephants.

Barberry Family

Fig. 269. A flowering Mayapple plant seen from below. Note the two leaves on this reproductive plant.

Fig. 270. A close-up of a Mayapple flower showing the globose ovary topped by the large stigma and surrounded by 12 stamens. Note that the anthers dehisce (open) longitudinally along their margins.

Mayapple

Podophyllum peltatum
Barberry Family (Berberidaceae)

Mayapple blooms in May throughout most of its range, but the fruit ("apple") doesn't ripen until August. The plant is an important source of compounds used in modern medicine.

Habitat: Moist, preferably open woods.

Range: Quebec to Minnesota, south to Florida and Texas.

I n late April small, green umbrellas poke from the ground in moist woodlands (fig. 271). These are the still furled leaves of Mayapple, a plant that grows in large colonies that are actually clones of genetically identical ramets (individual stems) arising from branching underground rhizomes. If the "umbrella" is unfortunate enough to emerge from the soil just beneath a dead leaf with a hole in it, it may carry that leaf upward as it grows and then remain imprisoned in its stranglehold (fig. 272). As the Mayapple leaves unfurl (fig. 273; a single one on juvenile plants and two on mature plants), they expand to a width of 8 to 10 inches. Only plants with two leaves are reproductive, producing a single flower at the divergence of the leaf stalk (fig. 269).

Fig. 271. The leaves of Mayapple emerge from the ground like furled green umbrellas.

133

Barberry Family

Fig. 272. (Left) This Mayapple plant arose from the ground beneath a fallen leaf that had a hole in it. The leaf was carried upward by the growing Mayapple plant, which is now prevented from unfurling its own leaf by the dead leaf.

Fig. 273. (Right) A Mayapple leaf beginning to expand.

The flowers are lovely but are often missed by passersby because they are hidden beneath the large, umbrella-like leaves. The sepals occur in two whorls of three, each whorl with different-sized sepals that are quickly shed, sometimes even before the bud opens (fig. 274). There are six to nine broad, white petals. Most species of *Podophyllum* have 6 stamens, but in *P. peltatum* there may be 12 to 18 broad stamens that dehisce by vertical slits along their outer margins (fig. 270). The large green ovary is round with a prominent white stigma at its apex. It develops into an oval yellow fruit when mature. Mayapple flowers are usually self-incompatible, that is they cannot be successfully fertilized with their own pollen, and they have few insect visitors; thus, relatively few plants produce fruit. Of the various types of bees that have been observed collecting pollen, bumblebees are the most likely to be effective pollinators because they move from clone to clone. Introduced honeybees, the second most common visitors, are more likely to visit flowers within only a single clone, essentially transporting self-pollen from one genetically identical flower to another, which will not result in the production of a fruit. Rarely, in some colonies, there are plants that *are* self-compatible, and a fruit will develop as a result of pollen having fallen from the anthers onto the stigma of the same flower. Seed production by self-pollination can be advantageous for a plant that receives few visits from potential pollinators, and perhaps this trait might eventually become more prevalent in the species.

Fig. 274. (Left) The six sepals of this Mayapple flower bud are of two sizes. The larger ones are about to fall off.

Fig. 275. (Right) The lovely pink flower and magenta stigma of *Podophyllum peltatum* forma *deamii*, native to a restricted area of the Midwest.

Fig. 276. (Left) Mayapple spreads by underground rhizomes, forming dense clonal stands that make an attractive ground cover from spring until midsummer. **Fig. 277.** (Right) A Mayapple leaf with a striking mottled red and green pattern.

Fig. 278. (Left) Flowers of *Podophyllum mairei*, which is native to China. **Fig. 279.** (Right) Mayapple shoots just beginning to emerge in early spring.

A form of Mayapple with pale-pink flowers and maroon-purple fruits (fig. 275) is found in a limited part of the species' range. Originally collected from Indiana, the pink-flowered form, *P. peltatum* forma *deamii*, has been found growing from Pennsylvania to Missouri. Additional forms include *P. peltatum* f. *biltmoreanum*, with orange fruit; *P. peltatum* f. *callicarpum*, with pink fruit; and *P. peltatum* f. *polycarpum*, with multilobed fruit. With its broad, long-lasting leaves and colonial habit, Mayapple makes an attractive ground cover in semishaded areas with moist soils (fig. 276); this is particularly true of clones having plants with an attractive mottled red and green pattern (fig. 277). Some of the Asian species also have attractive leaves and/or flowers (fig. 278), making them desirable for garden use.

If you look closely at the leaves in a colony of Mayapple, you will notice that the shape of the leaf on a single-leaved plant differs from that of the leaves on two-leaved plants. When the bud for the current year's growth was being formed during the previous summer, it had already been "programmed" to be either a one- or a two-leaved plant in the following year, a "decision" most likely based on the amount of carbohydrate stored in the plant's underground rhizome. Come spring, these buds expand, appearing first as small, pointed, white shoots breaking through the ground (fig. 279). The single-leaved plants have leaf blades attached to their petioles (leaf stalks) at a point on the center of the blade (fig. 277), an arrangement referred to as peltate. Plants destined to be two-leaved, and thus reproductive, have leaf blades that are

Barberry Family

Fig. 280. A two-leaved Mayapple plant with a flower bud at the junction of the two leaves. Note that the leaves are less lobed on the sides that are closest to the bud, unlike the more symmetrical single-leaved plant shown in figure 277.

attached at a point closer to their margins. This modification results in the flower bud having enough space to develop without impeding on, or being impeded upon by, leaf expansion (fig. 280).

While examining the leaves, you may also notice that some have yellow-orange spots on the leaf surface, which is evidence that a fungus has infected the leaf. The two main species of fungi that affect *P. peltatum*

are *Septotinia podophyllina*, which attacks new leaves, and *Puccinia podophylli*, a rust that forms orange pustules on leaves of differing ages (figs. 281, 282, 283). Unlike the *Puccinia* rust that attacks spring beauty, *P. podophylli* does not need an alternate host and thus can move more easily from one Mayapple plant to another. It is particularly lethal to seedlings.

The seedlings are slow to mature, taking from four to five years to develop the horizontal rhizome from which will arise the aerial parts of the plant and the contractile roots that anchor the plant in the ground (fig. 284). Only the youngest node on a rhizome produces a shoot, which is enclosed in protective scalelike leaves called cataphylls. The cataphylls often persist at the base of the aerial stem as it emerges in spring (fig. 285). Most reproduction is asexual—from proliferation of the underground rhizomes, which are only two to three inches below the soil surface. Thus, a large patch of Mayapple is, in fact, genetically, a single plant that has spread outward from one original plant over a period of several decades.

Podophyllum is considered to be an anomalous dicot, like some members of other primitive families (e.g., Ranunculaceae and Papaveraceae). Although Mayapple is a dicotyledonous plant, the vascular tissue

Fig. 281. (Left) Leaves of *Podophyllum peltatum* infected with the fungal rust, *Puccinia podophylli* that covers the underside of a leaf and is growing along its margin.

Fig. 282. (Upper right) The orange pustules are not visible on the upper surface of the leaf; only yellow discoloration indicates their presence.

Fig. 283. (Lower right) Unlike smuts, the rust affects only the leaves and does not become systemic in the plant. The leaves emerge without rust the following spring, but may be affected again if spores remain in the area.

Fig. 284. The base of a Mayapple stem with the soil cleared away to show the rhizomes and roots.

Fig. 285. Persistent cataphylls, which once covered an underground bud, remain on the base of the newly emerged stem of Mayapple.

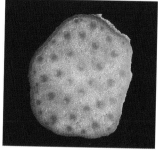

Fig. 286. A cross-section of a stem of Mayapple showing the arrangement of the vascular bundles scattered throughout the pith as seen through a microscope at 10x power.

in its stems has certain characteristics that resemble the vascular plan of monocots. In most dicots, the vascular tissue flanks a cambium layer that forms a ring around the circumference of the stem. In monocots, the vascular tissue is scattered in discrete bundles throughout the stem, and there is no cambium. By contrast, in *Podophyllum*, although vascular tissue bundles are scattered throughout the stem, each bundle is sheathed in its own cambium (fig. 286).

The name given to the plant by Linnaeus in *Species Plantarum* was meant to be descriptive of the leaves: *podos*, which is Greek for "foot," and *phyllon*, from the Greek for "leaf" (because of its resemblance to the webbed foot of an aquatic bird). Prior to the acceptance of Linnaeus's nomenclatural system, the plant had been given the name *Anapodophyllum canadense*, meaning "duck-foot-leaf from Canada" (actually a somewhat more precise description), by Mark Catesby, an English naturalist who collected plants and animals in eastern North America during the first half of the eighteenth century. Linnaeus considered Catesby's name for the plant too long and shortened the genus to *Podophyllum*. He also changed the species name to *peltatum* (from the Latin *peltatus*, "shield-shaped"), thereby further describing the leaf. At the same time, Linnaeus named what he viewed to be another species of *Podophyllum*, *P. diphyllum*. Thirty-nine years later, this species was determined not to belong in the genus *Podophyllum* after all and was renamed by Benjamin Barton as a new genus, *Jeffersonia* (see fig. 424).

Mayapple caught the attention of early explorers, including Captain John Smith, who compared the fruit to a lemon, and Samuel de Champlain, who wrote that the Huron Indians ate the fruit (a two-inch-diameter yellow berry) of the plant, the taste of which de Champlain compared to that of a fig. By the mid-1600s, the plant was already being grown in England and France.

Not only do *people* enjoy the ripe fruit (to my mind, the taste is most reminiscent of a tropical fruit, the cashew apple, or perhaps a litchi), but they are also relished by box turtles (*Terrapene carolina*; fig. 287). I always wondered how the turtles could reach the fruits, which are borne a foot or so above the ground. However, when observing the plants in August, I noticed that many of them, weighed down by the ripening fruit, were nearly prone on the ground (fig. 288). Box turtles are the only documented seed dispersers, but it may be assumed that other animals—bears, raccoons, or skunks—could take advantage of this easily accessible treat. Seeds that have passed

Barberry Family

Fig. 287. A close-up view of a box turtle (*Terrapene carolina*), the principal disperser of Mayapple seeds.

through the digestive system of a turtle have been shown to be almost twice as successful in germinating when compared with those that have not passed through the alimentary tract of a turtle (85.5% compared with 45%). Turtles can cover a distance of 40–60 meters a day, and, because the seeds spend an average of seven days in the turtle's gut, they can be carried some distance from the plant before being excreted; dispersal distances of up to 215 meters have been documented.

When ripe, the fruits produce a strong "fruity" aroma discernable from several feet away. Fruits usually have only a few fully developed wedge-shaped seeds (but potentially up to 50) surrounded by fleshy arils (fig. 289). Although the flesh of the ripe fruit of

Mayapple is described in many published references as edible, and even as delicious, I would recommend caution in consuming them. All other parts of the plant—seeds, leaves, rhizomes, and even the *unripe* fruit—are extremely poisonous. The toxicity of the unripe fruit protects it from being eaten before the seeds are mature and ready for dispersal.

Despite the toxicity of the leaves, at least two caterpillars have evolved to be able to consume the toxic leaves without harm to themselves: the green larva of a tortricid moth, *Clepsis melaleucana*, and the brightly colored larva of the nymphalid butterfly known as the variegated fritillary, *Euptoieta claudia*.

Native Americans utilized almost all of the plants around them in some way, and Mayapple was no

Fig. 288. (Left) A mature-fruited Mayapple plant that has fallen over, allowing the fruit to touch the ground, where it is readily accessible to turtles. **Fig. 289.** (Right) A ripe Mayapple fruit that has been cut open to show the wedge-shaped seeds.

Fig. 290. Leaves of a Mayapple plant that has been browsed by deer.

exception. Mayapple was valued for its medicinal properties, primarily as an emetic and for treating cases of intestinal worms. As with most medications, the dosage is important; the toxicity of the chemicals in *Podophyllum* is such that Native Americans chose it as an effective means of committing suicide. The plant was later—in my lifetime—one of the principal ingredients in a patent medicine known as Carter's Little Liver Pills (still sold, but with the word "Liver" removed from the name, because the pills showed no beneficial effect upon the liver). Unlike many other herbal remedies that have undergone scientific investigation for efficacy and failed, Mayapple is a species that has been confirmed to have true medicinal value in modern pharmacology. The active phytochemical in Mayapple is podophyllotoxin, from which are derived two semisynthetic drugs, etoposide and teniposide, both important in treating several types of cancer. The drugs are produced under a number of trade names, the best known of which, Vespesid (etoposide), is marketed by Bristol-Myers Squibb. In particular, etoposide has been highly effective in treating cases of small-cell lung cancer and testicular cancer. Lance Armstrong, perhaps the best-known survivor of testicular cancer, is one of the success stories of this plant-derived drug. Other cancers treated with etoposide include melanoma, Kaposi's sarcoma, and lymphomas. Teniposide (Vumon; VM-26) is used less often, mainly in

the treatment of lymphomas. Both drugs work by blocking DNA replication in dividing cells. In addition, podophyllin resin and podofilox, both from the rhizomes of Mayapple, are used effectively in treating genital warts, which are benign skin lesions caused by the human papillomavirus, but which, untreated, may undergo cancerous transformation. The efficacy of the drugs lies in their ability to cause cell death during mitosis.

Most podophyllotoxin used in the pharmaceutical trade today comes from an Asian species, *Podophyllum emodi*, which is indigenous to the Himalayas. Harvesting the underground rhizomes of this species to obtain the drug precursor results in the destruction of the plants, and overharvesting of the species to satisfy the demand for podophyllotoxin has led to its being declared endangered in its native range. The threat of losing this valuable resource has spurred the investigation of other species in the genus, including the North American *P. peltatum*, as possible alternative sources. While the level of podophyllotoxin found in *P. peltatum* is only about half that of *P. emodi*, it is found in all parts of the plant, including the leaves. Thus, the potential exists for *P. peltatum* to be grown and harvested in a sustainable way. If only the leaves of Mayapple were harvested, leaving the perennial rhizomes in the soil to produce another crop of leaves the following year, the harvesting would not destroy the plants. To allow the plant to photosynthesize and replenish its food stores for continued growth, the leaves would have to be harvested toward the end of the growing season. The amount of podophyllotoxin in Mayapple varies among populations, and studies are underway to select clones with high levels of this chemical for cultivation. In observing the Mayapple plants in my backwoods, I find that they are not generally eaten by deer until the end of the season (August), when both the fruit and some of the leaves can disappear overnight (the fruit also could have been eaten by other animals, but the leaves show distinct evidence of browsing by deer; fig. 290). This makes me wonder if the plants translocate the chemicals from the leaves to the rhizomes before becoming dormant during the fall and winter months. If this were the case, commercial harvesting of the leaves would have to be accomplished prior to this relocation of the valuable chemicals.

Saxifrage Family

Fig. 291. A dense patch of miterwort in an Adirondack forest growing with tall white violet.

Fig. 292. Two flowering stalks of miterwort. Fruits that develop from the flowers on the leaning stalk must orient themselves upward prior to seed maturity.

Miterwort

Mitella diphylla
Saxifrage Family (Saxifragaceae)

Miterwort (also known as bishop's-cap) is named for the resemblance of its two-peaked fruits to the hats (known as miters) worn by bishops of the Roman Catholic Church. The fruits look more like an earlier version of the miter that was shorter than those worn today. Similarly, the scientific name of the genus is from the Latin *mitra*, which, in turn, is derived from the Greek for "headdress" or "turban," and *-ella*, the Latin diminutive ending, thus "little headdress." "Wort" is an Old English word derived from *wyrt*, meaning "plant."

Habitat: Rich woods, especially slopes, with alkaline soil.

Range: Most of the eastern half of the United States except for Maine, Florida, and Louisiana; also in Quebec and Ontario.

As presently considered, the genus *Mitella* has two centers of diversity: the Pacific Northwest of the United States and eastern Asia. One species,

Mitella nuda, has a circumboreal distribution, occurring in the northern part of the range covered by this book as well as in Japan and Russian Siberia. However, the species composition of the genus is likely to change once molecular research has been conducted. At various times in the past, some species currently included in *Mitella* have been placed in different genera, and since there are no characteristics that unify the 20 or so species of *Mitella*, the genus is likely to be split into segregate genera again. The first species of *Mitella* to be described (by Linnaeus in 1753) was *M. diphylla*, from the eastern United States Thus, if the genus were to be split, the eastern North American *M. diphylla* would remain as a species of *Mitella*, most likely joined by the only other species occurring in the Northeast: *Mitella nuda* (naked miterwort). The two species, although quite different in appearance and habitat, are the only two in the genus that have 10 stamens—as compared with 5 in the remaining species of the genus. They also share similar chemistry.

Miterwort is one of my (many) favorite wildflower species. Easily dismissed as just a small plant with little white flowers growing on the dark forest floor

141

Saxifrage Family

Fig. 293. Miterwort plants scattered on the forest floor. Their tiny flowers often go unnoticed.

(fig. 293), it demands closer attention. If you take the time to kneel down to examine the flowers with a magnifying lens, you are sure to be delighted by their delicate beauty. In overall form, the flower of miterwort resembles a five-pointed snowflake (fig. 294). There are between 5 and 20 snowflake flowers on each flower stalk. Each flower is cuplike, with five tiny (two-millimeter long) petals arising from the rim of the cup—thus the need for a hand lens. The petals are finely dissected into upward-pointing segments that overlap with those of neighboring petals to produce a lacelike pattern. The plants may grow in scattered fashion in the forest or in closely associated colonies (fig. 291).

The flowering stalks arise from the center of a basal rosette of semi-evergreen lobed leaves similar in appearance to those of a red maple tree. Located approximately at the midpoint on the flower stalk is a pair of smaller leaves that are sessile (or nearly so) on the stalk (fig 295). It is the presence of these two leaves that prompted Linnaeus to use the epithet *diphylla*, meaning "two leaves" in Greek.

By contrast, the other species of *Mitella* in the Northeast, *M. nuda*, received its epithet to denote the lack of leaves on the flower stalk, making it thus "nude." The two species differ in several other aspects as well: *M. diphylla* is a larger plant with white, cup-shaped flowers, whereas the flowers of *M. nuda* are green with flattened corollas, more like a saucer than a cup (fig. 296). The flower stalks and the individual pedicels of *M. nuda* are slenderer than those of *M. nuda*, and the petal segments of *M. nuda* are as fine as hairs, spreading from the main axis of the petal at almost right angles, as opposed to the ascending angles seen in flowers of *M. diphylla*. The flowering stalks of *M. nuda* generally have fewer flowers (2–13 as compared with 5–20 in *M. diphylla*). The two species display strong habitat differences as well. *Mitella nuda* is an inhabitant of northern, wet coniferous forests and bogs, whereas *M. diphylla* has a broader latitudinal range and a greater tolerance for various forest and soil types; it is found with greater frequency on logs and at the base of trees. Miterwort and naked miterwort seldom coexist because of their diverse habitat preferences, but occasional hybrids, known as *Mitella intermedia*, have been found in Wisconsin and New York, indicating that cross-pollination between the species does occasionally occur. The ability of the two species to hybridize is a further indication of their close affinity. All species of *Mitella* are diploid (have the normal number of chromosomes), but in the case of *M. nuda*, only the Eurasian plants are diploid, whereas those from North America are tetraploid (having four sets of chromosomes). *Mitella diphylla* and *M. nuda* are both perennial; have leaves and stems covered with hairs (some glandular) (fig. 297); possess two carpels, two styles, and two stigmas; and have dehiscent capsular fruits.

As might be expected of flowers exhibiting different morphologies, the pollination systems of *Mitella* species differ as well. The white, cup-shaped flowers of *M. diphylla* are visited by small bees (e.g., halictid bees and small carpenter bees) and syrphid flies, all of which take nectar from a ring of glandular tissue located just below the stamens on the interior of the cup. In doing so, their mouthparts brush against the

Fig. 294. A close-up of the delicate beauty of a miterwort flower. Note the upwardly angled segments of the fimbriate petals.

stamens, and pollen is thus transported to other flowers. The flies may also consume some of the pollen, and bees collect it to feed to their larvae. The glandular ring dries up once the ovary begins to enlarge, and the lacy petals drop soon after pollination has been accomplished. In a study of several species of Saxifragaceae, including *Mitella*, in Japan, Yudai Okuyama and colleagues found that those plants with green saucer-shaped corollas (including *M. nuda*) were visited and pollinated by fungus gnats. Fungus gnats breed in the same dark, moist areas in which many species of *Mitella* grow. Since fungus gnats tend to be active only at dawn and dusk, their role as pollinators may previously have been overlooked. Although only one to three fungus gnats visited each inflorescence in a day, they all had pollen grains attached to their bodies, and over 63% of the flowers set fruit—evidence that the gnats are efficient pollinators.

Perhaps even more unusual than gnat pollination is miterwort's method of seed dispersal. Unlike the seeds of many spring ephemerals of the Northeast, those of miterwort and naked miterwort do not have elaiosomes (food bodies to attract ants, which act as dispersal agents). Rather, the stalks of the miter-shaped fruit capsules change in orientation on the flower stalk as the seeds develop so that the fruits are all oriented with their line of opening facing upward, even if the main flowering stem has been bent over (fig. 292). One capsule never overshadows another beneath; in this way raindrops are not impeded from striking the capsules below. Once the seeds are mature, the seam between the two stigmas splits widely to expose the shiny black seeds (fig. 298). The seeds are small and light in weight, but not so light that they are dispersed by wind. Instead, the seeds remain in the capsules until it rains and then are splashed out of the capsule whenever a raindrop happens to land in the open capsule—this dispersal mechanism is termed splash-cup seed dispersal. The capsules dehisce when they are still green and turgid, providing a firm container for the seeds until dispersal occurs. In many species, the open capsules are flattened cups, but in *M. diphylla*, the capsules look like little boats (fig. 298).

The distance traveled by the seeds is dependent upon both the size of the raindrop and the distance that it has fallen before landing in an open fruit of *Mitella*. When the drop hits the fruit, it breaks into several smaller droplets, each of which may carry with it up to several seeds. Experiments, both in the field and in the lab, show that the maximum dispersal distance by this method is about a meter. This method of seed dispersal is an effective means for short plants to disperse their seeds away from the parent plant. Splash-cup dispersal is found in other plant families as well, including some species of gentians (*Gentiana*) and speedwells (*Veronica*). The same means of dispersal is present in bird's nest fungi, in which the

Fig. 295. The paired, sessile leaves on the flowering stalk of *Mitella diphylla* that give the plant its name.

Saxifrage Family

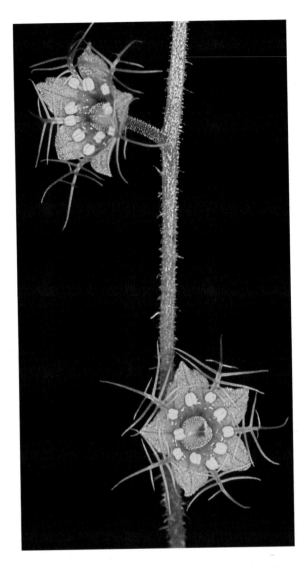

Fig. 296. A close-up view of two flowers of *Mitella nuda* showing the flattened, saucer-shaped flowers. Note the hair-like petal segments that are at almost right angles to the main axis of the petals, in contrast to those of *M. diphylla* that are at an oblique angle.

(Massachusetts) followed the regeneration of forested plots that had been decimated by an intense hurricane in 1938. After 50 years the forest had regained some semblance of its former stature and diversity, but certain species did not recover as well as others, among them *M. diphylla*, *Pyrola* spp., and *Polygala paucifolia*.

In trials where *Mitella* was tested for its potential in forest understory restoration, researchers Scott Ruhen and Steve Handel found that the species fared poorly when planted in locations subject to browsing by white-tailed deer. However, since miterwort survival was not much better when planted within exclosures designed to keep deer out, it was removed from consideration for restoration purposes. The result of this experiment shows miterwort's lack of resiliency to forest disturbance, whether natural or manmade. On the other hand, miterwort was one of several species to survive in the forest after invasion by alien honeysuckle, *Lonicera tatarica*. Other forest understory herbs not eliminated by honeysuckle invasion (e.g., Christmas fern, hepatica, mosses, and wood ferns) share, in common with miterwort, an evergreen, or partially evergreen, life history that may allow them to photosynthesize during that part of the year when the honeysuckle is leafless.

The Iroquois Indians are reported to have used miterwort to induce vomiting, and the seeds were considered sacred by the Menominee, who swallowed them as part of their medicinal rituals. The Cree used crushed leaves of naked miterwort to treat earaches. Although it is not known whether any of the above uses was efficacious, the plants do have demonstrable astringent properties.

spore-bearing flattened "eggs" (peridioles) in the fungal cups (fig. 299) are splashed out of the "nest" by raindrops. Also, certain liverworts, such as *Marchantia*, whose minute asexual bodies (gemmae) develop into new plants after they are splashed out of gemma cups on the surface of the liverwort (fig. 300), employ the same dispersal method.

Miterwort does not respond well to disturbance. A long-term study conducted in the Harvard Forest

Fig. 297. (Left) The basal leaves of naked miterwort. Note the hairs that cover both leaves and flower stalks. **Fig. 298.** (Right) The open, boat-shaped fruits of *Mitella diphylla* are full of seeds that will remain in the capsules until dispersed by the force of falling raindrops, a mode of seed dissemination called splash-cup dispersal.

Fig. 299. (Left) The spore-bearing "eggs" (peridioles) in the cups of these bird's nest fungi will be dispersed by raindrops in the same splash-cup dispersal manner as the seeds of *Mitella*. **Fig. 300.** (Right) A liverwort, *Marchantia polymorpha*, with gemma cups on its surface that contain asexual gemmae that also will be splashed out of the cups by falling rain.

Broomrape Family

Fig. 301. A cluster of single-flowered stalks of *Orobanche uniflora*. This North American species of broomrape is the only member of the genus *Orobanche* to have a solitary flower.

Fig. 302. A close-up of the white flowers of one-flowered cancer-root. Note the purple glandular hairs.

One-flowered Cancer-root

Orobanche uniflora
Broomrape Family (Orobanchaceae)

One-flowered cancer-root is unique among the members of the large genus *Orobanche* (broomrape), in that it is the only species with a solitary flower. Cancer-root lacks chlorophyll; it is parasitic on various other plants from which it obtains water and nutrients.

Habitat: Moist forests, thickets and fields; streamsides.

Range: Most of North America north of Mexico (but also Baja California).

Although one-flowered cancer-root is not commonly encountered, it occurs in all states but one (Hawaii) and throughout most of Canada (excluding Labrador, the province of Manitoba, and the three Canadian territories—Yukon, Northwest, and Nunavut). In Mexico, it is found only in Baja California. One-flowered cancer-root is a member of the genus *Orobanche*. Other common names applied to this species are one-flowered broomrape and naked broomrape.

The generic name *Orobanche* is derived from the Greek *orobos*, the name for a legume that we call vetch (*Vicia*), and *anchein*, meaning "to strangle," for the effect of the parasite on the vetch. The epithet "uniflora," of course, refers to the single flower of this species. The common name applied to the genus, broomrape, is a translation of the Medieval Latin *rapum genistae*, referring to a tuber (*rapum*), and the legume genus known as broom (*Genista*) that is parasitized by *Orobanche rapum-genistae* (fig. 303). The reference to a tuber applies to the tuberlike connection (the haustorium) that develops between the parasite and the root of the host.

The Orobanchaceae family formerly included only plants that were holoparasites, that is, those that obtain all of their water and nutrients through

Broomrape Family

Fig. 303. *Orobanche rapum-genistae*, the species from which the name broomrape is derived, growing with its host, broom (*Genista* sp.). Photographed in Spain.

an estimated 600–800 species. The genus *Orobanche* is found throughout the North Temperate part of the world but is most diverse in the Mediterranean region. Of the world's estimated 4,200 species of haustorial parasitic plants, almost half are included in the newly expanded Orobanchaceae.

One-flowered cancer-root is an inconspicuous, but pretty, plant that is often hidden in the leaf litter of the forest floor or masked by taller herbaceous plants in more open areas. The aboveground portion, a mere 5–8 inches (12–20 centimeters) tall, is only the flower stalk, the true stem being much shorter and subterranean. A characteristic of holoparasites is that the vegetative parts have become reduced, and in cancer-root only a few scalelike leaves are present on the underground stem. The subterranean part of the plant is tuberlike (fig. 304), sometimes branching, with overlapping scalelike leaves (fig. 305) from which one to several flower stalks arise (fig. 301). Usually, all portions of the plant are white to yellowish-white, but particularly in the western part of its range, the corolla may be lavender or a deep purple. Flowers are about a half inch (1.5 centimeters) in length. The five lobes of the calyx are longer than its tubular portion, but the five lobes of the corolla are shorter than the curved corolla tube. The aerial parts of the plant are densely covered with white or purple glandular hairs—to the extent that white-flowered plants may appear lavender due to the profusion of purple hairs (fig. 302). In

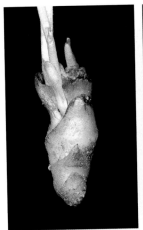

Fig. 304. (Left) The subterranean, tuberlike basal portion of one-flowered cancer-root. Fig. 305. (Right) The white, subterranean, scalelike leaves of one-flowered cancer-root.

the parasitization of other plants. However, the Orobanchaceae were always thought to be closely allied with certain members of the Scrophulariaceae, and recent molecular studies have confirmed this relationship. This new information has resulted in all 73 of the hemiparasitic genera of Scrophulariaceae (those that have chlorophyll and can photosynthesize but derive part of their nutritional needs through the parasitism of other plants) being transferred to the Orobanchaceae. One nonparasitic genus, *Lindenbergia*, was moved to the Orobanchaceae as well, based on its having many features in common with the parasitic genera (perpetually open stomata, the manner of opening of the flower buds, and the presence of similar chemical constituents). It is thought that the parasitic Orobanchaceae were derived from *Lindenbergia* or similar nonparasitic ancestors. The new, more inclusive Orobanchaceae includes almost 100 genera, many with only 1 to 5 species, but others, more cosmopolitan in scope, having many more species, including *Orobanche* with 150 and *Pedicularis* (see fig. 257) with

Fig. 306. Flowers of one-flowered cancer-root showing the yellow ridges in the throat of the corolla. The ridges may serve as nectar guides although few insects have been observed visiting the flowers.

the tubular throat of the flower are two raised, bright yellow ridges (fig. 306) that may function as nectar guides, although insects are rarely observed visiting the flowers. The style bends so that the stigma comes in contact with the anthers and picks up self-pollen (fig. 307). The flowers are most likely autogamous (self-pollinating), and some populations of cancer-root have been shown to be agamoogenetic (capable of producing seed without fertilization). As the fruit matures, the corolla becomes dry and brown yet remains attached to the developing fruit (fig. 308).

Fruits are capsules with numerous tiny seeds, most of which drift to the forest floor within a few inches of the plant, although some may be dispersed further afield by wind or incidental animal movement.

As a holoparasite, one-flowered cancer-root is entirely dependent upon other plants for its nutritional needs. The tiny seedlings, with their limited food reserves, must find a suitable host plant within a few days of germinating or die. However, ungerminated seeds may remain viable in the soil for up to 30 years. The search for a host is guided by chemical

Fig. 307. (Above) A flower of *Orobanche uniflora* that has been cut open to show how the style bends downward, allowing the stigmatic lobe to contact the anthers, where it may pick up self-pollen. **Fig. 308.** (Left) The dried, brown corollas of one-flowered cancer-root remain on the plant as the fruits develop.

Broomrape Family

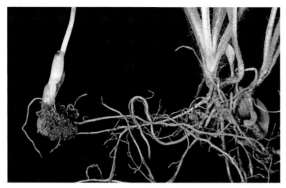

Fig. 309. A close-up of one-flowered cancer-root attached to the fibrous roots of *Hieracium* sp.

attractants (most commonly phenols) released by the growing roots of the host species. Attachment is always to a fibrous root, never a taproot. Once contact between parasite and host has been made, the hairs of the parasite root, just behind the area of contact, exude an adhesive substance that secures the attachment to the root of the host. Enzymatic action breaks down the cell walls of the host, and a tuberlike connection forms between the xylem of the two species that allows movement of water, minerals, and carbohydrates in one direction—from host to parasite. This connecting structure, comprising modified roots from both species, is called a haustorium.

In most cases, the haustorium of a parasite forms on the fibrous roots of the host (fig. 309), but in a few genera of other families (e.g., dodder, *Cuscuta* spp., in the morning-glory family), the connection is to the stem of the host. In some species, including *O. uniflora*, secondary haustoria form when the parasite contacts additional roots of the host. Haustorial parasitism, although associated almost exclusively with eudicot families (formerly termed dicots), involves fewer than 5% of those families (just over 1% of the species). The one quasi-exception is the relationship of the New Caledonian gymnosperm, *Parasitaxus ustus* (a member of the Podocarpaceae), to other members of the same family. The roots of *P. ustus* are always attached to another member of the same family but do not form a haustorium. Rather, a fungus that infects both species serves as an intermediary for the transfer of water and nutrients; thus, this relationship does not represent an instance of true parasitism. However, a surprising report in the Michigan Natural Features

Inventory claims that in Michigan *O. uniflora* is parasitic on juniper (*Juniperus*), a woody gymnosperm.

Some species of *Orobanche* are host specific, for example, *O. hederacea* is found only on English ivy (*Hedera helix*; fig. 310), but others may attack multiple unrelated species, sometimes having a preference for a certain host—clover broomrape (*O. minor*), an introduced species in the United States, has an affinity for red clover (*Trifolium pratense*; fig. 311) but also attacks other species. *Orobanche uniflora* is able to parasitize plants of many different genera, and even different families. Members of the aster family (Asteraceae) are frequent hosts of one-flowered cancer-root, as are species of *Sedum* (Crassulaceae) and members of the Saxifragaceae. In 2009, a new species of *Orobanche* was described from within the range of this book. Based on morphological differences and habitat preference, L. T. Collins and collaborators segregated *Orobanche riparia* out of the widespread, heterogeneous species, *O. ludoviciana*. The new species is parasitic on annuals in the aster family. I was curious to see what the host species was for the one-flowered cancer-root plants that I had photographed near my home in Westchester County, NY. Careful digging revealed a connection between cancer-root

Fig. 310. (Left) *Orobanche hederacea* on its exclusive host, English ivy (*Hedera helix*) in France. **Fig. 311.** (Right) *Orobanche minor*, an alien species introduced into the United States, parasitizing its preferred host, red clover (*Trifolium pratense*) in Delaware.

Fig. 312. (Left) An excavated plant of one-flowered cancer-root attached to its host, *Hieracium* sp. **Fig. 313.** (Right) The lavender-flowered *Orobanche ramosa* parasitizing the introduced yellow-flowered Bermuda buttercup (*Oxalis pes-caprae*) in Greece.

and a hawkweed (*Hieracium* sp.), a member of the Asteraceae (fig. 312).

Many species of *Orobanche* are considered to be noxious weeds because of their ability to devastate crop plants through their parasitism, but our native species, including *O. uniflora*, are exempt from this designation. One-flowered cancer-root does not attack crop plants and has a minor effect on the relatively unimportant weedy species that it does parasitize. However, worldwide *Orobanche* is considered to be one of the three most harmful genera of parasitic plants in terms of its economic impact. Several broomrapes that were accidentally introduced to the United States via contaminated seed have had a negative effect on important crop plants here, including hemp and tobacco. One of the worst of these alien invasives is *O. ramosa*, or branched broomrape, which is known to parasitize plants of at least 11 different families. A deceptively pretty plant with lavender flowers, it attacks a variety of economically valuable crops, among them tobacco, sunflower, tomato, hemp, cabbage, carrots, and eggplant. As a consequence, valuable minerals such as phosphorus and potassium are greatly reduced in the host, resulting in stunted growth and weakened stems. In its native Mediterranean setting, *O. ramosa* has shown its ability to attack even introduced species, such as the ornamental South African *Oxalis pes-caprae* (Oxalidaceae),

Fig. 314. The destructive result of a heavy infestation of *Orobanche ramosa* on *Oxalis pes-caprae*. The host plant has been all but eliminated. Photographed in Greece.

known as Bermuda buttercup (strangely named as it is neither from Bermuda nor in the buttercup family; fig. 313), devastating the host when the level of parasitism is high (fig. 314). This adaptability to new hosts is found as well in *O. uniflora*, which, in the state of Georgia, has begun to utilize as a host the introduced Brazilian catsear (*Hypochoeris brasiliensis*), a member of the Asteraceae.

Some host species have shown resistance to attack by parasitic plants, but to date it has not proven easy either to identify the factors responsible for conferring resistance or to isolate them for the purpose of incorporation into economically important crop species. Herbicidal control has had limited success, but treatment with high concentrations of the fungus *Fusarium* has shown some promise.

Jack-in-the-pulpit Family

Fig. 315. Skunk cabbage spathes growing in the mossy hummocks of a swamp.

Fig. 316. The snow surrounding this flowering skunk cabbage has melted due to the absorption of the sun's radiation by the dark spathe, and perhaps also from the heat generated by the spadix. The round-leaved plant in front is moneywort (*Lysimachia nummularia*).

Skunk Cabbage

Symplocarpus foetidus
Jack-in-the-pulpit (or Aroid) Family (Araceae)

Like Jack-in-the-pulpit, the flowers of skunk cabbage are arranged on a fleshy spadix enclosed by a sheathing bract called a spathe. Despite its unpleasant smell, skunk cabbage is a welcome harbinger of spring.

Habitat: Swamps and low, moist ground (fig. 315).

Range: Southern Canada to North Carolina, west to Minnesota and Iowa.

The first wildflower to bloom in the Northeast is skunk cabbage, a plant that I have found in flower as early as February. The emergence of the green-to-purple spathes, sometimes even poking through the snow (fig. 316), is something that I look forward to each year. It gives me an incentive to get out into the woods while snow still covers the ground, and it provides a sense of hope that spring really is on the way. As with other members of its family (the aroid, or Jack-in-the-pulpit, family), the floral structure of skunk cabbage consists of two parts, the flower-bearing spadix and the hoodlike spathe that surrounds it. To my eye, the spathes are quite beautiful, with an organic, sinuous shape that is almost sculptural, somewhat reminiscent of a miniature work by Henry Moore (fig. 317). Both the color (varying from yellow-green to deep maroon, or a mixture of the

Fig. 317. The sculptural forms of skunk cabbage spathes.

153

Jack-in-the-pulpit Family

Fig. 318. (Left) A pale-colored spathe variant of *Symplocarpos foetidus*. Note the cone of leaves emerging in front of the spathe on the right. **Fig. 319.** (Right) A spadix of skunk cabbage with flowers in the female phase. The spadix has been cut in longitudinal section to show the fusion of the ovaries.

two) and the way that the spathe opens (either left to right or the reverse; fig. 318; contrast with fig. 332) are genetically determined.

The scientific name of the genus, *Symplocarpus*, comes from the Greek *symploke*, meaning "connection," and *karpos*, meaning "fruit," because its fruits are fused together in the spadix to form a compound fruit (fig. 319). If bruised or crushed, the leaves and inflorescence emit a foul odor, the origin for the scientific epithet of the species, *foetidus* (from the Latin for "stinking") as well as the common name, *skunk* cabbage. Peter Kalm, Linnaeus's student who was sent to America to look for useful new plants complained in *Travels in North America*, "Among the stinking plants this is the most foetid; its nauseous scent was so strong that I could hardly examine the flower; and when I smelled it a little too long my head ached" (p. 256). Probably due to the offensive odor as well as to

Fig. 320. Skunk cabbage flowers in the male phase studded over the ball-like spadix. Note the pollen that has accumulated in the base of the spathe.

Fig. 321. (Top) Flowers with reddish-maroon tepals (four per flower) transitioning from the female to the male phase. Note the stigma protruding in the central flower and surrounded by four stamens that are about to emerge from the flower. **Fig. 322.** (Above) Flowers with creamy yellow tepals that are at the beginning of the male phase. Anthers are exerted from the flowers but have not yet opened.

154

Fig. 323. Two pale green plants of *Symplocarpus foetidus* that have emerged above ground in autumn. They will remain in this state until the longer days of February and March trigger them to resume growth.

the irritating crystals of calcium oxalate in the leaves, herbivores generally avoid skunk cabbage. However, I once observed Canada geese eagerly eating the leaves in early spring, and squirrels are reported to nibble the spadix. Another common name for the plant is bear cabbage. In a study published in the *Canadian Journal of Zoology* in 2001, black bears emerging from their long winter hibernation fed almost exclusively on skunk cabbage, with the exception of those years when acorns were still available from a highly productive crop the previous fall. Even in times of acorn plenty, 52% of the bears' diet was composed of skunk cabbage, despite the fact that acorns are more nutrient rich, containing up to 10% fat, compared with only 0.2% in skunk cabbage.

Calcium oxalate crystals are found in all genera of the Araceae. In skunk cabbage they take two forms: raphides, which occur in bundles of parallel, needle-like crystals, and druses, which are conglomerates of several crystals fused around a nucleus and shaped like an irregular, spiky ball. If skunk cabbage is eaten, the calcium oxalate causes a severe burning sensation in the mouth, throat, and esophagus and can result in an inability to speak or even in swelling of the throat. *Dieffenbachia seguine*, a familiar houseplant of the same family, is known as dumb cane or mother-in-law plant because it possesses these same properties. The raphides in skunk cabbage are contained in three different types of cells; some raphides are grooved so that in cross section they resemble small dumbbells. It

is said that even crushing the leaves may cause a burning sensation in the skin of some people, but I have not found this to be so. Despite the noxious properties of this species, it was used medicinally by Native Americans to treat a variety of illnesses, and it is also listed as a wild food in the *Peterson Guide to Edible Wild Plants*. Peterson states that the leaves and roots must be thoroughly dried and then reconstituted to rid them of the calcium oxalate. It is also claimed that cooking the leaves in several changes of water removes the cause of the burning sensation. However, according to information reported in Sue Thompson's treatment of skunk cabbage in the *Flora of North America*, the crystals are *not* destroyed by heat, and it is thought that the burning sensation might be caused by a compound other than calcium oxalate; a proteolytic enzyme is suspected as the possible cause in *Dieffenbachia*. I cannot imagine why anyone would want to go to the effort necessary to render skunk cabbage edible, and I strongly discourage its use as a food. In addition,

Fig. 324. Skunk cabbage spathes that are still closed in early March.

Jack-in-the-pulpit Family

Fig. 325. (Left) This spadix is still completely covered with flowers in the female (pistillate) stage. The anthers of the male flowers will soon begin to emerge beginning at the top of the spadix. The spathe has been partially cut away.

Fig. 326. (Right) The topmost flowers on this spadix have already finished releasing their pollen, the central ones are currently releasing pollen, and the lowest ones are still in the female phase. The spathe has been partially cut away to better show the spadix.

skunk cabbage has sometimes been confused with another plant of swamps, false hellebore (fig. 128), which can prove deadly if ingested.

To see the flowers of skunk cabbage, one must look inside the hood, or spathe. The 50–100 tiny flowers, consisting of only the essential reproductive parts surrounded by four small tepals, are studded in a spiral pattern over the ball-like spadix (fig. 320). The tepals may vary in color from maroon to creamy white (figs. 321, 322). When looking at the flowers, take the opportunity to smell them as well. If you have been careful not to break or bruise the spathe, you may be pleasantly surprised to detect a faintly sweet aroma. I notice this particularly when the flowers are in the female phase. The fetid smell associated with skunk cabbage is emitted only if the plant tissue is bruised. The spadix and its short stalk develop underground in summer and remain enclosed within the protective spathe. In some cases the tightly closed spathes push their way above ground in late summer or autumn (fig. 323); some may even open then, but most remain in the closed state throughout the winter (fig. 324); once the days have begun to lengthen they resume growth and open.

The flowers of skunk cabbage are bisexual, but sequentially so. The first flowers to open are those at the top of the spadix. The female part, a tiny pink style, topped by a fringed white stigma, is exposed first (figs. 325, 326, 327), followed by the four stamens (figs. 328, 329). Thus, when the upper flowers are in the male phase and are releasing pollen, the lower flowers are still in the female phase and can be dusted with pollen from above. However, it appears that skunk cabbage

cannot self-pollinate; it must be cross-pollinated in order to produce fruit. Pollen released by the anthers falls to the base of the spathe and accumulates there (figs. 320, 330); visiting insects may become covered with it as they crawl about the base of the spathe and carry the pollen when they move to another plant.

Amazingly, the fleshy spadix, only an inch or so in diameter, is capable of producing heat through a rapid method of respiration (the metabolic burning of carbohydrates through the process of oxidation). The

Clockwise from top left **Fig. 327.** A close-up of pistillate-phase flowers. **Fig. 328.** A side view of pistillate flowers showing the thick, pinkish styles and white-fringed stigmas. **Fig. 329.** A close-up of male flowers showing four anthers (each anther is composed of two anther sacs). **Fig. 330.** Pollen accumulated in the base of a spathe. Note that the two visible lower flowers are still in the pistillate stage.

Fig. 331. Three spathes that have been cut open to reveal the flowering spadices within. Note the thick spongy walls of the spathes that help to conserve the heat generated by the spadices.

temperature inside the spathe is thus warmed sufficiently enough that early-season bees and flies can take refuge there to warm their flight muscles and then continue on to other plants. Heat can also volatilize the chemicals that produce aromas attractive to insects. Early insect visitors may gather pollen, an important food resource, and in so doing effect pollination. Because of the paucity of insects in late winter, pollination occurs infrequently and skunk cabbage produces few fruits. In fact, in a 1998 Canadian study of heat regulation in skunk cabbage, only 11 invertebrates, most of them spiders, were found in the 195 flowering spathes examined. The result of the Canadian study contrasts sharply with the observation of an early American botanist, William Trelease, who in 1879 reported seeing many (nonnative) honeybees collecting pollen from the flowers early in the season and hordes of tiny flies a couple of weeks later. The spongy tissue of the spathe (fig. 331) serves well to insulate the spadix and retain the warmth that it generates. This may help to protect the inflorescence from frost damage when temperatures dip below freezing during the flowering period, but prolonged subfreezing temperatures can result in the demise of the inflorescence.

The spadix is able to maintain its temperature at about 20°C (68°F) and may exceed the ambient air temperature by as much as 25°C (77°F) for a period of two to three weeks. If the ambient temperature drops below 3°C (37.4°F), the plant can shut down the heating mechanism until the air temperature rises again. The source of the "fuel" consumed in this process is the reserve of starch stored in the rhizome. The dark, heat-absorbing spathe, perhaps in conjunction with the heat generated by the spadix, can cause the snow surrounding the plant to melt (fig. 316). An actual evolutionary benefit of heat production has not been documented but could have had significance early in the evolutionary history of the species, which at that time most likely inhabited tropical regions of the world. Some members of this primarily tropical family produce heat to volatilize chemicals that attract their pollinators, often beetles.

At flowering time, skunk cabbage leaves are still tightly wrapped around each other in conelike structures adjacent to the spathes (fig. 318) or even still below the ground. They begin to unfurl as the spathes wither (fig. 332) in the warmer temperatures of late April and May, opening in a spiral fashion (fig. 333).

Fig. 332. The leaves of skunk cabbage begin to enlarge after flowering.

Jack-in-the-pulpit Family

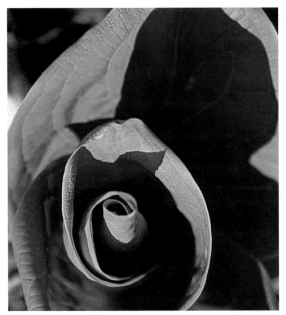

Fig. 333. As skunk cabbage leaves enlarge, they unfurl in a spiral fashion.

Fig. 335. Skunk cabbage plants line a stream bringing life to the forest in early spring.

Fig. 334. Skunk cabbage with its leaves nearly fully expanded carpets a swamp in early May.

The leaves can grow to be three feet or more in length and a foot wide, quickly carpeting swamps and wet forests (fig. 334) and lining stream banks (fig. 335) with a luxuriant green blanket that enlivens the early spring landscape. Skunk cabbage plants are drawn progressively deeper into the soft, muddy wetland soil by a series of strong, fleshy, adventitious roots that alternately grow and contract, pulling the plant further into the soft substrate (figs. 336, 337). Thus, the plants are strongly anchored in the soil and very difficult to dig out. Although skunk cabbage is a monocot, like lilies and grasses, its leaves are broad rather than linear, and they do not have the parallel venation typical of monocot leaves. Rather, the veins branch much like those of dicotyledons (fig. 338). The flowers, as well, differ from most monocots in that their parts are in fours rather than threes (figs. 321, 322). By mid-August, almost any trace of the lush green leaves has disappeared from the swamp. As with the spathes, the leaves lack fibers and do not have a tough waxy cuticle, and thus, wither and disappear quickly. As the leaves decay, they serve as a breeding ground for several species of small flies, many in the genus *Drosophila*, which most likely feed on bacteria.

Fig. 336. A partially excavated skunk cabbage plant with its long contractile roots splayed out over the muddy soil. It took three hours to fully excavate the plant.

The few fruits are seldom seen because they develop at ground level, hidden by the leaves. In one study, botanist John Small found that the percentage of inflorescences that matured into fruits was higher for plants growing in swampy forest habitat compared with those growing in an open marsh. The fruit (actually an infructescence of several fruits) is composed of many berries up to a half inch in length, each with a single seed (fig. 339). You can search for them in June by pushing the large, heart-shaped leaves aside, or wait until the leaves have begun to die back in midsummer, and then look carefully for the green-to-brown, ball-like fruits that lay camouflaged on the wet brown soil (fig. 340). Although the fruits decay, the seeds remain hard and viable through the winter. As evidenced by piles of horded seeds, rodents are thought to play a role in seed dispersal. Whole seeds have also been found in the crop of a pheasant, a game bird introduced to North America.

Formerly, *Symplocarpus* was considered to be a monotypic genus; however, three additional species are currently known, all native to eastern Asia. Many other plant genera share this long-range disjunct distribution, among them *Podophyllum* (Mayapple),

Fig. 337. A close-up of skunk cabbage roots showing the series of ridges that encircle the roots and are formed when the roots contract to pull the plant deeper into the soil.

Jack-in-the-pulpit Family

Fig. 338. The venation of the leaves of the monocotyledonous skunk cabbage is branched, much like that of the leaves of dicots.

Fig. 340. The grenade-like fruit of skunk cabbage remains long after the leaves have withered and disappeared. This fruit was photographed in August before it was fully mature.

Caulophyllum (blue cohosh), and *Jeffersonia* (twinleaf), with some of these genera having their origins in Asia and others in North America. The odd, widely separated distribution of *Symplocarpus* may have resulted from a once-widespread common ancestor that became extinct in intervening areas; the remaining disjunct plants then evolving into different species.

In the western United States, another member of the Araceae is also known by the common name of skunk cabbage. This skunk cabbage is a member of the genus

Fig. 339. An immature fruit that has been cut to show the developing seeds inside.

Fig. 341. Leaves and inflorescence of *Lysichiton americanus*, a western skunk cabbage that has an elongate spadix and a yellow spathe.

Lysichiton, which differs from *Symplocarpus* in having a more elongate spadix on a long stipe that is not fully enclosed by the more membranous spathe. *Lysichiton* (from the Greek *lisis*, "dissolve," and *chiton*, "tunic"), refers to the tuniclike spathe that quickly withers after flowering. The spathe of *Lysichiton americanus* is bright yellow and is more open than that of *Symplocarpus* (fig. 341). It produces an aroma that is attractive to the beetles that serve as its pollinators. As with *Symplocarpus*, there is another species of *Lysichiton* in Asia, the white-spathed *L. camtschatcensis* (fig. 342). It is suggested that both genera originated in eastern Asia and migrated across the Bering land bridge in the late Tertiary period.

Fig. 342. The white-spathed Asian counterpart to western skunk cabbage, *Lysichiton camtschatcensis*.

Montia Family

Fig. 343. A plant of *Claytonia virginica* showing the narrow, almost grasslike, leaves.

Fig. 344. Virginia spring beauty carpeting a grassy area adjacent to a woodland.

Spring Beauties

Claytonia virginica and *Claytonia caroliniana*
Montia Family (Montiaceae)

Spring beauty is one of the earliest spring bloomers in the Northeast. It carpets woodland edges and, occasionally, grassy fields with its white to pink flowers. Whether white or pink, the flowers always have deeper pink lines that serve as nectar guides. The genus *Claytonia* has recently been transferred from the portulaca family (Portulacaceae) to the montia family (Montiaceae) according to the APG.

Habitat: *C. virginica*—rich woods and fields; *C. caroliniana*—cool woods.

Range: *C. virginica*—from Nova Scotia to Minnesota, south to Georgia, Louisiana, and Texas. *C. caroliniana*—from Nova Scotia to Minnesota and south along the mountains to North Carolina, Tennessee, and northern Georgia.

Although spring beauty is a small plant with grasslike leaves (fig. 343), it can be quite conspicuous in early spring when it carpets large areas in or near the edges of woods (fig. 344). Its scientific name, *Claytonia virginica*, commemorates John Clayton, a 1700s clerk to the county court in Gloucester County, Virginia. Clayton came to colonial America from England as a young man and soon befriended Mark Catesby, the English naturalist and artist (see the chapter on Mayapple). Clayton became an enthusiastic plant collector in his new home colony of Virginia, and after Catesby returned to England, Clayton sent his plant collections to him for further study. Catesby often forwarded Clayton's collections to other European

Fig. 345. A herbarium specimen of *Claytonia virginica* collected by John Clayton and designated as a syntype (© The Natural History Museum, London).

Montia Family

Fig. 346. An especially deep pink-flowered specimen of Virginia spring beauty (*Claytonia virginica*). These are recently opened flowers with anthers releasing pollen; the style will open later to expose the three stigmatic surfaces.

botanists, among them, J. F. Gronovius, who, without Clayton's approval, preempted him in publishing a flora of Virginia that was based on Clayton's specimens and written documentation. Linnaeus also studied many of Clayton's collections and based 400 new species on them—including the new genus and species, *Claytonia virginica*—in his 1753 publication *Species Plantarum* (fig. 345).

The flowers of spring beauty are found in a range of colors from white through various shades of pink, often in the same population. It is curious that even within a single population you can find such a range of colors. In general, where a range of colors coexist, if a plant of one color is more successful at reproducing, it should eventually become dominant and result in the elimination of the other colors. However, this is not the case with spring beauty. Frank Frey, while a graduate student at Indiana University, investigated the reasons behind this phenomenon and came to some interesting conclusions. He found that plants with deeper-colored flowers (fig. 346) produced more seeds, an indication that they were perhaps more successful in attracting pollinators. But Frey determined that there is also a negative correlation between pink flowers and reproductive success. Slugs preferentially ate the leaves of pink-flowered plants, and plants that lost more than 50% of their leaves to herbivores were less likely to survive. Flower color is a result of a combination of factors, among them soil composition and the amount of sunlight. Also important are the floral color-producing chemical compounds within the plant. A red pigment, cyanidin, occurs in varying quantities in spring beauty. It interacts with two chemicals, both flavenols (kaempferol and quercetin—the latter recently in the news because of the controversy about its efficacy as an athletic supplement), to produce a range of pink to white flowers. Plants with a high percentage of flavenols produce white flowers. It is the presence of the flavenols that serves as a deterrent to herbivory. Thus, in years when slug damage is high, white-flowered plants are more successful in reproducing. Yet another factor comes into the equation—*Claytonia* is also parasitized by a

Fig. 347. (Left) *Claytonia virginica* with a leaf attacked by a fungal rust (*Puccinia mariae-wilsoniae*). **Fig. 348.** (Right) The deformed stem and flowers of Virginia spring beauty that have been parasitized by a rust.

Fig. 349. (Left) A small fly visiting a flower of spring beauty to collect nectar. **Fig. 350.** (Right) *Claytonia virginica* flowers showing the pink lines and yellow spots that serve as nectar guides for visiting insects.

rust (a type of fungus) called *Puccinia mariae-wilsoniae* (formerly known as *P. claytoniata*), which preferentially attacks the white-flowered plants, causing bright orange spots on the leaves and/or flowers (fig. 347) and sometimes seriously deforming the plant (fig. 348). *Puccinia* is a large genus that includes several rusts that parasitize economically important plants as well as our native Mayapple (*Podophyllum peltatum*—see figs. 281, 282, and 283). Thus, in *Claytonia*, selection pressures are working at cross-purposes: in years of high herbivory by slugs (usually years with high rainfall), white flowers are more successful at producing seeds; in years when herbivory is diminished but fungal infection is high, pink flowers are more reproductively successful. The sporadic success of pink- and white-flowered plants promotes the perpetuation of a variety of color forms.

The flowers of spring beauty open when the temperature exceeds 11°C (52°F), a temperature at which some of their visitors (flies) are capable of flight (fig. 349). Small native bees, spring beauty's primary pollinators, need temperatures of 13°C (55°F) for flight. Bumblebees, with their robust, hairy bodies, can fly at temperatures lower than 5°C (41°F), but they rarely visit the flowers of spring beauty because the small amount of nectar produced is not adequate to support their energy requirements. Insect visitors to *Claytonia*, both bees and flies, are seeking pollen and/or nectar. They are attracted by a contrasting pattern produced by petals, which absorb UV light, and filaments, which reflect it. In addition, the pink veins on the white or pink petals and the yellow spots at the base of the petals (fig. 350) serve to

Fig. 351. A flower of spring beauty that is in the female phase. The style apex has split to expose the three stigmatic surfaces, and the stamens have reflexed back onto the petals.

guide insects to the nectar source at the base of the filaments. The pink anthers release pollen on the first day that the flower opens, when the stamens are still tightly adpressed to the style and the stigma is yet not receptive. On the second day, the stamens bend away from the style and down onto the petals, and the style splits in three at its apex to expose the stigmatic surface that is now ready to receive pollen (fig. 351). Depending on temperature, the flower may remain in the female phase for up to a week. The separation of male and female phases helps to ensure that pollen is not transferred to the stigma of the same flower. Like many early bloomers, spring beauty closes its flowers at night, when insects are unlikely to be flying about, and during inclement weather, when the nectar could be diluted by rainwater.

The amount of sugar in the nectar produced by *C. virginica* falls within the range required by medium- to short-tongued bees and flies. *Andrena erigeniae*

Montia Family

Fig. 352. (Left) An andrenid bee at the entrance to her nest. **Fig. 353.** (Right) A portion of a community of andrenid bee nests in spring. A bee is just visible in the entrance to the nest on the right.

is the most common bee visitor and forages almost exclusively on *Claytonia*, both for nectar and, more important, for pollen, the sole source of food for its annual brood of larvae. The ranges of *C. virginica* and *A. erigeniae* are almost congruent. *Andrena erigeniae* is a solitary bee, but it nests gregariously, making dozens of small vertical nesting tunnels in areas that may encompass several square meters of woodland (figs. 352, 353). Females of the species must make between three and five trips to collect enough *Claytonia* pollen to make a three- to four-millimeter spherical pollen ball that they place into a side chamber off of the main nesting tunnel. A solitary egg is laid on the pollen ball. This process is repeated several times over the next few weeks, with each pollen ball and egg placed in a separate, and deeper, side chamber. When the eggs hatch, the larvae feed on the provisioned pollen. In late summer they pupate within the chambers and then emerge in fall as adults, but they spend the winter underground. Some larvae do not survive because fly eggs, deposited in the bees' chambers, develop more rapidly than the bees' eggs, and the earlier-hatching fly larvae consume all of the pollen resources.

The bee fly, *Bombylius major* (see fig. 91), is the second most common visitor to the flowers of spring beauty and is almost as effective as a pollinator. Bee flies are broad bodied and hairy with a long, straight proboscis used for sipping nectar. Since *C. virginica* is a widespread and common species, it serves as an important resource for small bees and flies in early spring. Over 100 different species of insects have been observed visiting the flowers of spring beauty, 58 of them bees, including 17 species of andrenids (fig. 354), and 35 flies. Although *Claytonia* did not evolve with honeybees, these introduced bees are now frequent visitors and effective pollinators. Wasps and ants also are observed to take nectar from the flowers (figs. 355, 356).

Initial flowering appears to be triggered by temperature. The earliest flowers to bloom (those lowest on the flowering stalk) are less successful in producing seeds since there are fewer pollinators flying when temperatures are still cool. Similarly, late-blooming flowers do not mature many seeds, but for a different reason: by the time they flower, the increased shade of the leaf cover from the tree canopy above inhibits the leaves of spring beauty from being as effective in photosynthesizing, thus limiting the plant's resources for seed development. On the other hand, early and late in the season, when there are fewer flowers in bloom,

Fig. 354. A bee of the genus *Andrena* collecting pollen from the anthers of spring beauty.

Fig. 355. A wasp using its long proboscis to sip nectar.

the insects that *do* visit will most likely travel greater distances between flowers, thereby moving the pollen further from its source and increasing gene flow. Thus, it is advantageous for the plant to produce flowers even during periods when seed production is reduced because it results in greater genetic diversity.

Spring beauty is truly ephemeral in that it produces its leaves and flowers early in the season and then quickly withers, leaving nothing visible above ground. From flower to seed may occur in as little as two weeks, although another two weeks may elapse until the mature seeds are dispersed. It generally takes four years for a plant to reach reproductive maturity, and only plants with two leaves have the resources necessary to produce flowers. The leaves are present when the canopy above is devoid of foliage (fig. 357), allowing the leaves to capture the sun's energy to manufacture carbohydrate. The short-lived leaves take up and sequester nutrients from the soil (e.g., nitrogen) and then release many of these valuable nutrients back to the soil as they senesce. Excess carbohydrate is stored in the underground tubers to be utilized for early growth the following spring (fig. 358). Contractile roots grow downward from the tuber, securing it more securely in the soil. The small round tubers of spring beauty are edible, much like other more familiar underground storage organs, such as potatoes, carrots, beets, and turnips. In fact, another common name for spring beauty is fairy spuds, for their resemblance to miniature potatoes. Baked until soft, they taste much like potatoes,

but their small size makes the meal hardly worth the effort. As always, care must be exercised when consuming wild foods, first to determine that proper identification is made (there are many plants with poisonous underground parts), and second to ensure that harvesting is done with conservation of the plant in mind. The conservation status of the species must be known and the viability of the population in the area assessed.

As the seeds develop, the flower stalks (pedicels) bend downward. When the capsules are fully mature, the three valves curl inward (fig. 359), putting pressure on the shiny black seeds and causing them to be explosively shot as far as two feet from the plant. Rarely do all six ovules in an ovary mature into seeds. Like many other of our spring flowers, the seeds of *Claytonia* are equipped with a small fleshy body

Fig. 356. The ant "stealing" nectar is an ineffective pollinator.

Fig. 357. Spring beauty in flower with a background of leafless trees behind.

Montia Family

Fig. 358. The small storage tuber of spring beauty with roots and stems arising from it.

Fig. 359. Three fruits of spring beauty, each still enclosed by its two persistent sepals; the fruits have already dehisced and ejected their seeds.

Fig. 360. Two seeds of spring beauty, each about one millimeter in size; the small white areas on the seeds are the elaiosomes.

elaiosome and discard the seed. Thus, the seeds have "found a way" to get themselves dispersed at some distance from the parent plant. The seeds do not germinate until fall, or sometimes not until the following spring.

Claytonia virginica is known for having a highly variable number of chromosomes, an indication of multiple genotypes. Even within the same plant, the chromosome number may differ in the leaf as compared with the roots, or some cells in the tuber many have the "normal" number of chromosomes ($n = 8$), whereas other cells may have many additional chromosomes. *Claytonia* plants growing under a forest canopy are primarily diploid and must complete their life cycle quickly, before the canopy shade becomes too dense. Those growing in weedy edges often have higher numbers of chromosomes (ranging up to $n = 191$) and a longer flowering period. Perhaps the variety of genotypes allows for greater adaptability in those plants with additional chromosomes.

In the northern part of our range and following the Appalachian Mountains south, one is more likely to encounter a second species of spring beauty, *Claytonia caroliniana*. This species differs from *C. virginica* principally in having broader leaves with a more distinct petiole and more deeply pink flowers (fig. 361). The two spring beauty species are rarely found growing together, but when they do co-occur, hybrids are occasionally found. Since there is little morphological difference between the two species, ribosomal DNA has been used to differentiate between them as well as to detect hybrids of the two species. Another method of detecting hybrids is to add a stain to the pollen. The pollen of hybrids does

called an elaiosome, which ants find to be an attractive edible (fig. 360). As with bloodroot, Dutchman's breeches, and trillium, ants carry the seeds back to their nests, where they then consume the lipid-rich

Fig. 361. Carolina spring beauty with strongly marked flowers. Note the broad leaves that narrow into a petiole that differentiate this species from the Virginia spring beauty.

Two yellow-flowered variants of spring beauty are found in the Northeast, both attractive but each quite different from the other. The first, found in Maryland and Pennsylvania, appears the same as typical *C. virginica* in every way except that it has light to medium yellow petals; the petal veins and anthers are pink as in *C. virginica* (figs. 362, 363). These plants can be found intermixed with "normal" *C. virginica* and are considered to be merely a form of that species and classified as *C. virginica* forma *lutea* (meaning "yellow"). The second yellow-flowered *Claytonia*, known only from New Jersey and growing in exceptionally wet areas, is quite different. The petals are bright yellow, sometimes even tending toward orange (fig. 364), and at first glance the flower may be mistaken for a buttercup (fig. 365). The petal veins are generally the same

not stain as darkly as that of pure species (an indication of decreased fertility).

The Carolina spring beauty was not described until 50 years after Linnaeus's naming of *C. virginica*. It was named in 1803 by the French royal botanist, André Michaux. Michaux had been sent to the United States by King Louis XVI in 1785 to search for plants that might be of economic use in France. He spent 12 years in botanically unexplored territory, collecting plants from Canada through the eastern part of the United States to Florida. Michaux described many species new to science—among them, *C. caroliniana*. He sent seeds of many North American species back to France and was also responsible for introducing plants from afar into the United States, including the gingko tree and the crape myrtle.

Fig. 362. Flowers of *Claytonia virginica* forma *lutea* with pale yellow petals marked with pink veins and pink anthers. The lower flower is in the male (first day) phase, and the two upper flowers are in the female phase.

Montia Family

Fig. 363. A close-up view of a flower of *Claytonia virginica* forma *lutea* with a deeper yellow color and bright pink contrasting lines and anthers. Although the anthers are pink in both forms of *C. virginica*, the pollen is creamy white (see the pollen in the corbiculae of the bee in fig. 354).

color as the petals (but sometimes tinted with orange) and thus do not stand out like the pink veins of *C. virginica*); the anthers and pollen are white. These plants are found isolated at some distance from populations of white- or pink-flowered *C. virginica*—never intermixed. The combination of these factors—the color difference in petals and pollen, isolation from "normal" *C. virginica*, and a preference for extremely wet habitat—have resulted in this yellow morph of *Claytonia* being elevated above the level of form to the status of variety. In a 1992 publication, David Snyder, the New Jersey State Botanist, described this spring beauty as *Claytonia virginica* var. *hammondiae*. Other botanists, including the authors of a recent (2006) monograph on the genus *Claytonia*, consider *C. virginica* to be a highly variable species, and they include the two yellow color morphs within the basic species description rather than as forms or varieties.

A new species of *Claytonia* has recently been described from areas just beyond the geographic range covered by this book. In 2006, plants in what had long been considered to be outlying populations of *C. caroliniana* were classified as *C. ozarkensis*, based on differences in the leaves and the habitat of the new species. The white- to pink-flowered Ozark spring beauty lives in cracks and fissures in dry

Fig. 364. Strongly yellow-orange flowers of *C. virginica* var. *hammondiae*. Note the white pollen in the newly opened top flower.

Fig. 365. Flowers of *Claytonia virginica* var. *hammondiae* with bright yellow petals, tending toward orange at the base, and white anthers.

sandstone bluffs in only three counties in Arkansas and (rarely) in southern Missouri and eastern Oklahoma. Its leaves have markedly long petioles and relatively short, broad blades. There are also several sepals rather than the standard two found in the two eastern species of spring beauty. When the plant is in fruit, the pedicels turn toward the bluff, often actually inserting the fruits directly into a fissure, where, it is presumed, the seeds are dispersed. As the species is known from only nine localities, the authors have recommended that it be considered for endangered-species protection status.

Broomrape Family

Fig. 366. A plant of *Conopholis americana* in flower. Each tubular white flower emerges above a tan bract.

Fig. 367. The remnants of squawroot fruit stalks at the base of a black oak tree in autumn.

Squawroot

Conopholis americana
Broomrape Family (Orobanchaceae)

Squawroot is different enough in appearance from most flowering plants that some people have mistaken it for a fungus.

Habitat: Rich woods with acidic soils, usually under oaks.

Range: Nova Scotia to Florida, west to northern Michigan, Wisconsin, Illinois, and Alabama.

The genus *Conopholis* was established in 1825 when a German botanist, K.F.W. Wallroth, segregated it out of *Orobanche*, where it had originally been placed by Linnaeus. Squawroot is an odd plant: lacking chlorophyll and true leaves (fig. 366), it is thus unable to produce its own food. It is a plant of forests inhabited by acid-loving species and generally grows beneath or near oak trees, which it parasitizes to obtain its nutritional needs. Groups of thick, fingerlike stalks rise from an underground tubercle in midspring. The stalks bear small, creamy-white tubular flowers that are seldom seen by the casual observer. The fleshy stalks range in color from creamy yellow to tan to brown, depending on the time of year, and are covered in overlapping scales arranged somewhat like those of a pinecone, hence the generic name, *Conopholis*, from the Greek *conos*, meaning "cone," and *pholis*, meaning "scale." This resemblance to a pinecone is particularly apparent in autumn, when the dried inflorescences have turned brown (figs. 367, 368); those that remain into winter are shriveled and black. The flower stalks are 5–8 inches in height with a dense raceme of flowers blooming initially at the base and ultimately covering most of the stalk. The flowers are small (8–14 millimeters long) with a toothed calyx and a two-lipped tubular flower whose upper lip curves slightly downward over the three-parted lower lip. The opening of the flower buds of squawroot is unusual in that the two lower side lobes of the corolla enclose the upper lobe in bud and open first. A small bract is present at the base of each individual flower stalk.

Reproduction in squawroot occurs exclusively by seed, yet the flowers contain no nectar and have no

Broomrape Family

Fig. 368. The dark brown remnants of a clump of squawroot inflorescences in late autumn, when their resemblance to a group of pinecones is evident. Note the presence of oak leaves from species in both red and white oak groups.

discernable scent with which to attract pollinators; published reports of insect visitation are rare. It is thought that the few bumblebees observed as floral visitors were collecting the sticky exudate of the stigma. However, as evidenced by the large number of seeds produced (about 500 per fruit with a potential of 100,000 for an average plant! fig. 369), self-pollination must occur. To verify squawroot's ability to self-pollinate, experiments were done in which inflorescences were bagged before the flowers opened in order to exclude any visitors from reaching the flowers; over 85% of the flowers still set seed (a percentage almost equal to those that were left uncovered). Each flower has four stamens that protrude from its upper lobe (fig. 370) as well as a thick style and stigma (fig. 371). The open anthers were observed to be in contact with the stigma just before the corolla opens and could thus effect pollination at that time. There are even reports that the flowers on an occasional aberrant flower stalk, one that never pushes through the surface of the ground (fig. 372), still open and set fruit with viable seed.

The seeds of squawroot are tiny (only up to one millimeter in diameter) but comparatively large for members of its family (Orobanchaceae). Such small seeds have few stored resources and must quickly find a source of nutrients in the surrounding soil or they will perish. It is thought that they will germinate only when in the vicinity of a root tip of an oak that is infected with mycorrhizal fungi. Most studies have shown that squawroot parasitizes oaks exclusively in the red/black group. Excavations of squawroot plants in an area with multiple individuals allowed researchers to trace their connections to the roots of host species. It was found that the actual attachments were only on species in the red/black oak group (e.g., *Quercus rubra* and *Q. velutina*), even if the tubercles were in contact with the roots of other species, including white oak (*Q. alba*). In one exception to this, the author of a study published in 1929 claimed to have encountered a tubercle of *Conopholis* on the root of a member of the white oak group (*Q. bicolor*). Given the difficulty of tracing a tiny root tip back to its parent tree when the roots of several species are entangled in the forest soil, there is room for possible error in this observation. However, there has been some success

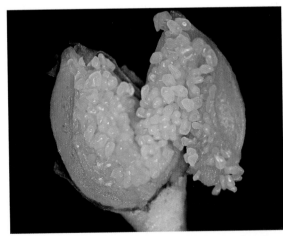

Fig. 369. An immature fruit of squawroot that has been split open to reveal the numerous ovules that will ripen into seeds.

Fig. 370. (Left) Squawroot inflorescences with flowers at their peak (full anthesis). Note the protruding stamens.

Fig. 371. (Right) The tip of a squawroot inflorescence that is past flower. Note the persistent styles and the few remaining dried stamens.

in cultivating *Conopholis americana* from seed on host plants of the white oak group; in this case, it is thought that the mycorrhizal fungal associate might be the more important component of the partnership, with squawroot seedling survival attributable to its presence. As stated earlier, *Conopholis* belongs to the Orobanchaceae, a family of plants almost all of whose members are parasitic to some degree. *Conopholis* is generally considered a holoparasite, one that is entirely dependent upon oak trees for its nutrition. Other genera in the family with this lifestyle include *Orobanche* (fig. 301) and *Epifagus* (beechdrops). However, members of those two genera have a direct connection to the photosynthetic host, whereas squawroot parasitizes only the *mycorrhizal* roots of oaks. Thus, it is difficult to say whether squawroot is truly a holoparasite on the oak or whether it is dependent on the fungal mycorrhizae as intermediaries to transport the nutrients from the oak.

A number of genera in the Orobanchaceae, many of them formerly in the figwort family, Scrophulariaceae (e.g., *Castilleja* and *Pedicularis*; fig. 257), are hemiparasites. These plants have chlorophyll and are capable of producing at least some of their own carbohydrate, but they are dependent upon their connection with a host plant for the balance of their nutritional requirements. In some cases, the hemiparasites can produce adequate photosynthate for their needs and rely on the host species solely for water,

nitrogen, and dissolved minerals. The decision to move the hemiparasitic "scrophs" from the Scrophulariaceae to the Orobanchaceae was made only recently and was based on information from the analysis of DNA sequences of a broad array of species in the formerly more inclusive figwort family.

Some parasitic species are host specific, meaning that they can form a parasitic association with only one species, for example, beechdrops (*Epifagus virginiana*) with American beech trees (*Fagus grandifolia*); others may parasitize a group of related species, as with squawroot (*Conopholis* spp.) and oaks (*Quercus* spp.),

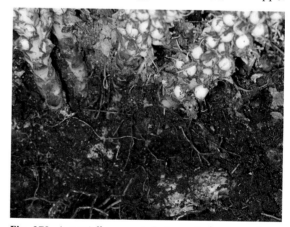

Fig. 372. A partially excavated plant of squawroot showing a partially uncovered subterranean inflorescence in the lower part of the photo.

Broomrape Family

Fig. 373. (Left) Inflorescences of squawroot with flowers that are not quite fully open. Note the tan scales that subtend the flowers.

Fig. 374. (Right) A plant of *Conopholis alpina* in bud. Note how similar in appearance this species is to *C. americana* in figure 373. Photographed in Costa Rica.

and still others can parasitize members of a number of different families, for example, cancer-root (*Orobanche uniflora*; fig. 301), which utilizes various genera of the aster family as well as herbaceous species from other families as hosts.

There are only two species of *Conopholis*, and there is no overlap of their ranges: *C. americana* (fig. 373) is native to the eastern United States, and *C. alpina* (fig. 374) is found in the southwestern United States, Mexico, and Central America. The two species look very much alike. Aside from their geographic locality, they are best told apart by small differences such as the length of the corolla tube, which in *C. americana*, is up to 14 millimeters long, as compared with that of *C. alpina*, which may reach 20 millimeters; or the style, which is often persistent (and reflexed downward) in fruit in the eastern species (fig. 375) but is deciduous in *C. alpina* (fig. 376).

The seeds of squawroot germinate if they are in the vicinity of the growing root of a host species (probably in response to a chemical stimulus produced by the host), and they then begin to grow into the host tissue. The junction where the parasite seedling comes into contact with a small, mycorrhizal root tip of the host species is called a haustorium. The mycorrhizal fungi absorb water and nutrients from the host and transfer them to the parasite. In general, once the oak root has been parasitized, it ceases to grow in length.

The parasitic stem tissue then undergoes a period of rapid proliferation, and the host tissue does so to a lesser extent at the site of penetration, so that it partially surrounds the parasite. An outgrowth of the host xylem (vascular tissue that transports water and nutrients) penetrates the parasite's tissue and connects to the xylem of the parasite, allowing for the passage of water and nutrients from host to parasite. To facilitate transpiration, members of the Orobanchaceae

Fig. 375. (Left) A close-up of the immature capsules of *Conopholis americana*. Note the persistent styles that have bent downward over some of the fruits. **Fig. 376.** (Right) An infructescence of *Conopholis alpina*. Note the lack of persistent styles, a feature that distinguishes this species from *C. americana*. Photographed in Costa Rica.

Fig. 377. The fruiting stalks of squawroot resemble small corncobs and are eaten by bears, hence the common name, bear-corn.

have stomata that remain open continuously, a feature common in parasitic species, which thus benefit from the increased movement of water from the host to the parasite. The fleshy subterranean structure is composed primarily of parasite tissue and is generally referred to as a tubercle (or alternatively as a nodule, gall, or tuber). In the squawroot/oak association the tubercles are usually located about six inches beneath ground level and may reach a diameter of up to 34 millimeters before they begin to senesce. When many tubercles grow in close proximity, they may fuse to form a large subterranean body reaching up to five meters across. As a defensive measure, the oaks produce tannins that infiltrate the tubercle and can ultimately cause its death as a result of slow poisoning

or by the clogging of its vascular tissue. *Conopholis* plants are known to live for about 10 years, with a maximum recorded age of 13 years (based on counting the annual rings of the host root). The first 4 years are spent developing underground, the next 4–5 as reproductive individuals, and the final 2 years as senescent plants. Most of the seeds of squawroot fall from the capsule onto the nearby soil, guaranteeing close proximity to a host. The same host may be parasitized repeatedly over its long lifetime without apparent harm. In addition to a nearby host, *Conopholis* seeds require loose, rich soil for proper germination and development.

In the Smoky Mountain region, black bears emerging from hibernation eat the flowering shoots of squawroot, which make up 10% of their total spring diet; the major part of the Smoky Mountain bears' summer diet consists of berries. However, in Virginia's Shenandoah National Park, squawroot composes 40% of the summer diet of black bears. A study of the nutritional properties of the squawroot shoots shows that they are high in fiber (45–62%), an important dietary component that helps the post-hibernation bear's alimentary system return to normal function. Bears continue to feed on squawroot throughout the season.

Not only bears feed on squawroot; white-tailed deer forage on the plants throughout the year as well. In the Southern Appalachians, samples from the stomachs of harvested spring-feeding deer showed that, although flowers of tulip trees (*Liriodendron tulipifera*) represented the deer's primary food, squawroot was an important secondary food. Squawroot seeds have also been found in the stomachs of mice. The consumption of squawroot fruit by mammals may result in long-distance seed dispersal.

Squawroot (so called perhaps for some undetermined medicinal use by Native Americans) is known by a few other common names throughout its range: cancer-root, for its purported use in treating that disease (perhaps because of the appearance of the tumor-like tubercles); bear-root, because of its consumption by bears; and bear-corn, for the appearance of the stalks when they are in immature fruit (fig. 377).

Bunch-flower Family

Fig. 378. Two flowering plants of painted trillium (*Trillium undulatum*) showing the magenta markings that "bleed" into the veins of the petals.

Fig. 379. Two flowering stems of purple trillium (*Trillium erectum*), probably arising from the same rhizome.

Trilliums
Purple Trillium, Large-flowered Trillium,
and Painted Trillium
Trillium erectum, Trillium grandiflorum,
and *Trillium undulatum*
Bunch-flower Family (Melanthiaceae)

Trilliums are native primarily to North America, with a few species in eastern Asia and one in the Himalayas. Because of their beauty, they are appreciated by wildflower lovers and gardeners alike. Like many other spring-flowering woodland herbs, their seeds are dispersed by ants, and in some cases, by wasps.

Habitat: Varies according to species, but generally moist woods, with painted trillium favoring wetter areas.

Range: Purple trillium—from Quebec and Ontario to Maryland and Ohio, south in the mountains to North Carolina, Georgia, and Tennessee. Large-flowered trillium—Quebec and Maine to Minnesota, south to Pennsylvania, Ohio, and Indiana, and in the mountains to northern Georgia and northeast Alabama. Painted trillium—Quebec and Ontario to New Jersey and Pennsylvania, south in the mountains to Tennessee and Georgia, and west to Michigan and Wisconsin.

As reflected in both its generic and common names, trillium has its parts arranged in threes, or in multiples of three—three leaves, three sepals, three petals, six stamens, three stigmas (fig. 380), and an ovary that has three compartments. Because of this, one common name that has been applied to various species of trillium is trinity flower. Another is birthroot (sometimes corrupted to "bethroot"), due to its use by Native Americans during childbirth. Like some other monocots discussed in this book (e.g., Jack-in-the-pulpit and skunk cabbage), the leaves of trillium are atypical of monocots in that they are broad and have a netlike system of veins.

Trillium species are herbaceous perennials that inhabit the ground layer of our forests and bloom in May, just as the trees are beginning to leaf out (fig. 381). Their three leaves are oriented parallel to the ground, enhancing their ability to intercept the sunlight that penetrates the canopy above. The leaves might be confused with those of Jack-in-the pulpit when the plants are not in flower, but the two can be readily distinguished by the alignment of the leaves: those of trillium are more evenly arranged, such that the tips of the three leaves could be said to point to

179

Bunch-flower Family

Fig. 380. A flower of purple trillium showing the three leaves, sepals, petals, and stigmas. The six stamens have just begun to open.

twelve o'clock, four o'clock, and eight o'clock (dividing a "clock-face" into three equal segments; fig. 382), whereas those of Jack-in-the-pulpit point more to twelve, three, and nine o'clock (fig. 383). As with everything in nature, there is some variation in this pattern, but a closer look at the veins of the leaf will resolve any indecision. The main veins of trillium leaves arch upward from the base of the leaf, whereas Jack-in-the-pulpit leaves have a single principal vein with parallel veins branching from it that extend to a vein that is close to and runs parallel to the margin of the leaf.

The aboveground portion of trillium arises from an underground rhizome that commonly produces just one stem a year, although a particularly robust rhizome might produce two, or rarely three, aerial stems with flowers. Only about 15% of plants in

a population have the necessary resources to produce more than a single stem. The rhizomes are well anchored in the ground by numerous roots that grow and contract, pulling the plant deeper into the soil. Robust plants that produce more than one flower are more successful in attracting pollinators and, hence, produce more seeds. Trillium rhizomes bear annual constrictions where each previous stem arose (fig. 384). A close estimate of a plant's age may be made by counting the annual constrictions, but in older plants the tip of the rhizome may have rotted away, obliterating evidence of the early years of growth. Using this method to estimate minimum age, plants in excess of 70 years of age have been documented.

Once established, trillium plants are long-lived, but they are slow to develop from seed. As shown by the lack of trillium regeneration in clear-cut forests, the seeds of trillium appear to have a short period of viability in the seed bank. Species in the eastern United States all require a two-year period before

Fig. 381. Purple trillium flowering as the canopy above is beginning to leaf out.

Fig. 382. (Left) Trillium leaves showing how the three leaves are evenly arranged on the stem. **Fig. 383.** (Above) A Jack-in-the-pulpit leaf with its three leaflets less equally arranged than the leaves of trillium. Note the parallel veins running from the central vein of each leaf to a vein that follows the margin of the leaf.

they produce aboveground stems and leaves. During the first year, the seedling develops a rhizome and roots, but its solitary cotyledon does not emerge until the following spring. A single, small oval true leaf is produced in the third year (fig. 385), and finally, by the fourth year (or beyond), the typical three-leaved plant appears. *Trillium erectum* is capable of reproducing when the plant is 6–7 years old, but *T. grandiflorum* must generally grow for 16–17 years before producing a flower in the wild. The leaf area and the volume of the rhizome are more important than age in determining whether a plant has enough energy stored to produce a flower. Because of the length of time required to raise a trillium to flowering size from seed, unscrupulous vendors of trillium species often sell plants that are dug from the wild. If you plan to include trillium in your garden, be certain to ascertain that your nursery source is following proper conservation protocols and selling only nursery-propagated plants (plants termed nursery grown may, in fact, be wild collected and then grown in a nursery setting). In the New England area, the New England Wild Flower Society (www.newfs.org) is a good source of seed-grown native plant material. A Google search for "nursery-propagated native plants" will locate sellers in other parts of the country.

The genus *Trillium* has a checkered history of familial membership, having been placed at various times in the Liliaceae, the Trilliaceae, and currently, based on molecular data, in the Melanthiaceae. Worldwide, there are 48–49 known species of *Trillium*: 42 from North America, with the greatest number of those (35) native to the East, and 7 in the western part of the continent. Five or 6 additional species are native to

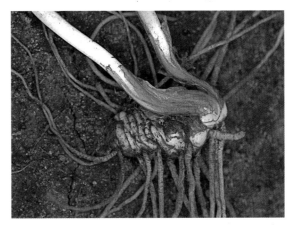

Fig. 384. A rhizome of purple trillium showing the annular constrictions, each indicating a year of growth. The roots growing from the rhizome are contractile, pulling the rhizome deeper into the ground. The age of this rhizome was gauged at 12 years. Note that the rhizome produced two stems.

Bunch-flower Family

Fig. 385. The single leaf produced by a three-year-old plant of *Trillium erectum*.

eastern Asia, and there is 1 Himalayan species. There is no geographic overlap of species. Europe has no native trilliums, and thus, trilliums are highly valued there for their rarity and beauty, even to the extent that they are sometimes stolen from botanical gardens.

The closest relative of trillium is the mostly Asian genus, *Paris*, which has one species that extends into Europe (*Paris quadrifolia*; fig. 386), but none in North America. *Paris* differs from *Trillium* in having narrower leaves in whorls of four or more, and sepals and petals numbering four to six. The inconspicuous, filiform petals are usually green. Most of the 30 species of *Paris* occur in China. In September 2010, researchers at Kew's Jodrell Laboratory announced the surprising discovery of the largest genome (amount of DNA in the nucleus of its cells) of any plant or animal on earth (to date)—almost 60 times the size of the human genome—in a species of *Paris*, *P. japonica*.

I have selected 3 of the 13 *Trillium* species that occur in our range to profile here. They were chosen because they are commonly encountered and are, to my eye, among the most beautiful and interesting members of the genus. Purple trillium (*T. erectum*) is common in moist woods on a variety of soils (fig. 379). The deep maroon-red flowers with widely spread petals produce no nectar. A white-flowered variety, with a dark maroon ovary (*T. erectum* var. *album*; fig. 387), may be found throughout the species' range but is rare except in the Smoky Mountains.

Large-flowered trillium (*T. grandiflorum*) is more frequently found in soils with a somewhat higher pH than those where *T. erectum* grows and is absent from areas with highly acidic soils. The petals of this nectar-producing, large-flowered trillium are snowy white (it is sometimes called white trillium) with their bases overlapping, so that the flowers appear funnel-shaped, and the ovary is mostly concealed (fig. 388). As the flowers of *T. grandiflorum* age, they become pale to deep pink (fig. 389), leading to possible confusion when trying to identify the species of this flower. Field guides generally show only the fresh, white stage of the flower. In certain parts of the eastern United States, *T. grandiflorum* carpets large areas of forest with newly opened white flowers mingled with the

Fig. 386. A flower of *Paris quadrifolia*, a Eurasian species that is a close relative of *Trillium* but has sepals and petals generally in fours and eight stamens.

Fig. 387. The white variety of purple trillium (*T. erectum* var. *album*) is more common in the Smoky Mountains. Note the dark ovary.

Fig. 388. In the more funnel-shaped flower of large-flowered trillium (*T. grandiflorum*), the ovary is almost hidden.

limp and translucent (fig. 394). The leaves of painted trillium, unlike the other two species treated in this chapter, have short petioles. All three of the species discussed here are members of what is called the pedicellate group of *Trillium*, meaning that the flowers are on short stalks (pedicels; fig. 395). The stalkless, or sessile-flowered, species such as toadshade (*T. sessile*) are not native to the northeastern part of the country

aging, but equally beautiful, pink flowers (fig. 390). An exception to this color form occurs in the Blue Ridge Mountains of Virginia, where large numbers of *T. grandiflorum* forma *roseum* are found with flowers that are pink even when newly opened (fig. 391).

Painted trillium (*T. undulatum*) grows in acidic soils in wet woods, bogs, and mountainous regions (fig. 392). Its leaves, especially in early spring, are a dark bronzy green. The petals of painted trillium flowers are white, like those of *T. grandiflorum*, but they are smaller, narrower, and stunningly "painted" with bright magenta chevrons at their bases, the magenta color bleeding outward into the impressed veins of the petals (fig. 393). The petals have wavy margins, the basis for the specific name *undulatum* (fig. 378). Once the flower has been pollinated, the petals become

Fig. 389. (Above) These aging flowers of large-flowered trillium have turned pink. **Fig. 390.** (Top right) A forest in Virginia carpeted with *Trillium grandiflorum*. **Fig. 391.** (Bottom right) The flowers of the pink form of large-flowered trillium (*Trillium grandiflorum* forma *roseum*) are pink from the time of opening.

Bunch-flower Family

Fig. 392. A painted trillium in the understory of a wet spruce-fir forest in the Adirondack Mountains of New York.

in the narrow sense (i.e., New England and most of New York, New Jersey, and Pennsylvania) but are quite common further south.

In general, insect visitation to trillium is minimal when compared with other members of the spring flora in Northeast forests. In fact, Frederick and Roberta Case, authors of the book, *Trilliums*, and growers of many species of trillium, state: "We have seen little published information on pollinators of trilliums," and "we have seldom seen pollinators on the flowers, except those of *Trillium nivale* . . . eagerly visited by small native bees and the honeybee" (p. 27). They also state, "Particularly on those species that produce fetid or putrid odors purported to attract carrion fly and beetle pollinators (*Trillium erectum, T. foetidissimum, T. stamineum*), we have seldom observed any insects visiting the bloom." This had been my experience as well; I had never observed insects visiting the flowers of any of the trillium species. As all the literature that I have read on pollination of the unpleasantly scented, carrion-colored purple trillium (another common, and appropriate, name for this species is wet-dog) mentions that flies are the most frequent visitors and likely pollinators, I decided one day to stake out a patch of purple trillium in Connecticut to see if I could observe any fly visitors. I did not wait long before visitors arrived—not flies, but small, native bees (fig. 396). Each spent up to a minute on a flower, manipulating the anthers and probing the base of the flower, their hairy bodies

carrying pollen when they left. Based on this very limited observation, there is perhaps more to learn about the pollination of this species. Another trillium visitor, this one a pest, is the larva of a tortricid moth that feeds on the leaves of trillium during part of its life cycle and may also destroy the flowers.

The large-flowered trillium is unscented but produces nectar that is sought by bumblebees, the effective pollinators of this species. Conflicting reports have been published regarding the self-compatibility of *T. grandiflorum* and *T. erectum*, that is, their ability to self-pollinate. Some observers have concluded that due to the limited number of visitations by pollinators, trillium must be capable of self-pollination.

Fig. 393. (Top) A close-up of the flower of painted trillium with magenta-colored chevrons that "bleed" into the veins of the petals. **Fig. 394.** (Above) The petals of painted trillium quickly wilt and become translucent soon after the flower has been pollinated.

Fig. 395. A side view of large-flowered trillium showing the pedicel (flower stalk) that holds the flower above the leaves. The flowers of some other species of trillium (e.g., *T. sessile*) arise directly at the level of the leaves.

However, in a recent paper, Tammy Sage and coauthors documented that mechanisms against self-pollination exist in both species. The stigmas are able to distinguish and inhibit the growth of their own pollen, thus preventing inbreeding and promoting out-crossing. If pollen from another flower germinates on the stigma, it begins growing a pollen tube down toward the ovary within a half hour, whereas pollen from the same flower (self-pollen) is either prevented from germinating or has its growth halted at an early stage, before it can fertilize an the egg in an ovule. However, the mechanism is not foolproof. Self-pollination does occur, especially in the wild, where up to a third of the ovules of *T. grandiflorum* and half of those of *T. erectum* were found, using genetic testing, to be fertilized with self-pollen. As the flowers of large-flowered trillium age, their stigmas reflex downward and come into contact with the anthers, allowing for occasional self-pollination. In both field studies and controlled pollination experiments, flowers that have been cross-pollinated are more successful reproductively—they produce a greater percentage of viable seed than do the self-pollinating plants. This "imperfect" system may, in fact, be a means of assuring that some seed will be produced when pollinators are scarce or even absent. I was unable to find any published information about the pollinators of painted trillium.

Large-flowered trillium is the favored trillium species of gardeners. Because of its beauty, it has been designated as the floral emblem of Ontario and the state wildflower of Ohio (the official state flower is still the nonnative red carnation). Large-flowered trillium is more prone than other species to develop aberrant flowers, either with an excess of petals resulting from the transformation of reproductive parts (fig. 397) or with color variations, such as green (fig. 398), or striped green and white, flowers. Such plant oddities command high prices at plant nurseries, where gardeners intent on having something "unusual" will pay as much as $100 for a mutant plant. These variations are caused by infection with a mycoplasma, an organism almost as small as a virus but free-living. The infections eventually weaken, and ultimately kill, the plant, making it bad practice to introduce such plants into the garden. The disease could spread to nearby plants in the wild (e.g., via insect vectors) and result in the destruction of native populations of trillium.

The fruits of the three species differ as well: those of purple trillium are rounded and red with six narrow wings (fig. 399) and have a sweet, fruity aroma; whereas when ripe, the fruits of large-flowered trillium are green (fig. 400) and somewhat six-angled;

Fig. 396. A flower of purple trillium being visited by a native andrenid bee. The bee was dusted with pollen that it will carry to another flower.

Bunch-flower Family

Fig. 397. (Left) Two plants of *T. grandiflorum* with doubled flowers that are caused by a mycoplasma. **Fig. 398.** (Above) A double-flowered *T. grandiflorum* with green petals. All of the reproductive parts have been converted into petals, rendering the plant unable to sexually reproduce.

and those of painted trillium are olive shaped, only slightly three-sided, and bright red (fig. 401).

The fruit of trillium is a berry with many small seeds, each with a fatty food body (elaiosome) attached (fig. 402). The fruits of trillium do not dehisce (split open) unless the pressure of their enlarging seeds is so great that they burst through the side of the fruit and drop to the ground in small clumps. More often, the point of attachment of the fruit becomes weak, allowing the entire fruit to fall to the ground, where it may break open or be burrowed into by insects seeking to obtain the elaiosome-bearing seeds. As discussed in the treatments of other species in this book, elaiosomes are the attractant for the dispersers (usually ants) of seeds of many spring-flowering plants, including those of trillium. About 75–80% of seeds remain where they fall, within 10 centimeters of the plant. Ants carry the rest to their nests, usually from 1 to 10 meters away, and chew off the elaiosomes. Fallen seeds discovered by ants are removed quickly, about a quarter of them within 90 minutes after falling; those not discovered by ants within the first three days remain where they fell, since the elaiosomes lose their attractiveness once they dry out. Deer mice and other small rodents prey upon the remaining seeds. In 2001, yellow jacket wasps (*Vespula* spp.) were observed carrying the seeds of trillium in the eastern United States (North Carolina) and consuming the oil-rich food bodies; wasp dispersal

for some western species had been documented previously. The wasps chew into the fruits to get the seeds and even steal seeds from ants that are in the process of carrying them to their nests. Dispersal by wasps, as contrasted to that by ants, results in the seeds being carried up to 20 meters from the source, a benefit for the plant. Harvestmen (daddy-longlegs) also feed on the elaiosomes. Investigators studying the chemistry of elaiosomes isolated two fatty acids that trigger certain behavior patterns in ants. Linoleic acid stimulates feeding behavior, and oleic acid induces carrying behavior; oleic acid in the elaiosome also serves as the chemical attractant for ants. The same oleic acid is

Fig. 399. A ripe red fruit of purple trillium with six ridges, or wings.

Fig. 400. An unripe fruit of large-flowered trillium with immature seeds. The fruit turns green when ripe.

Fig. 401. A plant of painted trillium with a mature red fruit. Note the short petioles of the leaves.

produced when ants die and begin to decompose. The carrying behavior instigated by the chemical prompts the ants to carry their dead out of the nest to nearby refuse heaps. Elaiosomes of all three species of trillium have amounts of oleic acid that are not substantially different, and all attract ants, but because the amount of total fat content in the elaiosomes of painted trillium is markedly less, fewer seeds of that species are taken by ants. Since wasps and harvestmen feed on dead insects, they are most likely attracted by the same scent of decomposition presented by the elaiosome. A paper published in 2009 by researchers at the University of California, Riverside suggests that there may be more to this necrophoresis process (the removal of the dead from communal nests) than the long-accepted explanation suggests. In their studies of Argentine ants, they noted that ants begin to carry their dead out of the nest almost immediately after death, before decomposition could have much effect. They found that oleic acid is *always* present in the ants and is not produced only as a result of decomposition. Rather, it is the rapid dissipation of two other chemicals in the cuticle of living ants that quickly "unmasks" the triggering aroma of oleic acid when the ants die. It will be interesting to see if similar results will be found in studies of ants in the Northeast.

Birds or mammals may well have been the original dispersers of trillium seeds, since the fruits of trillium

Fig. 402. An opened fruit of purple trillium. Note the cream-colored elaiosomes on the tan seeds.

are attractive (often red) and fleshy. Today deer inadvertently fill this role when they consume the whole plant, including the fruit and seeds, and "plant" the seeds in their droppings (this method of long-distance dispersal has been suggested as the means by which trillium gradually recolonized formerly glaciated areas). While such dispersal of seeds may be beneficial to the species, heavy browsing by deer has a strong negative effect on local trillium populations. As the deer population exceeds the carrying capacity of an area, overbrowsing results in the decline of trillium and other forest herbs.

Lily Family

Fig. 403. The outside of the tepals of trout-lily are brushed with red. Note the strongly mottled leaves.

Fig. 404. A particularly floriferous patch of trout-lily. Most colonies have few plants in flower.

Trout-lily

Erythronium americanum
Lily Family (Liliaceae)

Colonies of trout-lily brighten our northeastern wood-lands with their yellow flowers in early spring. Like other true ephemerals, the aboveground portion of the plant disappears by late spring when the canopy over-head has fully leafed out.

Habitat: Moist woods.

Range: Nova Scotia, New Brunswick, and Ontario to Minnesota, south to Florida and Alabama; more fre-quent in the East than in the South or Midwest.

In addition to trout-lily, this species is also known as adder's tongue, fawn-lily, and dog-tooth violet (a translation of the specific epithet, *dens-canis*, of the European species). Adder's tongue might have been bestowed upon the plant because of its mottled (snake-like?) leaves. John Burroughs, a nineteenth-century American naturalist and writer, felt that adder's tongue was an inappropriate name for such a lovely plant and suggested either fawn-lily, for its leaves spotted like the back of a fawn, or "Still better is the name 'troutlily,' which has recently been proposed for this plant. It blooms along the trout streams, and its leaf is as mottled as a trout's back" (p. 26).

Fig. 405. A culti-var ('Rose Queen') of the European species, *Erythro-nium dens-canis*.

Lily Family

Fig. 406. *Erythronium albidum*, the white trout-lily native throughout Ontario, the Midwest, and eastern United States (other than New England, the Carolinas, and Florida). Aside from the color of its tepals, white trout-lily differs from our yellow-flowered trout-lily in having recurved stigmatic lobes.

Fig. 407. *Erythronium toulumense* is a western species with multiple flowers on each scape. It is the parent of several cultivated hybrids.

Erythronium is a primarily North American genus of yellow- or white-flowered perennials, with a few exceptions: pink to purple flowers occur in the widespread European species, *Erythronium dens-canis*, and in a small number of western North American species. Linnaeus named the genus in 1753 for the European species, which explains the derivation of the generic name (from the Greek *erythros*, meaning "red," referring to the reddish color of the flowers). The common name of the European species, *dog-tooth* violet, is said to derive from its small, pointed, white bulb (like a

dog's tooth, hence *dens-canis*), but there is no physical resemblance to a violet. *Erythronium americanum* was described in 1808.

There are about 27 species in *Erythronium*, all of them North American with the exception of the above-mentioned *E. dens-canis* (fig. 405) and three former subspecies that have been segregated from it: *E. caucasicum*, *E. japonicum*, and *E. sibiricum*, each named for its place of origin. The majority of North American species are from the western United States and Canada, particularly California. Among the better known American species are the white trout-lily (*E. albidum*; fig. 406), a popular wildflower plant that is found in the eastern and central United States; the yellow- (or sometimes whitish-) flowered glacier-lily (*E. grandiflorum*), which blooms against the receding snows in the mountains of the western United States and Canada; the white-flowered avalanche-lily (*E. montanum*), which forms dense carpets in the alpine meadows of the Pacific Northwest; and the yellow Toulumne fawn-lily (*E. toulumnense*; fig. 407), from the Sierras of California. Although plants of the eastern species of trout-lily have only a solitary flower, those of the western species commonly produce scapes bearing multiple flowers. The last three species mentioned above are the source of several attractive garden hybrids. The leaves of the eastern and western species differ as well; those of the eastern species are either plain or have random whitish or deep red-brown mottling, whereas those of the western species, if not plain, have symmetrical streaking or veining.

Fig. 408. The three inner tepals (petals) of a flower of trout-lily showing the small "ears" at their bases.

Fig. 409. A wild tulip, *Tulipa saxatilis*, photographed in its native Greece, showing the similarity of this genus to the closely related *Erythronium*.

Four of the western species have flowers that range from pale pink to deep pink-purple, whereas all eastern species are yellow or white. Also, only one western species reproduces by producing stolons from its bulb, something that is common in the eastern species *E. americanum* and *E. albidum*.

Trout-lily is a typical monocot, with a single cotyledon (seed leaf), floral parts in threes or multiples of three, and leaves with parallel venation (the latter characteristic is not readily apparent in trout-lily leaves). As in many monocots, particularly those in the lily family, the perianth parts, composed of the outer two floral whorls, are nearly identical in appearance. In such cases, both the outer whorl of sepals and the inner whorl of petals are referred to as tepals. In *E. americanum*, there are small differences between the inner and outer tepals: the three outer tepals are usually brushed with red on their outer surfaces (fig. 403), and the three inner tepals have slightly flared margins at their bases, described as being auriculate, or "eared" (fig. 408). *Erythronium* is closely related to *Tulipa* (the genus of tulips), with which it shares several characteristics. The relationship with tulips becomes apparent when native species of Eurasian tulips are examined (fig. 409).

Fig. 410. Several plants of trout-lily with their flowers closed on an overcast day.

Fig. 411. A flower of trout-lily with its tepals fully reflexed on a sunny day. Note that three of the reddish anthers have already dehisced (one is shriveled), making their red pollen available; the three longer anthers will open on the following day.

Lily Family

Fig. 412. (Left) A native bee clinging to the stamens of trout-lily to collect pollen. Note that the stamens and pollen are yellow, rather than red, in these flowers and that the underside of the bee is heavily dusted with pollen. **Fig. 413.** (Right) A pollen-eating beetle, *Asclera ruficollis*, on a trout-lily flower. The beetle feeds on the pollen but also carries some of it to other flowers, thereby effecting cross-pollination.

Trout-lily flowers, as is the case with many spring bloomers, remain closed at night and on overcast days (fig. 410). When the sun appears, the tepals recurve fully so that the flower resembles a miniature Turk's cap lily in form (fig. 411). Nodding flowers such as trout-lily require a pollinator that is either able to hover in front of the flower or to hang from its tepals or stamens (fig. 412). In the case of trout-lily, it is the latter method that is utilized, primarily by bees. The anthers and pollen of *E. americanum* are dimorphic in color—red-brown in some plants and yellow in others (figs. 403, 412). The significance of this difference has not been established, and some researchers have even questioned whether the different color forms might represent different species. Recent research by Dr. Theresa Culley and her student, Richard Stokes, has shown that a normal number of fruits and viable seeds are produced from hand-pollinated crosses

between yellow-pollen plants and reddish-pollen plants. However, whether or not the resultant plants grown from those seeds will show one color to be dominant remains to be seen, because it will be several years until the young plants reach flowering stage. To date, Culley and Stokes have found no genetic differences between the two color forms. Their thinking is that the different color forms are a result of a somatic mutation within the clone.

Trout-lily has a very limited ability to self-pollinate, and lower seed production results from fertilization by self-pollen. However, a stigma that first receives self-pollen followed by outcrossed pollen will develop seeds fertilized by the foreign pollen and thus produce a higher number of seeds. For the most part, *E. americanum* is reliant upon pollinator visits to reproduce sexually. Among the insects observed visiting the flowers is the pollen-and-ovule-eating, red-necked

Fig. 414. A native bee foraging for nectar in the base of a trout-lily flower. In doing so, the bee clings to the stamens and gets dusted with pollen on its ventral surface.

false blister beetle, *Asclera ruficollis* (with black elytra and head, and dull red pronotum; fig. 413). The beetles become heavily dusted with pollen while feeding on the flowers and can serve as pollinators as well as predators of trout-lily. Several species of native bees—including *Andrena erythronii*, *A. carlini*, and queen bumblebees (*Bombus* spp.), as well as the introduced honeybee—are known pollinators, transporting the pollen on their lower (ventral) surfaces (fig. 412). Bee flies (*Bombylius* spp.) have also been observed visiting the flowers. All visitors collect nectar (fig. 414), and many collect pollen as well. Insects are attracted to flowers with greater amounts of nectar and/or pollen, and both of these pollinator attractants correlate positively with flower size. Plants with larger flowers are therefore more likely to attract pollinators and thus have their pollen disseminated. Consequently, the genes for larger flower size are more likely to be passed on to future generations, and new floral forms may develop in this manner.

Bees usually remove half of the available pollen in one visit, sometimes spending a long time at one flower, and even pausing during collection to groom themselves and pack the pollen into the pollen baskets (corbiculae) on their hind legs (fig. 415). Thus the plant's opportunity to disseminate its pollen to other flowers is limited because pollen packed into the corbiculae is not available for pollinating subsequently visited flowers. The negative consequence of such thorough pollen collection by bees is lessened by the availability of pollen on two sequential days. The anthers of the inner whorl dehisce shortly after the tepals open and reflex backward, while those of the outer whorl usually open a day later (fig. 411), thus, a bee will not be able to collect most of the plant's pollen during a single visit. The plant is thereby afforded at least two chances for

Fig. 415. A honeybee pausing during its visit to a trout-lily flower to transfer pollen into the corbiculae (pollen baskets) on its hind legs. Note that the hind legs, carrying brick-red pollen, are pulled forward so that the bee can move additional pollen from its front legs into the pollen baskets.

Lily Family

Fig. 416. Senescing yellow leaves of trout-lily at the end the aboveground phase of the plants' life cycle.

pollinators to transport pollen to different plants—preferably not in the same clone. Although one bee pollinator of *E. americanum* is named *Andrena erythronii*, it is not an obligate pollinator of trout-lily, which shares pollinators with other spring-flowering ephemerals such as Dutchman's breeches and toothwort. Fruits form quickly after pollination, with the entire aboveground period of the plant's life cycle lasting just two months. The plants enter dormancy once

Fig. 417. Nearly mature seeds of trout-lily, each with a small elaiosome at one end.

their leaves senesce (fig. 416), but it is a shallow dormancy that is broken when soil temperatures drop in late autumn. Throughout the winter, nutrients are translocated from the storage bulb to new roots and subterranean shoots, ensuring that the plant is ready to begin growth when the soil temperatures begin to rise in spring. The tightly wrapped cone of leaves pushes through the soil and leaf litter, sometimes even piercing leaves on the forest floor with its awl-like tip. Once established, the roots of some plants are quickly invaded by mycorrhizal fungi that sustain themselves during the winter months by utilizing carbohydrates stored in the trout-lily's bulb, thereby inhibiting the plant's root growth. However, with the arrival of spring, plants that have been invaded by mycorrhizal fungi benefit from the ability of the fungus to aid in

Fig. 418. Two plants of trout-lily dug from the ground to show all parts of the plants. Note that the flowering plant on the left has a long underground stem arising from the bulb, to which the two leaves are attached at ground level, and that there are no stolons. The young, single-leaved plant on the right has a short stem since the growing bulblet, though underground, was still close to the surface of the forest floor. It has the beginning of a stolon arising from the left side of the bulblet.

Fig. 419. A white "dropper" (stolon) growing from the underground bulb of a nonreproductive trout-lily plant. After penetrating the ground again, the dropper will produce a new bulblet at its tip.

the absorption of nutrients, resulting in a growth rate that is double that of plants not so "afflicted."

The crescent-shaped seeds of trout-lily are about three millimeters in length with an elaiosome attached to one end (fig. 417). Various species of ants disperse the seeds to their nesting sites. The seeds have delayed germination, waiting until autumn to send out a radicle (precursor of a root). The delay results in the seeds beginning growth in an undisturbed environment, since ants typically change their nest sites with some frequency and will no longer be churning up the soil in the area where the seeds were originally deposited. Seeds have a high germination rate (if they are not consumed by predators—primarily mice). During the first 48 hours, 25% of the newly fallen seeds are dispersed by ants and only 1% taken by predators (usually at night). After the first two days, ants take only a few seeds because the elaiosome quickly loses it attractiveness, and predators consume the majority of those seeds that remain. Ant dispersal of *Erythronium* seeds with elaiosomes is found only in species in eastern North America and Eurasia. The western U.S. species have hard, long-lasting seeds that remain in the opened cup-shaped capsules atop wiry stalks until they are shaken out by the wind or by a passing animal.

From a successfully germinated seed, a single, linear cotyledon emerges in early spring and senesces at the same time as the mature trout-lily plants, after the leafing-out of the trees above has closed the canopy. The following spring, the trout-lily's first true leaf will

be produced from the small bulblet that formed during the first year.

Young plants produce only one leaf. Not until the bulblet has reached sufficient size and worked its way deeper into the soil (as deep as 8–10 inches), will the plant have the resources to produce two leaves, and only then will it be capable of flowering. Although the leaves appear basal, growing at ground level at the base of the flowering stalk, they actually arise from a subterranean stem several inches above the bulb (fig. 418). The plants do not flower until they are at least four to seven years old, and then only if conditions are favorable. Unlike the small new bulblets that send out stolons (fig. 418), mature trout-lily bulbs produce offsets that are adjacent to the main bulb, as occurs in tulips.

Fig. 420. A colony of single-leaved, nonblooming trout-lily plants that most likely are all members of a single clone.

Lily Family

Fig. 421. A trout-lily flower from which all tepals but one have been removed to show the ovary, the style with its erect stigma lobes, and the remaining stamens.

Since trout-lily blooms when pollinator visits may be limited by poor weather conditions, vegetative reproduction is especially important. In *Erythronium* species that produce stolons, most reproduction is vegetative, and few flowers are produced. For the most part, the stolons are subterranean, but they sometimes appear above ground as thin white runners, looking much like strands of spaghetti creeping across the forest floor (fig. 419). They grow until the tip is able to "drop" down into the soil, where it will form a new bulblet (the stolons are sometimes referred to as "droppers" for this reason). Each new bulblet will repeat the process in subsequent years resulting in an ever-expanding clone of genetically identical sister plants (fig. 420). It is rare to find such patches with more than 1% of the plants in flower, but occasionally a particularly floriferous patch may be encountered (fig. 404).

Interesting chemical compounds have been isolated from the bulbs of *Erythronium*, the best known of which is tulipalin A, a compound with antibiotic properties that is capable of inhibiting the growth of both gram-positive and gram-negative bacteria. Subsequently, the compound was found in the bulbs of tulips as well and was determined to be the causative agent of an allergic reaction known in the horticultural trade as "tulip finger"—a redness and peeling of the skin caused by handling the bulbs of tulips (or of *Erythronium* and other related genera). Tulipalin A has now also been isolated from *Spiraea*, a member of the rose family, and is attributed with the ability to protect that species against insect attack.

The bulbs of *Erythronium* are of ethnobotanical use. Those of *E. americanum* were collected and eaten by various Indian groups in the East, and those of *E. grandiflorum* were particularly important as a winter staple in the Northwest and British Columbia, being preserved for long-term storage by a lengthy steaming and drying process. Bulbs of the Japanese species, *E. japonicum*, were formerly harvested and processed for their starch content to make a kind of flour called *katakuirko*, which was used in preparing tempura. The diminished availability of the wild bulbs and the

Fig. 422. *Erythronium americanum* in fruit. The fruit stalks are bent down by the heavy fruit so that they almost touch the ground. Note the white stolon that is visible in the leaf litter.

Fig. 423. Trout-lily plants growing in the semishade on the forest floor before the trees have leafed out in spring.

high cost of processing have resulted in the substitution of potato starch for this particular purpose. Some Native American medicinal uses are also reported for *E. americanum* (e.g., the crushed leaves were used as a poultice for skin sores and the bulbs taken as an emetic).

Trout-lily has two subspecies. Subspecies *americanum*, is widespread throughout the Northeast. It has a fruit with an apex that is either rounded or somewhat flattened, or that has a short point, a remnant of the stigma. The stigma lobes are erect and smooth (fig. 421). Subspecies *harperi* has a distinct point at the apex of its fruit, and its stigma lobes, rather than being erect, curve backward and are grooved rather than smooth. Subspecies *harperi* is found in the southern part of the

species' range—Tennessee, Alabama, Georgia, and Mississippi.

A second yellow-flowered species (*E. umbilicatum*) reaches the southern part of the area covered in this book. *Erythronium umbilicatum* differs from *E. americanum* in that it does not usually produce stolons or grow clonally. It also has spreading stigma lobes, and its fruits, with an indented apex (like an umbilicus), lie on the ground before dehiscing, as compared with those of *E. americanum*, which are usually held above ground (but sometimes are heavy enough to touch the forest floor; fig. 422). The two subspecies of *E. umbilicatum* differ in that subsp. *umbilicatum* has no stolons, and subsp. *monostolum*, just one. Like *E. americanum*, *E. umbilicatum* is an early ephemeral that blooms before the trees shade the forest floor (fig. 423). Three additional species are found at the western margin of the northeastern region: *E. mesochoreum*, from Indiana and Illinois; *E. rostratum*, from Ohio, Kentucky, Tennessee, and Missouri; and *E. propullans*, found only in Minnesota.

The lily family (Liliaceae), like the foxglove family (Scrophulariaceae), was formerly a large, diverse family that has now been severely "pruned." Many modern taxonomists agree that the Liliaceae now includes only 11 genera and 500–600 species whereas, formerly, 280 genera and about 4,000 species were recognized. Some genera previously in the lily family, such as *Trillium* (fig. 378) and *Uvularia* (bellwort), have been reassigned to at least 30 different families, with many of the placements still being debated; additional evidence will be necessary to determine the final family affiliations. *Erythronium* is among those genera that have remained in the lily family, along with the well-known true lilies (*Lilium*), tulips (*Tulipa*), and fritillarias (*Fritillaria*). Other northeastern members of the lily family are the aforementioned lilies (*Lilium*), bluebead lily (*Clintonia*), and twisted-stalk (*Streptopus*).

It is fortunate that trout-lily is not a plant favored by white-tailed deer. Deer may nibble at the emerging leaves, but because the animals tend not to consume the entire leaf, we may continue to enjoy this early sign of spring.

Barberry Family

Fig. 424. Twinleaf flowers blooming above their immature purple-tinged leaves.

Fig. 425. The leaves of *Jeffersonia diphylla* are greatly constricted at their center, giving them the appearance of green butterflies—or twin leaves.

Twinleaf

Jeffersonia diphylla
Barberry Family (Berberidaceae)

The common name of this species is descriptive, but it is inaccurate. Although the leaves of twinleaf appear to be two leaves that are mirror images of each other, each "pair" is actually a single leaf divided almost in two. Watch carefully for the flowers because they last for only a day or two. *Jeffersonia* is considered endangered in New Jersey and Georgia and threatened in New York and Iowa.

Habitat: Rich woods, especially with calcareous soil.

Range: Western New York and southern Ontario to southeastern Minnesota, south to Maryland, Alabama, and adjacent northwestern Georgia.

Thomas Jefferson is one of only two United States presidents to have a plant genus named for him, the other being George Washington, who is commemorated by the palm genus, *Washingtonia*. *Jeffersonia* was named for Jefferson not because of his political achievements, but rather to honor his deep love for, and knowledge of, natural history.

Like spring beauty, twinleaf was first discovered by John Clayton (see the chapter on spring beauties), whose nonflowering collection of the plant was sent to Linnaeus. Linnaeus determined the plant to be a new species of *Podophyllum* and gave it the name *Podophyllum diphyllum* in 1753. That name was used for nearly 40 years until, in 1791, a plant grown from a rhizome of twinleaf collected by the French botanist, André Michaux, flowered in the Philadelphia garden of William Bartram. Bartram and Dr. Benjamin Smith Barton, a professor of botany at the University of Pennsylvania, made the first drawings of the plant in flower, and Barton realized that Linnaeus' placement of the plant in *Podophyllum* was erroneous. In 1792, Barton proposed a new genus for the unique plant, naming it in honor of Thomas Jefferson, then secretary of state (Jefferson did not become president until 1801). Of all of the counties, cities (including the capital of Missouri), mountains, schools, buildings,

Barberry Family

Fig. 426. The flowers of twinleaf look superficially like those of bloodroot, but the leaves are very different.

streets, and ships named in honor of Jefferson, I like to think that he would have been most pleased to have been honored by having this plant genus named for him (and, perhaps also, the mineral, jeffersonite, which was discovered in 1822).

Jeffersonia soon became a popular plant in gardens, including Jefferson's own at Monticello. In one of Jefferson's detailed garden journals, he noted that in April 1807, seeds of *Jeffersonia* were planted in one of the oval beds that flanked the house. Twinleaf is still grown in the gardens at Monticello and blooms

Fig. 427. An immature, still folded leaf of *Jeffersonia diphylla*, with bright red-violet coloration.

Fig. 428. Two twinleaf plants that have recently emerged from the ground in early April.

Fig. 430. The soil has been removed from the base of two twinleaf plants in autumn to show the underground shoots of that will grow into new plants in spring.

Fig. 429. The yellow leaves of *Jeffersonia diphylla* as they appear when senescing in September.

Fig. 431. (Left) A twinleaf flower bud with its sepals still intact. **Fig. 432.** (Right) A small, native bee on a twinleaf flower bud. Note that all but one of the sepals has fallen.

at about the time of Jefferson's birthday, April 13. The Scottish plant collector, John Lyon, who had collected hundreds of twinleaf rhizomes at Harper's Ferry, Virginia, brought the plant to England in the early 1800s.

Twinleaf flowers bloom early, just before, or at the same time as, bloodroot (fig. 11). The white flowers of these two early bloomers are similar in appearance, and at first glance the two species might be mistaken for one another (fig. 426, and see fig. 15). The number of petals varies in both but is most commonly eight. The leaves, however, are distinctly different: those of twinleaf have very shallowly lobed margins and are sharply constricted at the middle, giving them the appearance of a butterfly in flight when the leaf is

fully expanded (fig. 425) or of a perched, magenta butterfly when the leaf is still folded and immature (fig. 427). In contrast, the bloodroot leaf has an overall kidney shape with a deeply lobed margin and very prominent veins on the undersurface (fig. 30). When bruised, the injured leaf of twinleaf exudes a clear sap, whereas the bloodroot leaf produces bright red sap.

Each twinleaf plant may have from four to eight leaves, which, as they emerge from the soil in early spring, are red-violet to maroon in color (fig. 428). When the flowers bloom, the leaves are still immature and shorter than the flower stalks; they later expand and can grow to 18 inches tall, which is as tall as, or taller than, the level of the developing fruits.

Barberry Family

Fig. 433. A close-up of a twinleaf flower showing the rolled up anther flaps on the stamens.

Jeffersonia leaves remain viable throughout the summer and begin to yellow and senesce only in September (fig. 429). By that time, the small buds for next year's growth will have formed just beneath the ground surface (fig. 430), where they will be ready to grow as soon as the days lengthen and temperatures rise the following spring.

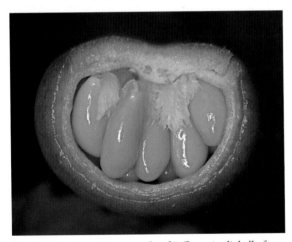

Fig. 434. An immature capsule of *Jeffersonia diphylla* from which the lid has been manually removed to show the immature seeds. Mice and other rodents often chew open the capsules to eat the immature seeds.

The sepals enclosing the flower buds of twinleaf are shed quickly (figs. 431, 432). The flowers, which only open on days when it is mild and sunny, are also very ephemeral, lasting for only one to three days before the petals are shed. Various types of bees (fig. 432) visit the flowers to collect pollen, pollinating the flowers in the process (twinleaf produces no nectar). The anthers open in an interesting way: small flaps roll upward like little awnings (fig. 433). With such a short life span the flowers must also rely on self-pollination. There seems to be no difference in the number of seeds produced by self-pollinated versus outcrossed flowers. Both methods are very effective and result in a high rate of seed set (90%), with larger plants producing the greatest numbers of seeds.

The only other member of the genus is twinleaf's closest relative, *Jeffersonia dubia*. As with *Arisaema* (Jack-in-the-pulpit), *Symplocarpus* (skunk cabbage), *Podophyllum* (Mayapple), and over 60 other genera in our Northeastern flora, the other species of *Jeffersonia* is native to eastern Asia. *Jeffersonia* shares another trait with many other of our spring woodland species

Fig. 435. Seedlings of *Jeffersonia* under the mature plants in spring. Some of the previous year's seeds were not dispersed by ants and germinated where they fell.

Fig. 436. Two capsules of twinleaf. The capsule on the left shows how the line of opening does not completely encircle the fruit.

Fig. 437. The capsules of twinleaf turn yellow-orange as they mature. This capsule has recently dehisced (opened).

Fig. 439. The reflexed margins of this old brown twinleaf capsule give it a helmetlike appearance. Note that one seed never fell from the capsule.

Fig. 438. Three mature reddish-brown seeds of twinleaf with their creamy-white fringed elaiosomes still intact.

in that its seeds bear fleshy elaiosomes and are ant dispersed (fig. 434). This mode of dispersal, termed myrmecochory (from the Greek *myrmex*, "ant," and *chorein*, "to wander"), results in the removal of the seeds to a site remote from the parent plant, thereby decreasing the chance of their being found by seed predators. Rodents will sometimes chew the capsules open before they dehisce naturally in order to eat the immature seeds; the rodents, usually mice, consume between 47% and 90% of the seeds. Small populations of twinleaf are not affected by rodent predation as adversely as are large populations and are thus better able to establish new plants from seed. Surviving seeds overwinter and germinate the following spring (fig. 435). Because of the heavy rodent-predation of seeds, most reproduction in large populations of twinleaf is vegetative, arising from the underground rhizomes. If rodent predation has not occurred, the seeds mature within the odd-shaped capsule (fig. 436) until the capsule turns yellow (fig. 437), at which time the lid opens, and the reddish-tan seeds (fig. 438) are spilled onto the ground. Once the seeds have fallen, ants gather them quickly in order to eat the attractive, fringed white elaiosomes while they are still fresh and nutritious. Ants disperse the seeds to germination sites that may, in fact, be more advantageous to the growth

Barberry Family

Fig. 440. (Above) The leaves of *Jeffersonia diphylla* (left) and *J. dubia* (right) planted together in a garden setting. The difference in shape is apparent here. Fig. 441. (Right) Plants of *Jeffersonia dubia* with unconstricted leaves and six-petaled lavender flowers, both features that differentiate this species from *J. diphylla*.

Fig. 442. (Above) The lovely, lavender flowers of *Jeffersonia dubia* make it an attractive addition to the early spring garden. Fig. 443. (Left) A leaf of *Jeffersonia dubia* that has retained some of its immature reddish coloration as it expands.

and survival of young seedlings. The empty pods turn brown, and the edges reflex back, leading to another common name for the plant, helmet pod (fig. 439).

The Asian *Jeffersonia*, *J. dubia*, is native to Korea, far eastern Russia, and Chinese Manchuria. It differs from *J. diphylla* in several ways, to the extent that some botanists favored placing it into a separate genus, *Plagiorhegma*. Two differences are most striking: the leaves of *J. dubia* are not deeply bilobed (fig. 440), and its flowers generally have only six petals and

Fig. 444. (Left) A capsule of *Jeffersonia diphylla* with a *horizontal* line of dehiscence indicating where the fruit opens when it is mature. **Fig. 445.** (Right) A capsule of *Jeffersonia dubia* with an *oblique* line of dehiscence indicating where the fruit opens when it is mature.

are lavender to purple (fig. 441). The colorful flowers are also longer lasting than those of *J. diphylla*, making it the preferred species for gardens (fig. 442). *Jeffersonia dubia* requires neutral or acidic soils rather than the calcareous soils favored by *J. diphylla* (however, my native twinleaf seems happy in the acidic soil of my garden). But the two species also share many features: early spring flowering, immature leaves that are a deep red-violet color (the leaves of *J. dubia* tend to keep some of this color as an iridescent sheen when they expand; fig. 443), quickly deciduous

sepals, seeds with fringed elaiosomes, and more or less oval-shaped capsules that open by an incomplete slit: horizontal in *J. diphylla* (fig. 444), but oblique in *J. dubia* (fig. 445).

Jeffersonia dubia is rare in Korea due to its widespread use as a medicinal herb. It was commemorated there on a postage stamp in 2001, part of a series of stamps featuring the endangered species of Korea. The American species, like almost all of our native species, was once used medicinally as well; another of its common names is rheumatism root.

Violet Family

Fig. 446. A plant of bird's-foot violet (*Viola pedata*) with bicolored flowers. Photographed in Virginia.

Fig. 447. A plant of round-leaved yellow violet (*Viola rotundifolia*) flowering as its leaves are still expanding.

Violets

Viola spp.
Violet Family (Violaceae)

Several violets are discussed here because I wanted to include species with flowers of each of the common colors: purple, yellow, and white. Local species mentioned are *Viola sororia* (dooryard violet), *Viola pedata* (bird's-foot violet), *Viola rotundifolia* (round-leaved yellow violet), *Viola pubescens* (downy yellow violet), *Viola canadensis* (tall white violet), *Viola striata* (creamy violet), and *Viola blanda* (sweet white violet). Some European violets of interest are also discussed: *Viola tricolor* (Johnny-jump-up) and *Viola odorata* (sweet violet).

Violets are among the best known of our spring wildflowers. They have played a significant role in history, literature, art, cuisine, perfumery, and horticulture.

Habitat: Depending on the species, habitats include moist woods (e.g., *V. canadensis* and *V. sororia*, which is also in wet fields and lawns), swamps (e.g., *V. cucullata*), mixed deciduous/coniferous woods (e.g., *V. rotundifolia*), dry fields and open woods (e.g., *V. pedata*), cool ravines and shady slopes in deep humus (e.g., *V. blanda* and *V. rostrata*), and rich woods or meadows (e.g., *V. pubescens*).

Range: Violets are found throughout North America.

Violets! What is it about these reputedly "shy" flowers that endears them to so many? Perhaps it is their modest appearance itself that charms. Nestled close to the ground, with flowers bowed among the leaves, violets compel one to look closely to appreciate their delicate beauty (fig. 448). After reading of the role played by violets in art, literature, and history, I shall forever think of them differently, remembering the romantic story of Napoleon and Josephine (see below) whenever I see them. Violets have been woven into so many facets of life throughout the ages that this essay has been lengthened to allow me to tell their story more fully.

Violets may be associated with meekness (so-called shrinking violets), but they are, in fact, quite hardy and well adapted for survival and reproduction in a variety of habitats. Although not the earliest of our native species to bloom, violets are one of our best known and most easily recognized wildflowers such that many people look to them as a sign that spring has arrived. Four states have chosen violets as their state flower: Illinois, Wisconsin, Rhode Island, and New Jersey.

The Violaceae is a large, cosmopolitan family, of which violets represent the largest genus, *Viola*. *Viola*

Violet Family

Fig. 448. Marsh blue violet (*Viola cucullata*) growing among bulblet ferns in a wet area.

is found primarily in temperate regions of the Northern Hemisphere and at higher elevations in tropical regions, with several species native to the Andes of South America (fig. 449). The family includes over 700 species of varied habit, including trees (fig. 450), shrubs, lianas (woody vines; fig. 451), and herbs. The approximately 400–600 species of *Viola* (depending on which taxonomist is providing the figures) are almost universally herbaceous (nonwoody), with just a few exceptional species that become somewhat shrubby (e.g., the endangered *V. oahuensis* in Hawaii).

Violets can be difficult to identify because so many species have more or less heart-shaped leaves and lavender- to purple-colored flowers. Our northeastern violets are of two forms: "stemless" plants, with both leaves and flowers arising from underground rhizomes and thus appearing not to have stems, and "stemmed" plants, with the leaves and flowers growing from recognizable aerial stems. That distinction is usually the first character one looks at when identifying violets. The size and shape of the leaves, stipules, and sepals and their hairiness or lack of it

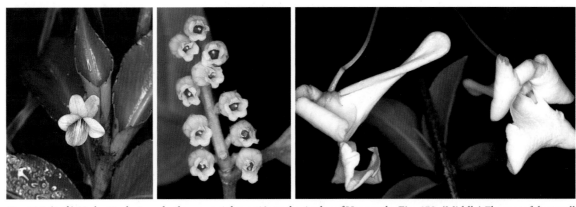

Fig. 449. (Left) *Viola stipularis*, an herbaceous violet native to the Andes of Venezuela. **Fig. 450.** (Middle) Flowers of the small tropical tree, *Rinoria pubiflora*, a member of the violet family. Photographed in French Guiana. **Fig. 451.** (Right) The large white flowers of *Corynostylis pubescens* a woody liana in the violet family, have a long, twisted nectar spur. Photographed in Amazonas, Brazil.

Fig. 452. (Left) A naturally occurring hybrid violet in Connecticut, possibly a cross between *V. canadensis* and *V. rostrata*. **Fig. 453.** (Right) A violet cultivar popular with gardeners, called *Viola sororia* "Freckles."

Fig. 454. A flower of dooryard violet with two petals removed so that the stamens and their orange anther appendages can be seen surrounding the style. Note the "beard" on the lower, right petal.

Fig. 455. Round-leaved yellow violets blooming in early spring before the overarching trees have leafed out.

must also be considered. Sometimes small details are important in distinguishing species; for example, noting whether or not the two or three lower petals are bearded (have clusters of hairs) and then determining if the hairs are pointed or clubbed plays an important role in violet identification. However, even the most careful observer may be stymied, because violets in the wild are notorious for hybridizing, so a plant may have characteristics of more than one species and not fit any one species description (fig. 452). Violet breeders take advantage of violets' tendency to hybridize and selectively cross species to obtain different colors or increased hardiness. Naturally occurring

oddities such as the polka-dotted *V. sororia* "Freckles" (sometimes called *V. cucullata* "Freckles"; fig. 453), are brought into cultivation and quickly become popular in the horticultural trade.

The flowers of violets are bilaterally symmetrical with two upper petals, two lateral petals, and a lower petal that serves as a landing platform for visiting insects. Additionally, the base of the lower petal is modified into a spur. Two of the five stamens have nectar-secreting appendages that extend back into the spur, where the secreted nectar accumulates. The anther connectives (tissue connecting the two pollen sacs of each anther) of violets have appendages at their apices that are pressed closely around the style

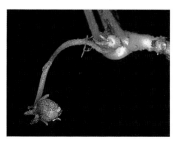

Fig. 456. A cleistogamous flower at the base of a hybrid violet plant that is a cross between *Viola sororia* and *V. cucullata*.

Violet Family

Fig. 457. A West Virginia white butterfly sipping nectar from a long-spurred violet (*Viola rostrata*).

(fig. 454). For the first few days that the flower is open, the appendages clasp the style. After the fourth or fifth day, they relax a bit, such that when an insect visits the flower and pushes against the style in its attempt to reach the nectar, the style presses against the appendages on one side (usually the upper side) causing a gap to form between the appendages and style on the other side. Loose pollen that has been trapped within this "cone" may then fall onto the insect (usually on its underside) and is carried on to the next flower. Many violets are commonly referred to as blue, but to my eye none are truly blue; rather, they appear to be various shades of lavender to purple (or violet), colors produced by a mixture of varying amounts of red with blue; the flowers of certain species may also be white, yellow, or pink.

In addition to the colorful violet flowers, most species of *Viola* have a second kind of flower that never opens and yet is capable of self-fertilization. The familiar, open (chasmogamous) flowers bloom early in the season before the sunlight is blocked by the forest canopy foliage (fig. 455). As light is diminished by the emerging overhead leaves, violet plants gradually cease production of their colorful flowers

Fig. 458. Two fruits of the American dog violet (*Viola conspersa*). The fruit on the left has already opened; that on the right has split but has yet to eject its seeds.

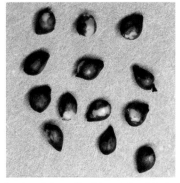

Fig. 459. Seeds of the tall white violet (*Viola canadensis*). Note the white elaiosomes on the seeds.

210

Fig. 460. (Left) A flowering plant of green violet (*Hybanthus concolor*), the only northeastern member of the violet family that is not in the genus *Viola*. **Fig. 461.** (Above) Sweet white violet (*Viola blanda*) is a clonal species growing on and near rotting wood.

and begin to produce cleistogamous flowers that look like unopened flower buds and have only rudimentary parts—a short style and two stamens with anthers that bear only a few pollen grains. Thus, if the open flowers have not received sufficient pollinator visits during a cold or rainy spring, the cleistogamous flowers serve as a secondary means of reproduction. Most of these "hidden" flowers are produced on stalks near the base of the plant (fig. 456), but in some species, especially those that grow in wet habitats, the cleistogamous flowers grow on aerial stalks and are thus not subject to rotting in the wet soil. In addition to this back-up means of seed production, in some species the senescing chasmogamous flowers are able to self-pollinate as their styles gradually bend downward until they are in contact with pollen scattered on the lowest petal. Plants resulting from the seeds of this additional back-up system are equally as fit as those formed from cross-pollinations, so there appears to be little negative effect from inbreeding in many species of violets.

Violets receive few visits from insects, but the diversity of recorded visitors is high and includes several species of bees, butterflies, flies, and wasps. In order to accommodate such a diversity of visitors, the flowers of some species change in shape and orientation over the life of the flower so that they are better adapted for one type of pollinator early in the flowering period and for another as the flowering period progresses. The principal pollinators are butterflies (fig. 457).

Fig. 462. (Left) A close-up of the flower and leaf of sweet white violet. Note that the basal lobes of the leaf almost touch each other.
Fig. 463. (Middle) Two views of the flowers of tall white violet (*Viola canadensis*): the frontal view shows the typical white "face" of the flower, while the side view shows the purple coloration on the undersides of the petals.
Fig. 464. (Right) A flower of tall white violet that is tinted lavender on the front side of the petals.

Violet Family

Fig. 465. (Left) Two flowers of the creamy violet (*Viola striata*). Note the lack of yellow at the base of the petals—one feature that differentiates the flowers of this species from those of *V. canadensis*. **Fig. 466.** (Above) A side view of the long-spurred violet (*Viola rostrata*) showing the exceptionally long spur.

Fig. 467. (Left) A flowering plant of downy yellow violet (*Viola pubescens*), one of the stemmed violets.
Fig. 468. (Top right) The underside of a leaf and the petiole of a downy yellow violet plant showing the hairiness of both.
 Fig. 469. (Bottom right) Senescing leaves of round-leaved yellow violet (*Viola rotundifolia*) in the fall. The leaves are about six inches (15 centimeters) in diameter and prostrate on the ground at this time of year.

The fruits of violets are three-chambered capsules (fig. 458). Once the fruit splits open along the three sutures, the edges of each valve squeeze inward until the seeds are "shot" out of the fruits, traveling, in some instances, a distance of more than five meters. A few species, including the European *V. odorata*, have lost this explosive means of dispersal, and their fruits merely open gently at ground level. In either case, ants serve as a secondary means of dispersal. Fleshy elaiosomes on the seeds (fig. 459) attract the ants, which may then carry the seeds away from the plant. The oil-rich elaiosome is eaten and the seed is discarded, perhaps to germinate in a new location. Such a bimodal system of dispersal is termed diplochory.

Fig. 470. (Above) A flowering plant of dooryard violet (*Viola sororia*), the most common violet of the Northeast. This species is an aggressive colonizer of lawns and gardens.
Fig. 471. (Right) A bird's-foot violet plant (*Viola pedata*) with pale lavender flowers growing in shale. The pronounced orange anther appendages are visible in the throats of the flowers.

In the 1991 revision of the *Manual of Vascular Plants of the Northeastern United States and Adjacent Canada*, Arthur Cronquist listed 29 species of violets as occurring in the Northeast, 22 fewer than in the first edition (1963) or in Fernald's eighth edition of *Gray's Manual of Botany*, which was published in 1950. Cronquist chose to "lump" (combine) several of those species into fewer, more broadly defined, species. As current taxonomists use new molecular tools to examine members of the genus more thoroughly, it seems likely that this number will increase once again. The only other species of Violaceae found in the northeastern United States is the green violet, *Hybanthus concolor*, which is taller than any of

Fig. 472. A deep lavender-flowered bird's-foot violet. Note the dissected leaves that are said to resemble the shape of a bird's foot.

our *Viola* species (up to a meter) and has many small green flowers in the leaf axils (fig. 460). The genus is unusual in this area, occurring primarily in warm to tropical regions.

Some violet species propagate themselves vegetatively. The sweet white violet (*V. blanda*) produces long stolons that may extend as far as 30 centimeters from the mother plant before producing a daughter plant. The daughter plants do the same, so that eventually, a clone of genetically identical plantlets may cover several square meters of forest floor. The mother plant dies after a few years, but the daughter plants continue to produce new offspring for another few years before they, in turn, die. A study done on how this species "moves" through the forest showed that new plantlets were more likely to be produced in proximity to a site with decaying wood (fig. 461), a probable source of nutrients that serves to direct the "flow" of the plant colony.

The leaves of sweet white violet are shaped like a rounded heart with a very narrow space between the basal lobes, which may even be in contact with one another (fig. 462). The short white hairs on the upper surface of the leaf bases are best seen by bending the leaf and looking closely at the profile of the folded part. *Viola blanda* is a stemless violet with leaves and

Violet Family

Fig. 473. A great spangled fritillary butterfly on red clover. The caterpillars of this and other fritillary species feed on the leaves and flowers of violets.

flower stalks arising from an underground rhizome. Despite the common name, I have detected little or no aroma from sweet white violets.

Tall white violet (*V. canadensis*) is one of the stemmed violets. It differs from all other northeastern white violet species in that its petals are white on the front (with a yellow base and purple lines on the three lower petals), while the back of the petals is either faintly or deeply tinged with purple (fig. 463). Occasionally, the purplish tinge may be noted on the front side of the petals as well (fig. 464). Some botanists hypothesize that this species may be in a transitional stage in the evolution of a white-flowered violet into one with purple flowers. Others have designated the two color morphs as varieties: var. *canadensis*, with white petals barely tinged with purple on the back, and var. *rugulosa*, with stronger lavender color on the back of the petals and sometimes on the front as well.

Even if the purple tinge is faint or lacking, the tall white violet may be easily distinguished from another white-flowered, stemmed violet, the creamy violet

(*V. striata*; fig. 465) by its stipules. Those of *V. striata* are toothed and green, like small leaves, whereas those of *V. canadensis* are smooth margined (entire), pale tan, and membranous in texture. These two white-flowered, stemmed violets do not hybridize with each other, but interestingly, *V. striata* does hybridize with purple-flowered, stemmed violets, among them the long-spurred violet (*V. rostrata*). The spurred petal in *V. rostrata* is the longest of any of our northeastern species, with the spur measuring up to two centimeters in length (fig. 466).

The downy yellow violet, *V. pubescens* (fig. 467), now includes what were once considered to be two distinct species: the previously known downy yellow violet, *V. pubescens*, and the smooth yellow violet, *V. pensylvanica*; both are now considered to be varieties of the former. *Viola pubescens* var. *pubescens* has hairy leaves and petioles (fig. 468), whereas var. *eriocarpa* (the former *V. pensylvanica*) is virtually hairless. Other differences, such as more numerous flower stems and fewer, narrower stipules in var. *eriocarpa* can also be used to distinguish between the two varieties.

Round-leaved yellow violet (*V. rotundifolia*) is one of the first violets to flower in the Northeast. It is a stemless violet that blooms when its leaves are still developing (fig. 447). As the season progresses, the leaves continue to enlarge, so that by midsummer they may have grown to 15 centimeters (6 inches) across and lie flat on the ground, persisting into the autumn when they turn yellow and die (fig. 469). The margins of the leaves are scalloped. This species varies little throughout its range and is not known to hybridize. With only six chromosomes, it is considered to be one of the more primitive species of violets.

Purple (including lavender) is the most common color of violets, and the purple-flowered dooryard violet (*V. sororia*; fig. 470) is the most common northeastern violet. Unlike *V. rotundifolia*, the dooryard violet is an extremely variable species in almost all aspects: size, leaf pubescence, and flower color. Dooryard violet is our most "weedy" violet, aggressively colonizing lawns and gardens, to the great consternation of gardeners and property owners.

Another of our "purple" violets, bird's-foot violet (*V. pedata*), is quite variable in flower color, ranging from pale lavender (fig. 471) to deep violet to strongly bicolored lavender and purple (fig. 446), with a far

Fig. 474. Two flowers of Johnny-jump-up (*Viola tricolor*) that show the variability in color found even in flowers on the same plant.

greater incidence of bicolored flowers in the southern part of its range. Both the common name and the species epithet, *pedata*, arise from the supposed resemblance of the deeply lobed leaves to a bird's-foot (fig. 472). Many other characteristics differentiate birds-foot violet from other species: it grows in dry sandy soil or crumbly shale rather than in the rich soils of mesic forests; its flowers are open and flat-faced, much like those of a pansy; the anthers project beyond the floral tube; and it produces no cleistogamous flowers.

Violets are the host plants for the caterpillars of fritillary butterflies (*Speyeria* spp.). Adult butterflies lay their eggs on or near the plants in late summer. The tiny larvae hatch and consume their egg cases, then drop to the ground where they survive the winter in the leaf litter without food. When the violet plants begin to produce new leaves the following spring, the caterpillars are on site and ready to begin eating. The beauty that these (often silver-spangled) butterflies add to the landscape allows us to forgive them their choice of menu (fig. 473).

Violets have served as symbols of faithful love, modesty, and royalty, and, as such, have found their way into literature throughout the ages. Almost everyone is familiar with the childhood Valentine verse:

> Roses are red,
> Violets are blue,
> Sugar is sweet;
> And so are you.

This all-too-familiar poem is based on an early English nursery rhyme: "The rose is red, the violet's blue, / the honey's sweet, and so are you," or more indirectly on *The Faerie Queene*, which was written by Sir Edmund Spenser in the sixteenth century: "She bath'd with roses red, and violets blew, / And all the sweetest flowres, that in the forrest grew."

A mid-sixteenth-century songbook, *A Handful of Pleasant Delights*, includes a poem on nosegays (cumbersomely entitled with a 28-word phrase) that attests to violets as a symbol of faithfulness:

> If violet is for faithfulness
> Which in me shall abide;
> Hoping, likewise, that from your heart
> You will not let it slide.

Fig. 475. A plaque at the Shakespeare Garden in Central Park, New York City, where plants mentioned in the works of Shakespeare are grown, including violets.

Violet Family

Fig. 476. A cultivated hybrid pansy (*Viola* × *wittrockiana*), developed by a complex series of backcrosses of *V. tricolor* with two other European species.

William Shakespeare mentioned flowers, including violets, in many of his works. Love-in-idleness, the plant credited in *A Midsummer Night's Dream* with the power to make a person "madly dote upon the next live creature that it sees," was, in fact, *V. tricolor* (fig. 474), a small European violet known also as heartsease, Johnny-jump-up, and wild pansy. The juice of this plant placed on the eyelids of the sleeping Titania was responsible for her falling in love with the ass-headed Bottom upon awakening. References to the violet's scent, color, and symbolism also appear in other of Shakespeare's works, among them, *Hamlet*, *Twelfth Night*, *King Richard II*, and *Pericles*. The commonly used phrase "to gild the lily" has its origins (although now altered from the original) in Shakespeare's *King John*:

> To gild refined gold, to paint the lily,
> To throw a perfume on the violet,
> . . . .
> Is wasteful and ridiculous excess.

The allusion to the violet for which perfume would be superfluous is a reference to the strongly scented Eurasian species, *V. odorata*, which will be discussed in greater detail below.

In 1916, the 300th anniversary of Shakespeare's death, a garden planted with flowers mentioned in Shakespeare's plays and poetry was dedicated in New York City's Central Park. Also planted there was a white mulberry tree that was a graft of a tree planted by William Shakespeare in 1602 in his own garden in Stratford-on-Avon; the tree was blown down by a storm in 2006. The garden in New York, which is located near West 81st Street and Central Park West, was redesigned and dedicated in 1989 and still exists today (fig. 475). Blooming violets can be found there in April and May.

Two hundred years after Shakespeare's death, the American poet, William Cullen Bryant, wrote eloquently of the violet in his 1814 poem "The Yellow Violet." The poem begins:

> When beechen buds begin to swell,
> And woods the blue-bird's warble know,
> The yellow violet's modest bell
> Peeps from the last year's leaves below.

Violets have been portrayed in art as well, appearing as one of the *mille-fleurs* (thousand flowers) in the background of two of the six tapestries known as *The Lady and the Unicorn*; they are depicted in a more naturalistic manner in the others. The series of six (plus a fragmentary seventh) exquisite tapestries is believed to have been woven in Flanders in the late fifteenth century. Flowers included in the tapestries are native to a wide area of Western Europe and are depicted so accurately that most are readily identifiable. Botanists at the New York Botanical Garden identified 115 (85%) of the species woven into the unicorn series and documented their findings in the *Journal of the New York Botanical Garden* in 1941. Other finely worked contemporary tapestries from the Netherlands depict *V. tricolor* in *The Unicorn Is Found* and *V. odorata* in *The Start of the Hunt*. Renaissance artists commonly painted violets at the feet of the Virgin Mary as a symbol of Mary's humility. The species chosen for this symbol was usually *V. tricolor*, because its three colors were seen to represent the trinity (a less common

Fig. 477. A flower of the white iris (*Iris florentina*), a European species, the rhizomes of which are used as the source of a violet-scented compound used in perfumery. Photographed in Greece.

name for *V. tricolor* is herb trinity). In the nineteenth century, violets appear as an accessory in portraits of women, garnishing both hats and bosoms (e.g., *Berthe Morisot with a Bouquet of Violets*, by Édouard Manet). With the burgeoning interest in natural history in Victorian times, violets were finally portrayed as the *principal* subject of works of art, such as those by French-born artist Paul de Longpre.

The role of violets in history begins with an ancient Greek myth that tells of their creation. Zeus had fallen in love with the young nymph Io, and to protect her from the wrath of Hera, his wife, he changed Io into a white heifer. When Io cried at the prospect of dining on grass for the remainder of her life, Zeus caused violets to grow where her tears fell, deeming the flowers a more fitting food for his lover. The Greek word for violet, *ion*, was derived from the name of this nymph.

The Athenians revered the violet, which served as a symbol of the city. Crowns of violet flowers were worn on special feast days, and doorways bore plaques inscribed with the word *ion*. Both the flowers and the leaves served as a source of food (the leaves eaten cooked or raw, and the flowers as a garnish) and drink (as a wine or syrup). Although violets were used on joyful occasions, they were also associated with mourning by the Greeks and, later, by the Romans. The name of the genus, *Viola*, is the Latin name for violets.

Empress Josephine, the first wife of Napoleon Bonaparte, was enamored of violets, particularly those that were sweetly scented; she always received a bouquet of them from Napoleon on their anniversary. However, Napoleon divorced Josephine when she had not produced an heir after 13 years of marriage. A year later he married the young Marie Louise, who quickly did provide him with the son he needed to perpetuate the Napoleonic dynasty. When Napoleon was banished to the island of Elba in 1814, he vowed to return to Paris in the spring, when the violets flowered. His followers adopted the violet as a symbol of loyalty to their ruler, referring to Napoleon as Caporal (Corporal) Violette. Indeed, Napoleon *did* escape from Elba and marched into Paris on March 20, 1815—on roadways supposedly strewn with violets by his followers. Women carried nosegays of violets in his honor and wore violet-colored gowns. Napoleon visited the final resting place of Josephine (who had died within weeks of his exile to Elba) and picked violets from her gravesite. His second reign lasted for only 100 days, until his defeat at Waterloo.

Fig. 478. A shelf of violet products for sale in Toulouse, France, including violet liqueur, violet mustard, and violet syrup.

Violet Family

Fig. 479. A package of crystallized violets, an important product of Toulouse, used to garnish baked goods.

Fig. 480. Cupcakes decorated with crystallized violets.

Napoleon was again banished—this time to the far-off oceanic island of St. Helena. At that time it was considered seditious in France to display images of Napoleon, or even of violets (or bees, another symbol of his reign). In 1821, the last word that Napoleon spoke on this deathbed was "Josephine," the name of his one true love. A lock of her hair and pressed violets were found in his locket. Following Napoleon's death his second wife, Marie Louise, retired to the Duchy of Parma (in northern Italy). She, too, favored violets, and Parma was famous for growing heavily scented double-flowered Parma violets.

The association of Napoleon with violets continued into the next generation. At the wedding of Napoleon's nephew, Napoleon III, to the empress-to-be Eugenie, the bride carried a wedding bouquet of violets, and upon his death, Napoleon III's casket was covered with violets. Napoleon III (Louis-Napoleon) was the son of Louis, brother of Napoleon I, and Hortense, the daughter of Josephine by her first marriage.

In addition to the aforementioned heartsease (*V. tricolor*) and the well-known sweet violet (*V. odorata*),

both of which are depicted in medieval tapestries, Europe has over 90 species of violets, notable among them the horned violet (*V. cornuta*), now a popular garden plant, in both Europe and the United States. In the early 1800s, English nurserymen experimentally crossed and backcrossed *V. tricolor* with the yellow-flowered *V. lutea* from central Europe and the purple-flowered *V. altaica* from Asia Minor; the result was the large-flowered pansy that is so ubiquitous in gardens today (*Viola × wittrockiana*; fig. 476). *Viola tricolor* provided the genes responsible for the different color patterns seen in the large, multicolored pansies. The various color combinations of *V. tricolor* are determined by five different genes and the diverse combinations of their dominant or recessive qualities. Pansies were introduced into France, and then into Belgium, where they became immensely popular by the late 1830s. They were then exported from Belgium to the United States in 1848. It was always thought that the colorful patterns of the flowers of wild pansy (*V. tricolor*) resembled little faces, and this trait was further emphasized in the cultivated pansy. The origin of the word "pansy" is from the French word for thought, *pensée*, because the little floral faces appeared to be thinking about something. Breeders have subsequently bred the "faces" out of some pansies and can now produce them in almost any solid color desired.

In the eighteenth century vendors sold bunches of violets on the streets of Paris. The preferred species was sweet violet (*V. odorata*), the flowers of which have a lovely fragrance. The flowers were gathered in the countryside and brought to Paris daily. By 1750, entrepreneurs realized that it would be more efficient to cultivate violets closer to Paris. This horticultural endeavor was successful, and by the early nineteenth century it had become common to grow violets in private gardens.

Viola odorata is renowned for the distinctive aroma of its flowers, leading to its use as both a fragrance and a flavoring. This species, along with two others, was long thought to be the principal contender for the role of ancestor of the famed double-flowered Parma violets. Like the double 'Multiplex' bloodroot flowers (fig. 24), Parma violets are not known in the wild, and all of their reproductive parts have been converted into petallike structures; the resulting flowers are full in appearance and generally have 20 "petals." They most likely have been perpetuated from a single mutant plant. The aroma of Parma violets is reputed to be even more fragrant than that of *Viola odorata*; it was their aroma that so enchanted Empress Josephine. Only in 2007 were the results of molecular research published, revealing that the true ancestor of Parma violets is *V. alba*, a widespread species with a range that extends the width of the Mediterranean, north to Scandinavia, and south to Crete. There are three geographic races, with molecular evidence showing that Parma violets arose from a widespread hybrid between intraspecific races of *V. alba*, most likely those from Italy and Turkey. Since the chasmogamous flowers of Parma violets have no functional reproductive parts, they are propagated by cuttings. The development of new cultivars must arise either from mutations in the flower buds or in the rarely produced self-pollinated cleistogamous

Fig. 481. Fresh, edible violet flowers and leaves brighten the frosting on this carrot cake.

flowers. The first historical mention of the fragrant, many-petaled violets in 1573 gave an origin for violets of this type as western Turkey. When they were introduced into Italy, they could have hybridized with the local *V. alba* subsp. *dehnhardtii*. An alternative explanation suggests that the double flowers were brought from Portugal to Naples in the first half of the eighteenth century, during the Bourbon dynasty. In any case, the flowers were brought from Naples to northern Italy, in the vicinity of Parma. Having this new knowledge on the origin of the Parma cultivar will assist violet hybridizers in more accurately selecting species to be used in producing new and interesting violets.

The compound responsible for the fragrance of sweet violets is ionone; it is described as sweet and powdery. The compound, a ketone, has an aroma which is said to saturate one's scent receptors to such an extent that once sensed, even fleetingly, it cannot be detected again until those receptors have recovered. Ionone is an important ingredient in the perfume industry and was originally obtained from violet flowers. Since only a few drops of the essential oil can be obtained from an acre of violets, it is prohibitively expensive. In 1893, the fragrance compound was isolated and the aroma synthesized. Today, methyl ionone and the less-expensive synthetic ionone, which was discovered at the same time, are widely used in fragrance. One of the best-known fragrances incorporating this aroma is Nina Ricci's *L'Air du Temps*. The scent of violets may also be obtained from the rhizome of certain European species of iris: *Iris germanica, I. pallida,* and *I. florentina* (fig. 477). The essential oil prepared from the dried iris rhizomes (known as orrisroot) is one of the most expensive natural ingredients because the harvested rhizomes require a five-year period to fully develop their aroma, and one ton of rhizomes yields only two kilograms of essential oil. Oil of orrisroot is just one of the costly ingredients used in the world's most expensive perfume, Clive Christian's No. 1, which sells for $2,150 an ounce (or $250,000 for 16.9 ounces in a Baccarat crystal bottle embellished with gold and diamonds, labeled Imperial Majesty). Orrisroot also acts as a preservative, enhancing the longevity of other scents. However, the actual violet plant still does play a role in perfumery:

Violet Family

Fig. 482. Violet flowers add color to a salad. Yellow or white violets may also be used.

violet leaves are utilized to produce a "green" or "grassy" aroma in some fragrances.

Violets are an important crop in southern France, with the area north of Toulouse being the prime growing area for both sweet violets and Parma violets. Toulouse, called the City of the Violet, is the major producer and exporter of violet products (fig. 478).

Fig. 483. A nosegay of flowers of *Viola odorata*, the "sweet violets" of Europe that were a favorite of Napoleon's Josephine. The surrounding leaves are from *Galax aphylla*, because the leaves of *V. odorata* are usually unattractive at the time of year that the flowers bloom.

Among the many items flavored with essence of violet are candies, including some candy-coated Jordan almonds; chewing gum; a liqueur, crème de violette; and edible crystallized violets. Toulousse is especially known for its decorative, crystallized violets, which are sugarcoated violets made by dipping the fresh flowers in beaten egg white and then sprinkling them with finely granulated sugar (fig. 479). Once they are completely dry, they will keep well in a sealed container for long periods of time. Crystallized violets are used primarily as a decoration for cakes and other baked goods (fig. 480).

Fresh violet flowers also make an attractive garnish for baked goods (fig. 481), or they can be used to add a touch of color to spring salads (fig. 482). The leaves of violets are rich in vitamins A and C and may be used as a garnish, eaten chopped in salads, or cooked like spinach. A purple-colored syrup is made by steeping violet flowers overnight in freshly boiled water, then adding twice the weight of the solution in sugar while stirring the mixture over heat until all the sugar is dissolved. The syrup adds a lovely note to beverages and fresh fruit (e.g., grapefruit). Interestingly, this syrup can serve as a pH test to determine whether something is acidic (low pH) or alkaline. The purple syrup turns red in the presence of an acid (e.g., lemon juice) and green in the presence of a base (e.g., baking soda). Strips of unsized, acid-free white paper may be dipped in the juice of crushed violets, dried, and kept in a sealed container to be used as a substitute for litmus paper.

The United States had its own self-proclaimed City of Violets on the east bank of the Hudson River—Rhinebeck, New York. Due to the poor economy at the beginning of the twentieth century, the estates of the region had fallen on hard times. A savvy entrepreneur, George Saltford, was the first to convert the unused estate greenhouses to the growing of violets that he imported from Europe—including a Parma cultivar called 'Marie Louise' (named for Napoleon's second wife). In the early 1900s, the double-flowered Parma violets were *the* flower for corsages, bouquets, and nosegays in New York City; sweet violets were also popular (fig. 483). Others soon entered the violet industry, and violets became the main source of income for Rhinebeck and the nearby towns of Poughkeepsie, Red Hook, and Milan until the 1920s.

Violets

Fig. 484. A street sign in Rhinebeck, New York, is one of the few reminders that this town was once the Violet Capital of the World.

Because the climate of the Hudson Highlands was too cold for outdoor cultivation of these violets, growers converted or erected hundreds of greenhouses heated by coal so that Parma and sweet violets could be grown year round. Thousands of violets were transported daily by rail to New York City and beyond. With the changing fashions after World War I, the popularity of these sweet flowers declined, and most growers went out of business. The decline continued throughout the Depression, but some celebrities, including First Lady Eleanor Roosevelt (herself a resident of the Hudson Highlands region) and Mrs. Vincent Astor, continued to wear and promote violets. By the 1960s the industry was all but dead. Today, little remains to remind one of this era of the "purple thunderstorm." The Museum of Rhinebeck History maintains the archives of the violet industry, and street signs in Rhinebeck commemorate the flowers (fig. 484). Many of the former violet greenhouses now grow other floral crops, but one grower, Richard Battenfeld, a descendent of a family of early violet growers, still plants a row of sweet violets each year out of a sense of tradition. Parma violets can be purchased in the United States today only from specialty nurseries.

In the 1880s one of New York City's venerable universities, New York University, adopted the violet as the symbol for its athletic teams, and the NYU Violets proudly bore this appellation for more than 100 years. The choice of violets for the team name and school colors (violet and white) is said to have originated from the violets that were planted surrounding the bases of the university buildings at the original Washington Square campus. In the 1980s it was felt that a more intimidating symbol was needed for its football team, and the NYU Bobcat was born. However, the NYU Violets is still the official name of many of the school's teams, and the bobcat mascot appears at games (and in graphic depictions) dressed in violet and white.

Violets served as a symbol of remembrance during and after World War I in Australia. The first annual Violet Day was held on July 2, 1915. Small bouquets of violets tied with purple ribbons proclaiming "In Memory" were sold on the streets to raise funds for a veterans club to be established for soldiers returning from the battlefield. Following the war, the custom continued as a means of honoring those who had died while serving their country. In this way, violets are analogous to the (artificial) poppies that symbolize Memorial Day in the United States. Violet Day was moved to August several years later and after World War II was expanded to commemorate the Australian dead of both world wars. More recently, the day has been all but forgotten.

The next time you encounter violets in the wild, take a moment to examine them closely and to recall their rich and romantic history.

Borage Family

Fig. 485. Virginia bluebells with a coiled inflorescence showing the change in floral color from pink buds to blue flowers.

Fig. 486. A bumblebee on an inflorescence of Virginia bluebells. Bumblebees are the most important pollinators of Virginia bluebells.

Virginia Bluebells

Mertensia virginica
Borage Family (Boraginaceae)

Virginia bluebells exhibit two of the characteristics of many (but not all) members of the borage family: their flowers are borne on coiled inflorescences, and there is a color change from pink to blue as the buds mature. The flowers are particularly welcomed by spring wildflower gardeners for the contrast that their blue flowers provide to the typical spring palette of pinks, whites, and yellows.

Habitat: Semishaded areas in moist forests, especially along streams and on low slopes.

Range: Most of the Northeast and Midwest, but not in New Hampshire, Vermont, Connecticut, or Rhode Island; south to Georgia and Alabama; Ontario and Quebec in Canada.

V irginia bluebells, which are native to much of the eastern United States and Canada, have been a favorite of gardeners there since Colonial times. Soon after the seeds were taken to England, Virginia bluebells became a popular garden plant there as well. The true blue color of its flowers complements the pastel pinks, yellows, and whites of other spring-blooming wildflowers and bulbs. Virginia bluebells are easy to grow; they readily self-seed and also may be divided in the fall. Peter Kalm (see the chapter on skunk cabbage) collected the species in Virginia, and it was subsequently named by Linnaeus as *Pulmonaria virginica* in *Species Plantarum* (1753). *Pulmonaria*, a related European genus in the Boraginaceae, is now commonly planted in American gardens. It was not until 1797 that the botanist Albrecht Roth erected the genus *Mertensia* for certain members of Linnaeus' genus *Pulmonaria*. The genus was named by Roth to honor a German botanist, Franz Carl Mertens (1764–1831), a professor of botany at Bremen University. (*Mertensia* is also the name of a genus of jellyfish named for K. H. Mertens, the son of F. C. Merten and also a naturalist, who described several species of jellyfish collected during a circumnavigation of Russia.) The epithet *virginica* was given by Linnaeus based on the collecting locality of Kalm's specimen—the colony of Virginia. Thirty-two years later, in 1829, another

Borage Family

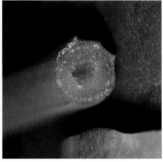

Fig. 487. Young leaves of Virginia bluebells emerge with a deep purplish-green coloration.

Fig. 488. A sectioned stem of *Mertensia virginica* showing the hollow core.

taxonomist, Christiaan Persoon, transferred Virginia bluebells to Roth's new genus as *Mertensia virginica*. Other common names for Virginia bluebells include eastern bluebells, Roanoke bells, and Virginia cowslip. Because Thomas Jefferson grew them in his gardens at Monticello, they were once known as "Jefferson's blue funnel flowers."

Virginia bluebells is a true spring ephemeral, emerging as dark purplish-green leaves (fig. 487) in early April and blooming before the trees leaf out. The purplish color is probably due to high levels of anthocyanins (red pigments) in the leaves. The leaves eventually become a clear green, and when the seeds mature, the leaves turn yellow and disappear completely by late June. Bluebells often form large colonies, carpeting hundreds of acres in certain woodlands in Virginia. Because of their partially hollow stems (fig. 488), the plants are delicate and will break easily if roughly handled. The lower leaves have long petioles, but the smaller, upper ones have either short petioles or none at all. The leaves are large (up to seven inches long) and somewhat soft and lax (fig. 489), reminding me of the ears of lop-eared rabbits. However, unlike rabbit ears, the leaves are hairless—an unusual condition in the borage family. Prominent, raised veins are evident on the underside (fig. 490), and small dots (punctations) are often visible on the upper surface (fig. 491).

Although the plants are attractive overall, it is the clusters of dangling blue, bell-like flowers (fig. 492) that make this plant a favorite. As is typical in Boraginaceae, the flowers are borne in a coiled inflorescence (fig. 493) that uncoils and lengthens into a graceful arch as the flowers mature. The plants may stay in flower for as long as four weeks, with individual flowers remaining open for four or five days. Like some other members of the borage family, for example, forget-me-not, viper's bugloss, and lungwort (*Pulmonaria*; fig. 494), the flowers of Virginia bluebells change in color as they age. Beginning as small pink

Fig. 489. A flowering plant of Virginia bluebells. Note the drooping leaves.

Fig. 490. The undersides of the leaves of Virginia bluebells have prominent venation.

Fig. 491. Young leaves surrounding an inflorescence of pink buds. Note the punctations (dots) on the exposed surface of the open leaf.

Fig. 493. A tightly coiled inflorescence of buds that is still partially surrounded by the young purple leaves.

Fig. 494. An inflorescence of a cultivated lungwort (*Pulmonaria*), a European member of the borage family with flowers that exhibit a pink-to-blue color change similar to that of *Mertensia virginica*, but the transition from pink to blue is more gradual.

Fig. 492. The fully opened flowers of Virginia bluebells are generally a light-to-medium blue as seen in this inflorescence.

buds, they turn pinkish-purple, and finally blue (fig. 485) approximately four to six hours before the flowers open. The color change is caused by changes in the pH of the cell sap. Most flowers are light blue at maturity, but plants growing in more acidic soils tend to have deeper-blue flowers. The combination of colors and the retention of flowers for two to three days after pollination occurs enhance the floral display, attracting more pollinators. Occasionally, some plants bear flowers that remain pink throughout their bloom period, and sometimes white-flowered plants (fig. 495) are found interspersed with the blue-flowered ones. The white-flowered plants often have lighter green leaves.

The corolla has a very narrow tubular portion that flares into a shallow five-lobed "bell" (fig. 496). Inwardly raised bumps (called fornices) occur at the junction of the tubular and flared portions. The five stamens are adnate (attached) to the corolla at this

Borage Family

Fig. 495. A white-flowered form of Virginia bluebells. Note that the leaves beneath the inflorescence are a lighter green than those of the normal blue-flowered *Mertensia virginica*.

Fig. 496. The bell-shaped blue flowers and developing pink buds of *Mertensia virginica*.

ones. The ovary develops into four rough-textured nutlets (fig. 498).

Several species of insects visit the flowers, but certain bees (e.g., bumblebees, honeybees, mason bees, and a few other types) have tongues long enough to reach the nectar that has accumulated at the base of the corolla tube. The bees not only drink nectar but also collect pollen both for themselves and to provision their nests. Bumblebees are the primary pollinators of Virginia bluebells (fig. 486). Short-tongued bumblebees, such as *Bombus affinis*, may slit the corolla tube at its base in order to "steal" nectar without entering the flower in the "proper" way. Large, black carpenter bees (*Xylocopa* spp.) also use this "illegal" method of obtaining nectar. In doing so, both robbers actually benefit the plant by transferring sizable amounts of pollen to the stigma when they inadvertently brush against it in the act of "robbing" nectar. Increased seed set as a result of nectar robbery is rare among plants but was found to occur in *M. virginica*. In addition, Bernd Heinrich and Peter Raven hypothesized that the greater seed set in plants that have been "robbed" of nectar may reflect increased pollination by the true pollinators, who must visit a greater number of the "pirated" flowers in order to obtain enough nectar to supply their energy needs. Along with Dutchman's breeches, Virginia bluebells is one of the most abundant (and therefore most important) nectar resources for early-season bumblebees. Other flower visitors that seek nectar from Virginia bluebells include bee flies, butterflies, sphinx moths, and skippers. Flower flies also visit, but only to feed on the pollen; they are not effective pollinators. The flowers, with concealed nectar at the base of a long tube, would be suitable for

same level. On the second day after the flower opens, the anthers, either yellow or brown, open to expose the creamy-white pollen. At the base of the tube is a slender white style that is surrounded by white hairs and arises from the four-lobed ovary (fig. 497). Eighty percent of flowers have long styles; the rest have short

Fig. 497. A sectioned flower of Virginia bluebells with half of the corolla and two stamens removed. Note the raised ridges (fornices) at the point where the tubular portion of the corolla flares; the yellow anthers that have not yet opened; the thin, white style; and the white hairs at the base of the tube.

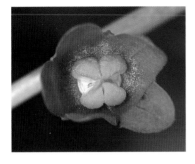

Fig. 498. A young fruit of *Mertensia virginica* with four rough-textured nutlets.

Fig. 500. The tall plants of mountain bluebell (*Mertensia ciliata*) grow along streams at high elevations in the western United States. This plant was photographed in Colorado.

hummingbird pollination, but their flowering period is often finished before ruby-throated hummingbirds return to the Northeast.

Mertensia is primarily a North American genus with about half of the approximately 45 worldwide species located in the western part of the United States. The greatest number of species is found in western Colorado. One coastal species, oyster plant (*M. maritima*), is found throughout the Northern Hemisphere along cold, northern coasts. Its common name alludes to the claim that its leaves taste strongly of oysters. Having never sampled the leaves, I cannot comment, but others say there is no true oyster flavor but rather that it is the mucilaginous texture of the leaves that is reminiscent of eating raw oysters (the same is said of the leaves of other species of *Mertensia*). The leaves, flowers, and roots of oyster plant are all eaten by the Inuit of Alaska. Although the plant grows in sand or gravel near the sea, with care it can be grown in nutrient-poor, sandy soils in rock gardens. It is attractive for this purpose because of its rosettes of otherworldly blue-green leaves and pale blue flowers (fig. 499) borne on long trailing stems. The flowers bloom

Fig. 499. A close-up of a flowering portion of oyster plant (*Mertensia maritima*) on a gravel beach in Newfoundland. Note the striking blue-green leaves and small blue flowers.

from summer into fall, longer than those of any other member of the genus. Only one other species, northern bluebell (*M. paniculata*), occurs in the Northeast, growing in damp north-woods regions of the northern Great Lakes and across Canada to Alaska.

Like most native plants, *M. virginica* and other species of *Mertensia* have a host of recorded medicinal uses by Native Americans; among them are the treatment of whooping cough, tuberculosis, and venereal disease. *Mertensia* was also used as an antidote for poisons. The leaves of mountain bluebell (*M. ciliata*; fig. 500), a tall western species growing along streams at high elevations, are reportedly edible and serve as an emergency food for hikers. The leaves are hairy and thus not very palatable, but, nevertheless, they are relished by livestock. The Cheyenne Indians made a tea of mountain bluebell to increase milk flow in nursing mothers. Despite its purported edibility and history of medicinal use, *M. ciliata* (along with other western species that have been investigated chemically) has been found to contain toxic levels of pyrrolizidine alkaloids. When given large doses of these compounds, rats developed pancreatic tumors. Once again, caution is urged before ingesting any wild plant.

Dutchman's Pipe Family

Fig. 501. A floral bud of wild ginger with the three sepal lobes just beginning to open. The leaves have not yet fully expanded.

Fig. 502. A ground level view of wild ginger showing the flowers that are hidden under the leaves when viewed from above.

Wild Ginger

Asarum canadense
Dutchman's Pipe Family (Aristolochiaceae)

The curious flowers of wild ginger go unseen by most who walk by the large patches of heart-shaped leaves. However, it behooves the interested observer to get down on his knees to seek out the flowers hidden under the leaves, for they are unlike any other found in the Northeast.

Habitat: Understory of (usually) rich deciduous forests.

Range: Throughout the eastern half of the United States other than Florida and Nebraska, and in New Brunswick, Quebec, Ontario, and Manitoba in Canada.

As stated above, the flowers of wild ginger deviate from the norm. Wild ginger is a dicot, yet its floral parts occur in threes (or multiples of three) like those of a monocot: three sepals, 12 stamens, and six styles fused into a column topped by six stigmatic lobes. Petals are lacking, but occasionally tiny (three-millimeter), pointed vestigial petals may be observed between the dark maroon sepal lobes. The flowers are borne at ground level, hidden beneath the plant's paired leaves that rise five to eight inches above on densely hairy stalks (fig. 502). One to three scale leaves (cataphylls) may be present at the base of the leaf stalks (fig. 503). The heart-shaped leaf blades are softly hairy, especially along the margins, and the exterior of the flower is thickly covered with coarse white hairs (fig. 504). What pollinators might be attracted to such a flower? This question has puzzled biologists for years, but no definitive answer has been found. The color of the sepals and their location in the leaf litter might lead one to think that flies would be likely visitors, perhaps mistaking the flowers for carrion. However, the flowers lack the characteristic putrid aroma of fly-pollinated species. Indeed, flies *are* said to visit the flowers in early spring, but only to

Dutchman's Pipe Family

Fig. 503. Plants of wild ginger with the surface level rhizomes exposed. Note the leaflike cataphylls at the base of the leaf stalks.

Fig. 505. Plants of wild ginger seen from below. Note the hairy leaf stalks.

seek shelter in the enclosed space of the fleshy sepals; they have not been documented as effecting pollination. Beetles and even slugs (!) have also been hypothesized as pollinators. In all of my times of looking for insect visitors in the flowers of wild ginger, I have only once found one—a small beetle (figs. 505, 506), and that only after the fact when I viewed the photo that I had taken of the plant. The fact that the stamens are appressed flat onto the flower's "floor" at the time that the flower first opens (fig. 507) would seem to indicate that the flower is "designed" to be cross-pollinated, since pollen from anthers in this position cannot reach the already receptive stigma. Therefore, a window of opportunity is open for pollen brought from another flower to effect cross-pollination. Only later, when the inner six stamens (fig. 508), and later the outer six (fig. 509), move upward to positions adjacent to the stigma, can the flower self-pollinate. The flowers are oriented downward, and thus it is easy for pollen from the dehisced anthers to fall upon the stigma once they have moved into the upright position. This type of backup system is common in flowers that may have limited opportunities to receive insect visitors, as happens in early spring. Experiments in which flow-

Fig. 504. The exterior of a wild ginger flower is covered with thick white hairs on the sepals and flower stalk. Note the long, pointed sepal lobes and the remnant of a cataphyll at the base of the stem.

Fig. 506. An enlargement of a wild ginger flower seen in figure 505, with a beetle in its base.

Fig. 507. An open flower of *Asarum canadense* in the early stage of anthesis when the 12 stamens are still appressed to the bottom of the floral tube. Note the six fuzzy stigmatic lobes, which are already receptive when the flower opens. Compare with figures 508 and 509.

Fig. 508. In this flower, six of the stamens have bent upright bringing their anthers adjacent to the stigmatic lobes allowing for possible self-pollination.

ers were bagged to prevent visitation by insects that could possibly transport pollen have demonstrated that the majority of such flowers produce seeds without the services of a pollinator; they are self-fertile.

After the ovules have been fertilized, the ovary begins to enlarge, but the appearance of the flower does not change markedly. The fruit splits open irregularly when mature, discharging its seeds into the surrounding leaf litter. As in many other spring ephemerals, the seeds of wild ginger bear oil-rich, fleshy elaiosomes that attract ants to disperse the seeds. Ants have been recorded as carrying the seeds of wild ginger up to 35 meters across the forest floor,

the longest distance known for ants to transport the seeds of any woodland herb. However, this mode of dispersal cannot possibly account for the great range expansion of wild ginger since the glaciers retreated. *Asarum canadense* was once totally eliminated from the northern part of its range by glacial ice that covered the land; since that time (ca. 16,000 years ago) it has recolonized an area extending northward for hundreds of kilometers from its former southern refuge at the terminus of the glacier. Michael Cain of New Mexico State University and his colleagues hypothesize that occasional, random, long-distance dispersal events must have occurred in order for the species to reach its current northern limit. Such events might include meteorological events such as tornados and hurricanes that blew the seeds (or fragments of the rhizomes) over long distances, or other chance occurrences, such as biotic transportation of seeds ingested by birds and subsequently excreted at some distance from their source or animal transport by external means, for example, seeds caught in mud clinging to the feet of birds or mammals that unknowingly carried the seeds with them as they traveled north. But reproduction by seed is low in any case; *A. canadense* is a clonal species and reproduces primarily by spreading rhizomes. A clone may cover sizable patches of the forest floor with a carpet of closely spaced, paired leaves that appear to be separate plants but are actually all connected underground and genetically identical (fig. 510). For this reason, wild ginger has found popularity in shade gardens, where it provides a dense, low-maintenance ground cover. The rhizomes spread horizontally just beneath the leaf litter and may be easily seen by brushing the forest duff away from under the leaves (fig. 503). This also affords one the opportunity to verify how the plant received its common name. Scratching a bit of the rhizome with a fingernail releases a pungent aroma reminiscent of the ginger used in cooking. In fact, wild ginger has served as a condiment for hundreds of years, used first by Native Americans and later by the colonists who learned of its use from them. It had many medicinal uses as well (but based on new information, these uses are strongly discouraged; see below). The apparently effective use of a related western species of *Asarum*, *A. caudatum* (long-tailed wild ginger), was reported in the 1806 journal of Meriweather Lewis. While he

Dutchman's Pipe Family

Fig. 509. In a later stage of anthesis, all 12 of the stamens are upright and adjacent to the stigmatic lobes.

and William Clark were exploring the Louisiana Territory, a member of their party suffered from a painful inflammation of his leg. A poultice of the roots and leaves of *A. caudatum* was applied and quickly provided relief.

In the 1990s, Swiss and Canadian researchers conducted pharmaceutical studies to ascertain the medicinal effectiveness of plants used by Native Americans. Nineteen species were tested for their antibacterial and antifungal properties, as well as for larvicidal and molluscidial activity. Various extracts of *A. canadense*, mostly from the rhizomes, were found to be effective in all of the above categories. Other investigations have shown that wild ginger also possesses anti-inflammatory properties (thus its effectiveness on the Lewis and Clark expedition) and can inhibit the effects of snake venom.

Despite its name, wild ginger is not even distantly related to the plant from which we obtain the popular ginger spice (a tropical monocot named *Zingiber officinale*). Wild ginger's long use as a flavoring and preservative for food, as well as in herbal medicine, is shared with other members of its genus around the world. In a 2008 document prepared by the United States Department of Health and Human Services, botanical products from *Asarum* and the related genus *Aristolochia* where shown to contain aristolochic acids—known carcinogens responsible for causing urothelial cancer and kidney disease. The use of these plants in weight-loss products in the 1990s

exposed many more people to the dangerous compounds, and in 2001 the FDA issued a warning about the hazards of consuming products containing aristolochic acids. Several other countries have outright banned their use.

These same toxic compounds serve to protect one of our favorite butterflies, the beautiful pipevine swallowtail (*Battus philenor*). Like the monarch butterfly, which is protected as an adult by the toxic compounds of milkweed that it consumed as a larva, the caterpillar of the pipevine swallowtail feeds not only on the leaves of various members of the genus *Aristolochia* (some species of which are called pipevines because of the shape of their flowers) but also on those of *Asarum*. The larva is not harmed by the toxic acids and sequesters them in its body, where they remain throughout its life. Also like the monarch, the pipevine swallowtail wears warning colors—orange dots on a black background as a caterpillar (fig. 511), and orange, yellow, and blue markings on its black wings as an adult (fig. 512). The bright, contrasting colors warn potential predators (mainly birds) of its toxicity.

In *Species Plantarum* (1753), Linnaeus provided the generic name *Asarum* as the Latinized form of *asaron*, a Greek name for a similar plant, and the specific name *canadense* to denote that the plant occurred in Canada. The name had already been in use in Europe for over a hundred years before Linnaeus officially named it, since the species had been

Fig. 510. A clone of wild ginger showing how the thick leaf cover can hide the flowers below.

Fig. 511. A pipevine swallowtail caterpillar feeding on a leaf of *Aristolochia*, a genus closely related to *Asarum*. Both genera are fed on by pipevine swallowtail larvae, and both contain aristololochic acid, a toxin that renders caterpillars that feed on the leaves unpalatable.

introduced to Europe as a medicinal plant in the late sixteenth century.

Although wild ginger grows well in the shaded forest understory, those plants receiving more light are less likely to be eaten by herbivores (e.g., snails and slugs). This might be a result of decreased photosynthesis by the plants that are heavily shaded. Such plants produce fewer carbohydrates than those that receive more of the sun's energy. Those carbohydrates that *are* produced are utilized for general growth and maintenance with little left for less critical functions—such as producing defensive compounds for protection against herbivory. At the end of the growing season, the leaves senesce, leaving only the rhizomes, with next season's buds already formed at their tips, to overwinter. This strategy permits the plants to

produce their flowers (one per plant) early the following spring, before the plants' leaves are fully developed. In bud, the tips of the three sepals meet in a valvate point (fig. 501). The shape and length of the free sepal tips is quite variable throughout its range, leading earlier botanists to think that there was more than one species, or at least a number of subspecies, involved. The genus *Asarum*, in the strict sense, has only 10–14 species worldwide, with 6 species in North America (all but *A. canadense* are located in the West), 1 species in Europe, and the remainder in Asia. Some botanists consider the strictly defined *Asarum* (with flowers having distinct sepals, connate [joined] styles, appendaged anthers, and an inferior ovary) as a section of a more broadly defined genus *Asarum*, which includes another 10 species that others place in the genus *Hexastylis* (with flowers having connate sepals, distinct styles, anthers without appendages, and superior [or partially inferior] ovaries). All species of *Hexastylis* are North American.

Fig. 512. Two mating pipevine swallowtail butterflies. Their bright contrasting colors advertise their toxicity to predators.

~ Glossary ~

Botany, like any discipline, has its own terminology. In many cases, there are not equivalent terms in everyday English, thus making explanation of some words necessary to enable the general reader to understand their meaning as used in this book. This glossary is meant to provide brief definitions of botanical and other terms that are used in the text and may not be familiar to the general reader.

achene: a small, dry fruit with a single seed that is attached to the fruit wall at only one point and is indehiscent

actinomorphic: capable of being divided into two equal parts along an infinite number of planes, as in the flower of a buttercup (is the equivalent of *radially symmetric*)

acute: pointed, as in the tip of a leaf in which the two sides form an angle of less than 90°

adpressed: tightly adjacent to each other, as in a calyx that closely surrounds an ovary

adnate: attached to another structure, as when stamens are attached to the corolla of a flower

adventitious roots: roots that arise from a part of the plant other than the primary root, for example, from a stem or corm

alkaloid: an organic, nitrogen-based compound found in plants that is often toxic but in some cases has important medicinal properties; generally serves as a botanical defensive compound against herbivores

aniline: an organic compound used in making dyes and plastics

andrenid: member of a family (Andrenidae) of solitary, native bees, many belonging to the genus *Andrena*

angiosperm: a flowering plant, the seeds of which are enclosed within an ovary

annual: a plant that completes its life cycle within one growing season; it does not persist to the following year

anther: the pollen-bearing part of a stamen

anther connective: the tissue that connects the lobes of an anther

anthesis: the time of opening of a flower

APG: Angiosperm Phylogeny Group, the organization responsible for summarizing plant-family classification based on current research

appendage: a secondary outgrowth of a primary plant organ that often extends beyond it, for example, the extensions of the anthers of *Viola* (violet)

aril: a fleshy outgrowth of the funicle (the structure that attaches the seed to the fruit wall); often attractive to an animal that disperses the seed

aroid: a member of the Araceae, or Jack-in-the-pulpit, family

auriculate: ear-shaped; often used to describe lobes at the base of a leaf or petal

autogamous: capable of self-fertilization

axil: the junction of the petiole of a leaf with a stem of the plant

banner: the uppermost petal of a legume flower (also called a standard)

basidiomycete: a type of fungus that produces its sexual spores on club-shaped structures called basidia; basidiomycetes include most of the more noticeable fungi such as mushrooms, bracket fungi, and puffballs

bearded: with a cluster of hairs, as on the petals of some species of violets

bilaterally symmetric: capable of being divided into two equal parts along only one plane, as in an orchid flower (is equivalent to *zygomorphic*)

bisexual flowers: having both male (stamens) and female (pistils) reproductive structures in the same flower

boreal: referring to regions of high northern latitude or to forests that grow in such regions

blade: the broad part of a leaf without the leaf stalk (petiole)

bract: a modified leaf in an axil from which a flower or inflorescence stalk arises

bulb: an underground storage organ composed of concentrically wrapped fleshy leaf bases

bulbil: a small, bulblike structure that is capable of producing a new plant asexually, and is usually formed in an axil

bulblet: a small bulb arising as an offshoot from a larger bulb

calcareous: containing calcium; alkaline, as applied to soil

calciphile: a plant that grows best in calcareous soils; "calcium-lover"

calyx: the outer whorl of floral organs, often green, that arise beneath the petals; a collective term for the sepals

cambium: an undifferentiated layer of cells within the stem of a plant that produces new tissues, including vascular tissue (xylem and phloem)

canopy: the uppermost layer of a forest, formed by the crowns of the trees

capsule: a dry fruit composed of two or more carpels that splits open at maturity

carbohydrate: the product made by plants through the process of photosynthesis and that is used to supply energy

Glossary

carpel: the basic unit of the female reproductive part of a plant (the pistil); a pistil may have one carpel or many

caruncle: a fleshy appendage to a seed arising from the point where the seed is attached to the funicle (is equivalent to *strophiole*); a type of elaiosome

cataphyll: a leaflike scale associated with a vegetative part of a plant

chasmogamous: applied to flowers that open and are accessible to pollinators

chlorophyll: the green pigment in plants that is capable of absorbing energy from the sun and using it to produce carbohydrates

chromosome: a threadlike body within the nucleus of a cell that contains the genetic material

circumboreal: throughout the boreal region that comprises the northern regions of Eurasia and North America; may refer to a floristic region or to a plant or animal found throughout the boreal regions of the Northern Hemisphere

circumpolar: throughout the polar regions of the Northern or Southern hemispheres

claw: the narrowed base of a petal, sepal, or bract

cleistogamous: applied to a flower that never opens; self-fertilized seeds result from pollination within the flower

clone (clonal): a population of plants that is the result of asexual reproduction; thus, the plants composing the clone are genetically identical

coniferous: referring to trees or shrubs having cones as the reproductive structures as in gymnosperms (e.g., pines and spruces)

connate: fused together, as in the similar parts of a flower (e.g., a corolla in which all the petals are fused into a tube or bell shape)

contractile roots: roots that grow in length and then retract, pulling the plant deeper into the soil

corbiculae: pollen-carrying modifications of the hind legs of some bees (pollen baskets)

corm: a fleshy subterranean storage organ composing the base of a stem

cormlets: small corms that grow from the base of a corm

corolla: the floral whorl of petals within the calyx; a collective name for the petals

corona: a modified crownlike floral structure located between the stamens and the corolla as in *Asclepias* (milkweed)

cotyledon: a "seed leaf" contained within the seed to provide food for the developing embryo; different in appearance from the plant's true leaves that develop later; usually solitary in monocots and paired in dicots

cross-pollination: pollination of a flower with pollen from another plant of the same species

deciduous: shedding foliage (or other organs) at the end of a growth period or season

dehisce: to split open at maturity allowing discharge of the contents, such as the seeds of a fruit or the pollen of an anther

diapause: a temporary pause in the development of an organism, especially in insects

dicotyledon (dicot): a plant with (generally) two cotyledons (seed leaves) in its seed, net-veined leaves, and flower parts most commonly in fours or fives

dioecious: the condition of bearing male flowers and female flowers on separate plants

dioecy: the state of being dioecious

diplochory: bimodal seed dispersal as, for example, in *Viola* (violet) in which the seed is first explosively ejected from the dehiscent fruit and is then carried further from the parent plant by ants

diploid: having two sets of chromosomes in the nucleus; the "normal" condition of nonreproductive cells

disjunct: the range of a species with populations that are widely separated geographically from others of the same species

dormancy: a period of inactivity, often said of a seed that must undergo specific conditions (e.g., cold, abrasion, water saturation) to trigger germination

doubled flowers: flowers having more than the usual number of petals; the extra petals are usually derived from stamens; as a result the many-petaled flower may be infertile

dropper: the (generally) subterranean rhizome of a plant such as *Erythronium* (trout-lily), that sometimes appears above ground before "dropping" down into the soil again, where its tip will develop into a new ramet (plantlet in the same clone as the parent plant)

druse: a mace-shaped aggregation of calcium oxalate crystals found in some plants, especially members of the Araceae; the sharp crystals may serve to deter herbivory

elaiosome: a general term for a seed appendage that is lipid rich and may be derived from different parts of the seed; depending on its origin, the elaiosome may be a caruncle (strophiole) or an aril

ephemeral: transient; short-lived

epicotyl: the upper portion of a plant embryo that develops into the stem

ethnobotanist: one who studies plants and their uses by humans

eudicot: meaning "true dicotyledon" and applied to a subgroup of dicotyledons that represent 70% of the dicots; members of the group have characters typical of dicotyledons and pollen with three pores. The remaining dicots are considered to be more primitive and are referred to as basal eudicots.

extrafloral nectary: a nectar-producing organ located on a part of the plant other than the flower

family: a level of taxonomic classification comprising genera with similar characteristics; related families are grouped into orders

fertilization: in botany, the union between a sperm cell released by a pollen grain deposited on a receptive stigma and an egg cell in an ovule of the flower

filament: the anther-bearing stalk of a stamen

flavonols: water-soluble pigments (including the red pigment anthocyanin) common in plants that have antioxidant properties and may provide health benefits in humans

follicle: a fruit that opens only along one line of dehiscence, as in milkweed (*Asclepias*), differentiating it from a pod that opens along two lines of dehiscence, such as a pea pod

form: anglicized version of the Latin *forma*; a level of classification within a species that recognizes minor differences from the species; may be abbreviated as "f." (e.g., *Claytonia virginica* f. *lutea*)

fornices: plural of *fornix*; inpushings at the junction of the tubular portion of a corolla with its flared portion, as seen in some members of the Boraginaceae

funicle: a cordlike structure that attaches an ovule or seed to the interior of a fruit

galea: the helmet-shaped upper lip of certain flowers, for example, *Pedicularis* or various species of the mint family

genera: plural of *genus*

genotype: the inheritable genetic information of cells that determines all aspects of an individual organism

genus: a level of taxonomic classification that includes species with similar characteristics; related genera are classified into families

germinate: emerge from a dormant state, as when a seed begins to develop into a plant

gymnosperm: a seed plant with its seeds borne naked on the scales of cones rather than enclosed within an ovary; compare with angiosperm

habit: the overall growth form of a plant

habitat: a particular type of environment regarded as the home of an organism

haustorium: the part of a parasitic plant that invades a host species and joins with the host's vascular tissue in order to procure nutrients from it (plural, *haustoria*)

hemiparasite: a plant that photosynthesizes but obtains some of its water and/or nutrients from a host plant (e.g., lousewort); compare with holoparasite

herbaceous: nonwoody, soft-stemmed

herbarium: a collection of dried and mounted plant specimens

herbarium specimen: a dried and pressed plant specimen that has been mounted on a large sheet of relatively thick, acid-free paper with a label telling when and where the plant was collected along with other relevant data

herbivory: the act of feeding on plants

hermaphroditic: having both sexes, as in a flower with both stamens and pistils (also called a perfect flower)

hilum: the scar left on a seed where the funicle had been attached

holoparasite: an organism that is completely reliant on a host species for its nutrients (e.g., squawroot); compare with hemiparasite

host-specific: living or feeding on a single host species

hummock: a small mound, such as a small area of land raised above the level of water in a swamp

humus: the rich layer of topsoil containing decomposing organic matter

hybrid: the offspring of the sexual union of two different species

hydathode: a pore of a leaf that is modified to exude water and sometimes dissolved minerals

indehiscent: not opening at maturity, as in a fruit

inferior ovary: an ovary in which all of the floral parts (i.e., sepals, petals, and stamens) are attached to the top of the ovary

inflorescence: an arrangement or grouping of flowers on a plant

infructescence: an arrangement or grouping of fruits on a plant

keel: the boat-shaped structure formed by the two lower petals of certain flowers (e.g., pea flowers)

ketone: a class of organic chemical compounds found in plants that are as diverse as acetone and fructose; they are often used as solvents, but they can also play important metabolic roles in the human body

labellum: the median petal of an orchid; it serves as a landing platform for insects, attracting them by virtue of (usually) being larger and variously embellished in structure and color; also called the lip

legume: a general name for a member of the pea family; a type of fruit, usually dry, that opens along two sutures

liana: a woody climbing vine; usually applied to such vines in the tropics

lignin: a complex chemical component of wood and of all vascular plant cell walls that provides mechanical strength

Glossary

Linnaeus, Carl: a Swedish botanist, zoologist, and physician who is credited with the creation of the system of binomial nomenclature used for naming all living things; in 1753 he published *Species Plantarum*, in which names were given to all plants then known by him

liverwort: a type of small, nonvascular plant, often with leaves in three ranks, sometimes deeply lobed, or with stem and leaves undifferentiated; such plants, along with mosses and hornworts, are called bryophytes

mesic: descriptive of a habitat that has a moderate amount of moisture

midden: a dump for the waste products of human or animal activity (e.g., applied to accumulations of shells that have discarded after consumption of their contents)

monocarp: a plant that flowers and fruits once in its lifetime and then dies

monocotyledon (monocot): a flowering plant whose embryo generally has only one seed leaf, whose leaves usually have parallel venation, and whose flower parts usually occur in threes or multiples of three

monoecious: the condition of bearing separate male (staminate) and female (pistillate) flowers on the same plant

monogeneric: referring to a plant family having only one genus

monograph: a taxonomic treatment of a distinct group of plants throughout its range; it may be a family, a genus, or another level of classification, such as subfamily or subgenus

monoterpene: a chemical compound found in the volatile oils of plants such as citrus; credited by some with anti-cancer properties

monotypic: referring to a family or a genus with only one species

morph: a plant or animal with a visual difference from others in the same population of a species

morphology: the form and structure of an organism and the study of same

morphological difference: a difference in shape or structure

mutualistic relationship: a symbiotic interaction between two organisms that benefits both

mycelium: the vegetative part of a fungus consisting of a mass of hyphae (branching threadlike strands) that is usually hidden underground or within a host plant

mycoplasma: very small bacteria that lack a cell wall; the cells are thus unaffected by antibiotics that target the synthesis of the cell wall

mycorrhizal: descriptive of the symbiotic union between a fungus and the roots of a plant

mymecochory: the dispersal of seeds by ants

necrophoresis: the removal of dead members of a colony from the nest by ants or other insects in order to maintain proper hygiene within the nest

nectar: a sugary liquid produced within flowers to attract pollinators or by other parts of the plant to attract insects that subsequently protect the plant from herbivores (see *extrafloral nectary*)

nectar guides: lines or other markings on a flower that are assumed to direct a pollinator to the reward (usually nectar or pollen)

nectary: a tissue or structure that produces nectar

obtuse: blunt, as in the tip of a leaf that is not sharply pointed; the two sides of the leaf meet at an angle greater than 90º

order: a level of taxonomic classification that includes families with similar characteristics

outcross: reproduction by individuals of the same species that are not closely related genetically

ovary: the part of a flowering plant that contains the ovules; the fertilized ovary becomes a fruit and the ovules become the seeds

oxidation: in plant metabolism, the process of utilizing glucose to produce carbon dioxide and water and to release chemical energy

palate: a raised portion of the lower lip of a two-lipped corolla that closes the throat of the flower, as in the flower of butter-and-eggs (*Linaria*)

panicle: a compound inflorescence in which the secondary branches arise from a central stalk and in turn give rise to additional such branches

parthenogenetic: capable of producing a new individual from an ovule without the benefit of fertilization

pedicel: the stalk of a flower

pedicellate: possessing a pedicel (flower stalk)

peduncle: the stalk of an inflorescence

peltate: descriptive of a leaf blade that is attached to its petiole at a point within its lower surface rather than at the margin

perfect flower: a flower having both stamens and pistils

perennial: a plant that lives for longer than two growing seasons and continues to grow after it has reproduced

perianth: the collective name for the calyx and the corolla

peridiole: a small packet containing spores, as found in bird's nest fungus (representing the "eggs" in the "nest") that is then splashed out of its cuplike enclosure by raindrops

petal: a unit of the corolla (the floral whorl between the calyx and the stamens); often serves to attract pollinators

petaloid sepal: a sepal that appears petallike, usually because it is colorful

petiole: the stalk of a leaf

pH: a unit of measurement of the acidity or basicity of a solution or of soil

phenolics: plant-produced, nitrogen-containing compounds that play a role in the plant's defense

photosynthate: the carbohydrate product produced by plants through the process of photosynthesis

photosynthesis: the process by which green plants produce carbohydrates from carbon dioxide and water using the sun's energy; oxygen is a byproduct

phylogenetic: adjectival form of *phylogeny*

phylogeny: a hypothesis about the evolutionary relationships of groups of plants and other living organisms, which includes hypotheses about their derivation from ancestral forms and relationships among its members

phytochemical: a chemical that occurs naturally in plants

pistil: the female part of a flower composed of the ovary, style, and stigma

pistillate: descriptive of a flower that has only functional female organs

pistillate phase: descriptive of a bisexual flower in which there is a transition from female to male (or the reverse), but where the flower is currently functioning in the female phase (stigmas are receptive, but anthers are not shedding pollen)

pistillode: a rudimentary, sterile pistil; found in staminate flowers

pollen: the microspores (male reproductive structures) of seed plants contained in the anthers

pollination: in flowering plants, the deposition of pollen on the stigma of the same or a different flower

pollinator: an animal that serves as a vector to transport pollen from the anthers of one flower to the stigma of another (or within the same flower)

proboscis: a long tongue of an insect—such as a bee, butterfly, or moth—used for sucking nectar from flowers

pronotum: the upper side of the prothorax (the segment of the thorax closest to the head) of an insect

quinone: an organic compound derived from aromatic compounds that plays a role in photosynthesis; some quinones are bioactive, and others are the source of dyes

raceme: an inflorescence with a single axis, the stalked flowers of which bloom from the bottom upward

radially symmetric: capable of being divided into two equal parts along many planes, as in a buttercup flower (is equivalent to *actinomorphic*)

radicle: the lower portion of an embryo that develops into a root

ramet: an individual member of a clone

raphide: a needle-shaped crystal, usually of calcium oxalate

receptacle: the expanded apex of a pedicel that bears the floral parts

receptive: the state of a stigma when it is conducive to germination of pollen that is deposited on it

recurve: to curve downward or backward

reflexed: bent sharply downward or backward

respiration: the process of burning sugars to yield energy for growth and reproduction

rhizome: a prostrate stem on or below the ground that sends off roots, vertical stems, and/or leaves

ribosomal DNA (rDNA): the DNA sequences that code for ribosomal RNA (ribosomes, which are made up of RNA, direct protein synthesis in living cells.)

rust: any of several species of fungi that parasitize plants, often resulting in great economic loss in affected crop plants; so called because the spore stage is often reddish-orange like metallic rust

samara: a dry, indehiscent winged fruit, such as produced by maples (*Acer*)

saponin: a chemical compound found in plants (e.g., *Saponaria*; common name, soapwort) and in some marine organisms that produces soaplike foaming when mixed with water and shaken

scape: the leafless stalk of a flower or inflorescence

scientific name: the two-word name of an organism—the binomial—which is based on Latin or the Latinized version of words in other languages

scroph: an abbreviated version of the plant-family name Scrophulariaceae, applied to members of that family

self-compatibility: the ability of a plant to fertilize the eggs in its ovules with sperm from its own pollen

self-pollination: the pollination of a plant with pollen from the same plant or another plant within a clone; this does not necessarily result in fertilization

senesce: to age

sepal: one unit of the calyx, the outer whorl of the perianth of a flower

serpentine: a green mineral, the presence of which in soil limits the ability of many species to grow there due to relatively high concentrations of certain metals such as nickel, manganese, and chromium

sessile: without a stalk, as in leaves or flowers

silique: an elongate, dry, dehiscent fruit having two chambers divided by a papery membrane (the replum); found in the mustard family (Brassicaceae)

somatic: descriptive of cells other than the reproductive cells (eggs and sperm)

spadix: a congested inflorescence of very small flowers that is surrounded by a spathe in the plant family Araceae (plural, *spadices*)

spathe: a large bract (modified leaf) that surrounds an inflorescence, as in *Symplocarpus* or *Arisaema*

species: (singular and plural) the basic rank of classification; may be further subdivided into subspecies, varieties, or forms (abbreviation: singular, *sp.*; plural, *spp.*); a plant species name consists of the generic name and the specific epithet

specific epithet: the second part of a binomial species name that denotes the species (e.g., in *Viola pubescens*, "*pubescens*" is the specific epithet)

Species Plantarum: a 1753 publication by Carl Linnaeus that is the basis for all validly published plant names at that time; the foundation for the binomial system of nomenclature

stabile: resistant to chemical change

stamen: the male part of a flower composed of the filament and pollen-bearing anther

staminal: composed of stamens as in a staminal ring made up of stamens fused at least at their bases

staminate flower: descriptive of a flower that has only functional male organs (stamens)

staminate phase: descriptive of a bisexual flower in which there is a transition from female to male (or the reverse), but where the flower is currently functioning in the male phase (stamens are shedding pollen, but stigmas are not receptive)

staminode: a sterile stamen (plural, *staminodia*)

statolith: an organelle found in the plant cells (including root-tip cells) of some plant species (e.g., *Hottonia inflata*) that makes and stores starch granules that are involved in the perception of gravity, ultimately resulting in the roots growing downward (gravitropism) and the shoots growing upward

stemless: without an apparent stem; in violets, those plants having leaves and flower stalks arising from the underground rhizome

stemmed: having a stem; in violets, those plants that, like most plants, have leaves and flower stalks arising from an aerial stem

stigma: pollen-receptive tissue located at the apex of the style (or directly on the apex of the carpel if the style is lacking)

stipe: a small stalk that supports another structure, such as an ovary; the petiole of a fern; the upright stem supporting the cap of a mushroom

stipule: a small, leaflike structure on the stem at the base of a leaf stalk

stolon: a prostrate stem at the surface of the ground that produces roots and stems at the nodes

stratification: a method of treating seeds with cold and moisture to simulate the winter conditions necessary to stimulate germination

strophiole: an outgrowth of the seed coat near the hilum (the equivalent of *caruncle*); a type of elaiosome

style: the part of the pistil between the ovary and the stigma

suberin: a waxy, waterproof substance found in plants; a main constituent of cork

subspecies: a population within a species that differs somewhat from the recognized species, but not enough to be classified as a separate species; abbreviated "subsp." or "ssp."

superior ovary: an ovary that is above the attachment of the sepals, petals, and stamens to the receptacle below

suture: a seam, as the line of dehiscence of a fruit

syntype: any of two or more specimens listed in a species description in which a holotype (the sole type specimen on which a species name is based) was not designated

syrphid fly: a member of the Syrphidae family of flies; many mimic small bees or wasps; often seen hovering at flowers to take nectar; also called hover flies or flower flies

systematics: the study of the diversification of life on Earth, both past and present, and the relationships of living things throughout time

tachinid flies: a group of parasitic flies that lay their eggs on another organism, often a caterpillar, which is then fed upon by the fly larvae until they emerge and the host dies

taxon: a named group at any level of classification, for example, a species, a genus, a family, etc. (plural, *taxa*)

taxonomist: one who studies taxonomy

taxonomy: the study and description of variation in the natural world and the subsequent classification and naming thereof

tepal: the unit of the perianth of a flower in which the sepals and petals are similar in appearance (e.g., lilies)

teratogenic: capable of causing anomalies in an embryo or fetus

tetrahedron: a polyhedron composed of four triangular faces forming a type of pyramid

tetraploid: having double the normal number of chromosomes

tortricid moth: a member of the Tortricidae family of moths, small moths whose larvae are leaf rollers or live inside of fruits or galls

translocate: in botany, the movement of water and dissolved carbohydrates through the phloem of a plant

tuber: an underground swollen stem that serves to store food for the plant

tubercle: a small rounded projection or knob

tubercule: a small, vegetatively reproductive structure formed in the leaf axils of lesser celandine; tuberlike, rather than comprised of leaf material as in the bulbils found in some lily species

type specimen: a specimen upon which a species name is based and from which at least a portion of the species description was made (other specimens many also be used for providing descriptive information)

USDA: United States Department of Agriculture

UV pattern: markings as on a flower that are only discernable under ultraviolet light or by insects that are able to see colors in this wavelength

variety: a population within a species that has minor differences that are more significant that those that denote a form, but less significant than those that would be used to determine subspecies (the delineation of the various ranks of classification is often subjective); abbreviated "var."

variegated: having streaks, spots, or patches of different colors as in green leaves that are marked with white

vegetative reproduction: a method of producing new plants other than by seeds, for example, by budding from rhizomes, tubers, or bulblets

venation: the arrangement of the vascular system (veins) of a leaf

zygomorphic: bilaterally symmetrical as in a flower that can only be divided into two equal, mirror images along one plane

References

The General References were consulted for background information and were referred to for multiple essays. They are not included again in the references for the individual species.

General References

Clemants, S., and C. Gracie. 2006. Wildflowers in the Field and Forest: Field Guide to the Northeastern United States. Oxford University Press, New York.

Fernald, M. L. 1950. Gray's Manual of Botany. 8th ed. American Book Company, New York.

Flora of North America Editorial Committee, eds. 1993–. Flora of North America North of Mexico. Oxford University Press, New York. http://www.fna.org/families (accessed 2010).

Foster, S., and J. Duke. 1990. Peterson Field Guides: Eastern/Central Medicinal Plants. Houghton Mifflin, Boston.

Gleason, H., and A. Cronquist. 2004. Manual of the Vascular Plants of the Northeastern United States and Adjacent Canada, 2nd ed. New York Botanical Garden Press, Bronx.

Hyam, R., and R. Pankhurst. 1995. Plants and Their Names: A Concise Dictionary. Oxford University Press, New York.

International Plant Names Index. http://www.ipni.org (accessed 2010).

Judd, W. S., C. S. Campbell, E. A. Kellogg, P. F. Stevens, and M. J. Donoghue. 2008. Plant Systematics: A Phylogenetic Approach. 3rd ed. Sinauer Associates, Sunderland, MA.

Lamoureux, G. 2002. Flore Printanière. Fleurec Éditeur, Saint-Henri-de-Lévis, Quebec.

Mabberley, D. J. 2008. Mabberley's Plant-Book. 3rd ed. Cambridge University Press, Cambridge.

Mehrhoff, L. J., and J. A. Silander, Jr. Invasive plant atlas of New England. http://nhii-nin.ciesin.columbia.edu/ipane (accessed 2009; site now discontinued).

Radcliffe-Smith, A. 1998. Three-Language List of Botanical Name Components. Royal Botanic Gardens, Kew, UK.

Stevens, P. F. 2001–. Angiosperm Phylogeny Website. Version 9, June 2008. http://www.mobot.org/MOBOT/research/APweb (accessed 2010).

Tropicos.org. Missouri Botanical Garden. http://www.tropicos.org (accessed 2010).

USDA, NRCS. PLANTS Database. http://plants.usda.gov/ (accessed 2010).

Usher, George. 1996. The Wordsworth Dictionary of Botany. Wordsworth Editions, Hertfordshire, UK.

Yao, Y.-F., Y.-Z. Xi, B.-Y. Geng, and C.-S. Lil. 2004. The exine ultrastructure of pollen grains in Gnetum (Gnetaceae) from China and its bearing on the relationship with the ANITA Group. Botanical Journal of the Linnean Society 146: 415-425.

Baneberries

Compton, J. A., A. Culham, and S. L. Jury. 1998. Reclassification of Actaea to include Cimicifuga and Souliea (Ranunculaceae): Phylogeny inferred from morphology, nrDNA ITS, and cpITS, and cpDNA trnL-F sequence variation. Taxon 47: 593–634.

Compton, J. A., and S. L. Jury. 1995. Lectotypification of Cimicifuga foetida. Taxon 44: 603–605.

Fernald, M. L. 1940. What is Actaea alba? Rhodora 42: 260–265.

Ford, B. A. 1997. Actaea. In Flora of North America North of Mexico, ed. Flora of North America Editorial Committee, 3: 181–183. Oxford University Press, New York.

Hanson, T., and E. B. Walker. Field Guide to Common Insect Pests of Urban Trees in the Northeast. Department of Forests, Parks and Recreation, Waterbury, VT. http://www.forestpests.org/vermont/ (accessed 2010).

Larsen, E. L. 1957. Pehr Kalm's Account of the North American rattlesnake and the medicines used in the treatment of its sting. American Midland Naturalist 57: 505–511.

Linnaeus, C. 1752. Genera Plantarum. 4th ed. Halle.

———. 1753. Species Plantarum. Stockholm.

———. 1767. Systema Naturae, 12th ed. Vol. 2. Stockholm. {YES}

Merriam, J. S. 1872. Actaea L. Bulletin of the Torrey Botanical Club 110: 298–303.

Montana Plant Life. 2009. "Baneberry, Actaea rubra (Ait.) Willd." http://montana.plant-life.org/species/actaea_rub.htm (accessed 2009).

Nova Scotia Museum. "The Poison Plant Patch." http://museum.gov.ns.ca/poison/default.asp (accessed 2009).

Pellmyr, O. 1985. The pollination biology of Actaea pachypoda and A. rubra (including A. erythrocarpa) in northern Michigan and Finland. Bulletin of the Torrey Botanical Club 112: 265–273.

Pellmyr, O., G. Bergstrom, and I. Groth. 1987. Floral fragrances in Actaea, using differential chromatograms to discern between floral and vegetative volatiles. Phytochemistry 26: 1603–1606.

References

Pellmyr, O., and L. B. Thien. 1986. Insect reproduction and floral fragrances: Keys to the evolution of the angiosperms? Taxon 35: 76–85.

Rathbone, E. 2009. "White baneberry: The eyes have it." Adirondack Almanac [blog]. http://www.adirondackalmanack.com/2009/08/white-baneberry-eyes-have-it.html (accessed 2009).

Skidmore College. "White baneberry." North Woods. https://academics.skidmore.edu/wikis/NorthWoods/index.php/Actaea_pachypoda_(White_Baneberry (accessed 2009).

Webster, C. R., M. A. Jenkins, and G. R. Parker. 2001. A field test of herbaceous plant indications of deer browsing intensity in mesic hardwood forests of Indiana, USA. Natural Areas Journal 21: 149–158.

Wilson, M. F. 1983. Natural history of Actaea rubra: Fruit dimorphism and fruit/seed predation. Bulletin of the Torrey Botanical Club 110: 298–303.

Bloodroot

Baskin, C. C., and J. M. Baskin. 2001. Seeds: Ecology, Biogeography, and Evolution of Dormancy and Germination. Academic Press, San Diego.

Densmore, F. 1974. How Indians Use Wild Plants for Food, Medicine and Crafts. Dover, New York.

Foster, H. L., and L. L. Foster 1990. Cuttings from a Rock Garden: Plant Portraits and Other Essays. Atlantic Monthly Press, New York.

Gates, B. N. 1940. Dissemination by ants of the seeds of Trillium grandiflorum. Rhodora 42: 194–196.

Hill, S. H. 1997. Weaving New Worlds: Southeastern Cherokee Women and their Basketry. University of North Carolina Press, Chapel Hill.

Kiger, R. W. 1997. Sanguinaria. In Flora of North America North of Mexico, ed. Flora of North America Editorial Committee, 3: 305. Oxford University Press, New York.

Lyon, D. L. 1992. Bee pollination of facultatively xenogamous Sanguinaria canadensis L. Bulletin of the Torrey Botanical Club 119: 368–375.

Mascarenhas, A. K., C. M. Allen, and M. L. Moeschberger. 2002. The association between Viadent use and oral leukoplakia—Results of a matched case-control study. Abstract. J. Public Health Dent. 62: 158–162. PubMed (PMD 12180043), http://www.ncbi.nlm.nih.gov/entrez/query.fcgi?cmd=Retrieve&db=PubMed&list_uids=12180043&dopt=Abstract (accessed 2009).

Meeker, J. W., J. E. Elias, and J. A. Heim. 1993. Plants Used by the Great Lakes Ojibwa. Great Lakes Indian Fish and Wildlife Commission, Odahna, WI.

Milius, S. 1998. Eating seeds shifts ant sex ratios. Science News 153: 184.

Moreman, D. E. 2000. Native American Ethnobotany, 3rd ed. Timber Press, Portland, OR.

Reed, D. W. "Bloodroot (Sanguinaria canadensis)." Wildflowers of the Southeastern U.S., 2binTheWild.com. http://2bnthewild.com/plants/H261.htm (accessed 2009).

Robertson, C. 1897. Seed crests and myrmecophilous dissemination in certain plants. Botanical Gazette 23: 288–289.

Rountree, H. C. 1989. The Powhatan Indians of Virginia: Their Traditional Culture. University of Oklahoma Press, Norman.

Sanders, J. 2003. Secrets of Wildflowers: A Delightful Feast of Little-Known Facts, Folklore, and History. Lyons Press, Guilford, CT.

Sheldon, J. W., M. J. Balick, and S. A. Laird. 1997. Medicinal Plants: Can Utilization and Conservation Coexist? Advances in Economic Botany 12: 1–104.

Spencer, W. P. 1944. Variation in petal number in the bloodroot, Sanguinaria canadensis. American Naturalist 78: 85–89.

Volkers, N. 2001. Ingredient in oral products linked to precancerous lesions. Oral Cancer News. http://oralcancernews.org/wp/ingredient-in-oral-products-linked-to-precancerous-lesions/ (accessed 2009).

Blue Cohosh

Audet, M., J. Gruert, D. Sunblad. 2009. "Black and blue cohosh to induce labor." Love to Know. http://herbs.lovetoknow.com/Black_and_Blue_Cohosh_to_Induce_Labor (accessed 2010).

Augustine, D. J., and P. A. Jordan. 1998. Predictors of white-tailed deer grazing intensity in fragmented deciduous forests. Journal of Wildlife Management 62: 1076–1085.

Beattie, A. J., and D. C. Culver. 1981. The guild of myrmecochores in the herbaceous flora of West Virginia forests. Ecology 62: 107–115.

Brett, J. F., and U. Posluszny. 1982. Floral development in Caulophyllum thalictroides (Berberidaceae). Canadian Journal of Botany 60: 2133–2141.

Cerner Multum. 2004. "Blue cohosh." Drugs.com. http://www.drugs.com/mtm/blue-cohosh.html (accessed 2010).

Dugoua, J.-J., D. Pem, D. Seely, E. Mills, and G. Koren. 2008. Safety and efficacy of blue cohosh (Caulophyllum thalictroides) during pregnancy and lactation. Canadian Journal of Clinical Pharmacology 15: 66–73.

Ganzera, M., H. R. W. Dharmaratne, P. D. Nanayakkara, and A. Kahn. 2003. Determination of saponins and alkaloids in Caulophyllum thalictroides (blue cohosh) by high-performance gas chromatography and evaporative light scattering detection. Phytochemical Analysis 14: 1–7.

Hannan, G. L., and H. A. Prucher. 1996. Reproductive biology of Caulophyllum thalictroides (Berberidaceae), an early flowering perennial of eastern North America. American Midland Naturalist 136: 267–277.

Jones, T. K., and B. M. Lawson. 1998. Profound neonatal congestive heart failure caused by maternal consumption of blue cohosh herbal medication. Journal of Pediatrics 132: 550–552.

Li, H.-L. 1952. Floristic relationships between eastern Asia and eastern North America. Transactions of the American Philosophical Society, n.s., 42: 371–429.

Loconte, H. 1997. Caulophyllum. In Flora of North America North of Mexico, ed. Flora of North America Editorial Committee, 3: 274–275. Oxford University Press, New York.

Loconte, H., and W. H. Blackwell, Jr. 1984. Berberidaceae of Ohio. Castanea 49: 39–43.

Moerman, D. University of Michigan–Dearborn. Native American Ethnobotany. http://herb.umd.umich.edu/ (accessed 2010).

St. Olaf College. 2003–2010. "Blue cohosh." Natural Lands. http://www.stolaf.edu/academics/naturallands/woodlands/ephemerals/blue-cohosh.html (accessed 2010).

Thompson, J. N., and M. F. Willson. 1979. Evolution of temperate fruit/bird interactions: Phenological strategies. Evolution 33: 973–982.

Ueno, H., N. Fumiyana, and H. Katakura. 1997. Genetic basis for different host use in Epilachna pustulosa, a herbivorous ladybird beetle. Heredity 78: 277–283.

University of Texas–Austin. "Caulophyllum thalictroides (L.)." Native Plant Database. Lady Bird Johnson Wildflower Center. http://www.wildflower.org/plants/result.php?id_plant=CATH2 (accessed 2010).

Wikimedia Foundation. 2010. "Caulophyllum thalictroides." Wikipedia. http://en.wikipedia.org/wiki/Caulophyllum_thalictroides (accessed 2010).

Blue-eyed Mary

Ahloowalia, B. S., and E. D. Garber. 1961. The genus Collinsia. XIII. Cytogenetic studies of interspecific hybrids involving species with pedicelled flowers. Botanical Gazette 122: 219–228.

American-Farina Enterprises. "Growing Instructions: Collinsia heterophylla." http://www.growinginstructions.com/fa149.html (accessed 2010).

Armbruster, W. S., C. P. H. Mulder, B. G. Baldwin, S. Kalisz, B. Wessa, and H. Nute. 2002. Comparative analysis of late floral development and mating-system evolution in tribe Collinsieae (Scrophulariaceae s.l.). American Journal of Botany 89: 37–49.

Baskin, J. M., and C. C. Baskin. 1985. Germination ecology of Collinsia verna, a winter annual of rich deciduous woodlands. Bulletin of the Torrey Botanical Club 110: 311–315.

Davis, L. R., and W. E. LaBerge. 1975. The nest biology of the bee Andrena (Ptilandrena) erigeniae Robertson (Hymenoptera: Andrenidae). Illinois Natural History Survey Biological Notes 95: 1–16.

Foster, H. L., and L. L. Foster. 1990. Cuttings from a Rock Garden: Plant Portraits and Other Essays. Atlantic Monthly, New York.

Hilty, J. 2002–2010. "Blue-eyed Mary." Illinois Wildflowers. http://illinoiswildflowers.info/woodland/plants/be_mary.htm (accessed 2010).

Kalisz, S. 1991. Experimental determination of seed bank age structure in the winter annual Collinsia verna. Ecology 72: 575–585.

Kalisz, S., D. Vogler, B. Fails, M. Finer, E. Shepard, T. Herman, and R. Gonzales. 1999. The mechanism of delayed selfing in Collinsia verna (Scrophulariaceae). American Journal of Botany 86: 1239–1247.

Kennedy, B. F., and E. Elle. 2008. The inbreeding depression cost of selfing: Importance of flower size and population size in Collinsia parviflora (Veronicaceae). American Journal of Botany 95: 1596–160.

Lankinen, Å., W. S. Armbruster, and L. Antonsen. 2007. Delayed stigma receptivity in Collinsia heterophylla (Plantaginaceae): Genetic variation and adaptive significance in relation to pollen competition, delayed self-pollination, and mating-system evolution. American Journal of Botany 94: 1183–1192.

Marcot, B. G. 2007. "Casual visitor or pollinator?" EPOW—Ecology Picture of the Week. http://taos-telecommunity.org/EPOW/EPOW-Archive/archive_2007/EPOW-070507.htm (accessed 2010).

McKenna, M. F., and G. Houle. 2008. Why are annual plants rarely spring ephemerals? New Phytologist 148: 295–302.

Pennell, F. W. 1935. Scrophulariaceae of Eastern Temperate North America. Academy of Natural Sciences of Philadelphia Monographs, no. 1, The Academy, Philadelphia.

Perutz, M. F. 1969. The structure of proteins as revealed by x-ray analysis: A contribution of physics to biology. Proceedings, American Philosophical Society 113: 247–264.

Province of British Columbia. 2003. "Blue orchard mason bee, Osmia lignaria." Apiculture Factsheet #506. Ministry of Agriculture and Lands. http://www.agf.gov.bc.ca/apiculture/factsheets/506_osmia.htm (accessed 2010).

Rafinesque, C. S. 1828. Gentiana collinsiana. In Medical Flora, 1: 231–232. Atkinson and Alexander, Philadelphia.

Robertson, C. 1891. Flowers and insects, Asclepiadaceae to Scrophulariaceae. Transactions of the Academy of Science of St. Louis 5: 569–598.

Sargent, C. S. 1905. Crataegus in eastern Pennsylvania. Proceedings of The Academy of Natural Sciences of Philadelphia 57: 577–661.

Shearwater Marketing Group. 2007. "Chinese Houses: Collinsia heterophylla." Enature.com. http://www.enature.com/fieldguides/detail.asp?allSpecies=y&searchText=Collinsia heterophylla&curGroupID=11&lgfromWhere=&curPageNum=1 (accessed 2010).

Tenaglia, D. 2007. "Collinsia verna Nutt." Missouriplants.com. http://www.missouriplants.com/Blueopp/Collinsia_verna_page.html (accessed 2010).

University of Wisconsin–Stevens Point. "Family Scrophulariaceae, Collinsia verna Nutt." Plants of Wisconsin. Robert W. Freckmann Herbarium. http://wisplants.uwsp.edu/scripts/detail.asp?SpCode=COLVER (accessed 2010).

Wikimedia Foundation. 2010. "Collinsia." Wikipedia. http://en.wikipedia.org/wiki/Collinsia (accessed 2010).

Celandines

Abu-Asab, M. S., P. M. Peterson, S. G. Shetler, and S. S. Orli. 2001. Earlier plant flowering in spring as a response to global warming in the Washington, DC area. Biodiversity and Conservation 10: 597–612.

Baskin, J. M., and C. C. Baskin. 1984. Germination ecophysiology of an eastern deciduous forest herb Stylophorum diphyllum. American Midland Naturalist 111: 390–399.

Benninger, J., H. T. Schneider, D. Schuppan, T. Kirchner, and E. G. Hahn. 1999. Acute hepatitis induced by greater celandine (Chelidonium majus). Gastroenterology 117: 1234–1237.

Biswas, S. J., and A. R. Khuda-Bukhsh. 2002. Effect of a homeopathic drug, chelidonium, in amelioration of p-DAB induced hepatocarcinogenesis in mice. BMC Complementary and Alternative Medicine 2: 4. PubMed Central (PMC107841), http://www.ncbi.nlm.nih.gov/pmc/articles/PMC107841/ (accessed 2010).

Blattner, F. R., and J. W. Kadereit. 1999. Morphological evolution and ecological diversification of the forest-dwelling poppies (Papaveraceae: Chelidonioideae) as deduced from a molecular phylogeny of the ITS region. Plant Systematics and Evolution 219: 181–197.

Brundrett, M. C., D. E. Estone, and C. A. Peterson. 1988. A berberine-aniline blue fluorescent staining procedure for suberin, lignin, and callose in plant tissue. Protoplasma 146: 133–142.

Buker, W. E., and S. A. Thompson. 1986. Is Stylophorum diphyllum (Papaveraceae) native to Pennsylvania? Castanea 51: 66–67.

Copeland, L. O., and M. B. McDonald. 2001. Principles of Seed Science and Technology. 4th ed. Kluwer Academic, Boston.

Hilty, J. 2002–2010. "Celandine poppy." Illinois Wildflowers. http://illinoiswildflowers.info/woodland/plants.cel_poppy.htm (accessed 2010).

Matos, O. C., J. Baeta, M. J. Silva, and C. P. Pinto Ricardo. 1999. Sensitivity of Fusarium strains to Chelidonium majus L. extracts. Journal of Ethnopharmacology 66: 151–158.

Missouri Botanical Garden. "Stylophorum diphyllum." Kemper Center for Home Gardening. PlantFinder. http://www.mobot.org/gardeninghelp/plantfinder/Plant.asp?code=M450 (accessed 2010).

Nearctica.com, Inc. 2003. "Celandine Poppy (Stylophorum diphyllum)." Nearctica. http://www.nearctica.com/flowers/papaver/Sdiphy.htm (accessed 2010).

Payne, N. 2010. "Wood poppy (Stylophorum diphyllum)." Canadian Wildlife Federation. http://www.cwf-fcf.org/en/resources/online-articles/news/wildlife/wood-poppy.html (accessed 2010).

Schlotterbeck. J. O. 1902. The color-compound of Stylophorum diphyllum and Chelidonum majus. American Journal of Pharmacology 74: 584–586.

Schlotterbeck, J. O., and H. C. Watkins. 1901. Contribution to the chemistry of Stylophorum. Proceedings of the American Pharmaceutical Association at the Forty-ninth Annual Meeting, 251–263, American Pharmaceutical Association, Philadelphia.

Schmeller, T., B. Latz-Brüning, and M. Wink. 1997. Biochemical activities of berberine, palmatine and sanguinarine mediating chemical defense against microorganisms and herbivores. Phytochemisty 44: 257–266.

Tenaglia, D. 2007. "Styloporum diphyllum (Michx.) Nutt." Missouriplants.com. http://www.missouriplants.com/Yellowopp/Stylophorum_diphyllum_page.html (accessed 2010).

University of Wisconsin–Stevens Point. "Family Papaveraceae, Stylophorum diphyllum (Michx.) Nutt." Plants of Wisconsin. Robert W. Freckmann Herbarium. http://wisplants.uwsp.edu/scripts/detail.asp?SpCode=STYDIP (accessed 2010).

Columbine

American Beauties. "Aquilegia canadensis 'Little Lanterns.'" American Beauties Native Plants. http://www.abnativeplants.com/ (accessed 2009).

Burroughs, J. 1906. Bird and Bough. Houghton, Mifflin, New York. Available at http://books.google.com/books?id=F98-AAAAIAAJ&printsec=frontcover&source=gbs_ge_summary_r&cad=0#v=onepage&q&f=false (accessed 2010).

Brunet, J. 2009. Pollinators of the Rocky Mountain columbine: Temporal variation, functional groups and associations with floral traits. Annals of Botany 103: 1567–1578.

Eckert, C. G., B. Ozimec, C. R. Herlihy, C. A. Griffin, and M. B. Routley. 2009. Floral morphology mediates temporal variation in the mating system of a self-compatible plant. Ecology 90: 1540–1548.

Fenster, C. B., G. Cheely, M. R. Dudash, and R. J. Reyolds. 2006. Nectar reward and advertisement in hummingbird-pollinated Silene virginica (Caryophyllaceae). American Journal of Botany 93: 1800–1807.

Freeman, M. B. 1976. The Unicorn Tapestries. Metropolitan Museum of Art, New York.

Griffin, S. R., K. Mavraganis, and C. G. Eckert. 2000. Experimental analysis of protogyny in Aquilegia canadensis (Ranunculaceae). American Journal of Botany 87: 1246–1256.

Herlihy, C. R., and C. G. Eckert. 2005. Evolution of self-fertilization at geographical range margins? A comparison of demographic, flora, and mating system variables in central vs. peripheral populations of Aquilegia canadensis (Ranunculaceae). American Journal of Botany 92: 744–751.

———. 2007. Evolutionary analysis of a key floral trait in Aquilegia canadensis (Ranunculaceae): Genetic variation in herkogamy and its effect on the mating system. Evolution 61: 1661–1674.

Hodges, S. A., M. Fulton, J. Y. Yang, and J. B. Whittall. 2003. Verne Grant and evolutionary studies of Aquilegia. New Phytologist 161: 113–120.

Hilty, J. 2002–2010. "Wild columbine." Illinois Wildflowers. http://www.illinoiswildflowers.info/woodland/plants/wild_columbine.htm (accessed 2009).

Jürgens, A., and S. Dötterl. 2004. Chemical composition of anther volatiles in Ranunculaceae: Genera-specific profiles in Anemone, Aquilegia, Caltha, Pulsatilla, Ranunculus, and Trollius species. American Journal of Botany 91: 1969–1980.

Macior, L. W. 1966. Foraging behavior of Bombus (Hymenoptera: Apidae) in relation to Aquilegia pollination. American Journal of Botany 53: 302–309.

Miller, R. 1981. Hawkmoths and the geographic patterns of floral variation in Aquilegia caerulea. Evolution 35: 763–774.

Payson, E. B. 1918. The North American species of Aquilegia. Contributions from the United States National Herbarium 20: 133–157.

Rook, E.J.S. 2002. "Aquilegia canadensis: Wild columbine" Flora, Fauna, Earth, and Sky—The Natural History of the North Woods. http://www.rook.org/earl/bwca/nature/herbs/aquilegiacan.html (accessed 2009).

Tamm, S., and C. L. Gaas. 1986. Energy intake rates and nectar concentration preferences by hummingbirds. Oecologia 70: 20–23.

Whittall, J. B., and S. A. Hodges. 2007. Pollinator shifts drive increasingly long nectar spurs in columbine flowers. Nature 447: 706–709.

Whittemore, A. T. 1997. Aquilegia. In Flora of North America North of Mexico, ed. Flora of North America Editorial Committee, 3: 249–258. Oxford University Press, New York.

Wisconsin Department of Natural Resources. 2009. "Columbine dusky wing (Erynnis lucilius)." Wisconsin Department of Natural Resources. http://dnr.wi.gov/org/land/er/biodiversity/index.asp?mode=info&Grp=9&SpecCode=IILEP37140 (accessed 2009).

Dutchman's Breeches

Blanchan, N. 1900. Nature's Garden. Garden City Publishing, Garden City, NY.

Cheney, R. H. 1946. Medicinal herbaceous species in the north-eastern United States. Bulletin of the Torrey Botanical Club 73: 60–72.

Herron, J. W., and D. E. LaBore. 1972. Some plants of Kentucky poisonous to livestock. College of Agriculture, University of Kentucky, Lexington. http://www.ca.uky.edu/agc/pubs/id/id2/id2.htm (accessed 2009).

Huang, J.-H., and G. A. Johnston. 1990. (+)-Hydrastine, a potent competitive antagonist at mammalian GABAA receptors. British Journal of Pharmacology 99: 727–730.

Lamoureux, G. 2002. Flore Printanière. Fleurec Éditeur, Saint-Henri-de Lévis, Quebec.

Linnean Society of London. The Linnean Collections. http://www.linnean-online.org/ (accessed 2009).

Lukes, Roy. 2003. Nature-wise: Bleeding hearts are an old favorite. Door County Advocate, May 2, 2003.

Macior, L. W. 1970. The pollination ecology of Dicentra cucullaria. American Journal of Botany 57: 6–11.

MacLean, D. B., and V. Snieckus. 1998. R. H. F. Manske: Fifty years of alkaloid chemistry. In The Alkaloids: Chemistry and Biology, ed. G. A. Cordell, 50: 3–59. Academic Press, San Diego.

Marinelli, J., ed. 2005. Plant. DK Publishing, New York.

Stang, David. 2004–2009. "Dicentra cucullaria." ZipcodeZoo.com. http://zipcodezoo.com/Plants/D/Dicentra%5Fcucullaria/ (accessed 2009).

Stern, K. R. 1961. Revision of Dicentra (Fumariaceae). Brittonia 13: 1–57.

———. 1962. The use of pollen morphology in the taxonomy of Dicentra. American Journal of Botany 49: 362–368.

Tebbitt, M. C., M. Lidén, and H. Zetterlund. 2008. Bleeding Hearts, Corydalis, and Their Relatives. Timber Press Portland, OR.

UIUC Veterinary Medicine Library. "Dutchman's breeches & squirrelcorn (Dicentra cucullaria (L.) Bernh. & Dicentra canadensis (Goldie) Walp." Plants Toxic to Animals. http://www.library.illinois.edu/vex/toxic/dutchman/dutchmn.htm (accessed 2009).

Wen, J. 1999. Evolution of eastern Asian and eastern North American disjunct distributions in flowering plants. Annual Review of Ecology and Systematics. 30: 421–544.

Early Meadow-rue

Bierzychudek, P. 1982. Life histories and demography of shade-tolerant temperate forest herbs: A review. New Phytologist 90: 757–776.

Casselman, B. "Meadow-rue." Bill Casselman's Canadian Word of the Day and Words of the World. http://www.billcasselman.com/canadian_garden_words/meadow_rue.htm (accessed 2010).

Charters, M. L. California Plant Names: Latin and Greek Meanings and Derivations. A Dictionary of Botanical and Biographical Etymology. http://www.calflora.net/botanicalnames/index.html (accessed 2010).

Di Stilio, V. S., and C. Connelly. 2007. Genetic underpinnings of shifts in pollination-related floral phenotypes in Thalictrum. Abstract of talk presented at the Plant Biology and Botany 2007 Joint Congress, Chicago, IL. July 7–11, 2007. http://2007.botanyconference.org/engine/search/index.php?func=detail&aid=1933 (accessed 2010).

Di Stilio, V. S., E. M. Kramer, and D. A. Baum. 2005. Floral MADS box genes and homeotic gender dimorphism in Thalictrum dioicum (Ranunculaceae)—A new model for the study of dioecy. Plant Journal 41: 755–766.

Melampy, M. N., and A. M. Hayworth. 1980. Seed production and pollen vectors in several nectarless plants. Evolution 34: 1144–1154.

Park, M. M., and D. Festerling, Jr. 1997. Thalictrum. In Flora of North America North of Mexico, ed. Flora of North America Editorial Committee 3: 258–271. Oxford University Press, New York.

Pogue, M. G. 2005. The plusiinae (Lepidoptera: Noctuidae) of Great Smoky Mountains National Park. Zootaxa 1032: 1–28.

Poulton, J. E. 1990. Cyanogenesis in plants. Plant Physiology 94: 401–405.

Schaffner, J. H. 1925. Experiments with various plants to produce change of sex in the individual. Bulletin of the Torrey Botanical Club 52: 35–47.

———. 1927. Sex-limited characters in heterosporous sporophytes. Ohio Journal of Science 27: 19–24.

Seigler, D. S. 1976. Plants of the northeastern United States that produce cyanogenic compounds. Economic Botany 30: 395–407.

Steven, J. C., and D. M. Waller. 2004. Reproductive alternatives to insect pollination in four species of Thalictrum (Ranunculaceae). Plant Species Biology 19: 73–80.

———. 2007. Isolation affects reproductive success in low-density but not high-density populations of two wind-pollinated Thalictrum species. Plant Ecology 190: 131–141.

Wagner, D. L. 2005. Caterpillars of Eastern North America. Princeton University Press, Princeton, NJ.

Walck, J. L., C. C. Baskin, and J. M. Baskin. Seeds of Thalictrum mirabile (Ranunculaceae) require cold stratification for loss of nondeep simple morphophysiological dormancy. Canadian Journal of Botany 77: 1769–1776.

Wikimedia Foundation. 2010. "Glycoside." Wikipedia. http://www.wikipedia.org/wiki/cyanogenic_glycoside#Cyanogenic_glycosides (accessed 2010).

Wodehouse, R. P. 1936. Pollen grains in the identification and classification of plants. VII. The Ranunculaceae. Bulletin of the Torrey Botanical Club 63: 495–514.

Early Saxifrage

Aiken, S. G., M. J. Dallwitz, L. L. Consaul, C. L. McJannet, L. J. Gillespie, R. L. Boles, G. W. Argus, J. M. Gillett, P. J. Scott, R. Elven, M. C. LeBlanc, A. K. Brysting and H. Solstad. 1999–. "Saxifraga oppositifolia L." Flora of the Canadian Arctic Archipelago: Descriptions, Illustrations, Identification, and Information Retrieval. Version 29 April 2003. http://www.mun.ca/biology/delta/arcticf/ (accessed 2010).

Harris, M. 2003. Botanica North America. HarperResource, New York.

Hyam, R., and R. Pankhurst. 1995. Plants and Their Names: A Concise Dictionary. Oxford University Press, New York.

Köhlerin, F. 1985. Saxifrages and Related Genera. Trans. D. Wiastanley. Timber Press, Portland, OR.

Lehmkuhl, F., and S. Liu. 1994. An outline of physical geography including Pleistocene glacial landforms of Eastern Tibet (provinces Sichuan and Quighai). GeoJournal 34: 7–30.

Levin, M. H. 1960. Studies on the ecological life history of Saxifraga virginiensis. Bulletin of the Torrey Botanical Club 87: 348–360.

Small, J. K. 1896. New and noteworthy species of Saxifraga. Bulletin of the Torrey Botanical Club 23: 362–368.

Soltis, D. E., and P. S. Soltis. 1997. Phylogenetic relationships in Saxifragaceae sensu lato: A comparison of topologies based on 18S rDNA and rbcL sequences. American Journal of Botany 84: 504–522.

Sterns, E. E. 1887. Some anomalous forms of Saxifraga virginiensis. Bulletin of the Torrey Botanical Club 14: 122–125.

Stubbs, C. S., H. A. Jacobson, E. A. Osgood, and F. A. Drummond. 1992. Alternative Forage Plants for Native (Wild) Bees Associated with Lowbush Blueberry,

Vaccinium spp., in Maine. Maine Agricultural Experiment Station Technical Bulletin 148, Univ. of Maine, Orono.

Thoreau, H. D. 1906. Journal. Vol. 5. March 5–November 30, 1853. The Writings of Henry David Thoreau. Houghton, Mifflin, and Company, Boston. Available at http://www.walden.org/documents/file/Library/Thoreau/writings/Writings1906/11Journal05/Chapter2.pdf (accessed 2010).

Tyndall, R. W., and P. M. Farr. 1989. Vegetation structure and flora of a serpentine pine-cedar savanna in Maryland. Castanea 54: 191–199.

Weinmann, F., and D. Giblin. 2009. "Saxifragaceae (Saxifrage Family)." Cascadia. A Checklist of the Vascular Plants of Washington State. http://biology.burke.washington.edu/herbarium/waflora/checklist.php?Family=Saxifragaceae&view=list (accessed 2010).

Westgaard, K. B., M. H. Jørgensen, T. M. Gabrielsen, I. G. Alsos, and C. Brochmann. 2010. The extreme Beringlan/Atlantic disjunction in Saxifraga rivularis (Saxifragaceae) had formed at least twice. Journal of Biogeography 37: 1262–1276.

Whitty, J. 2008. "Thoreau's wildflowers wilt in warming climate." Mother Jones. October 27, 2008. http://motherjones.com/blue-marble/2008/10/thoreaus-wildflowers-wilt-warming-climate (accessed 2010).

False Hellebore

Bender, M. H., J. M. Baskin, and C. C. Baskin. 2000. Age of maturity and life span in herbaceous, polycarpic perennials. Botanical Review 66: 311–349.

Bergmann, E. D., Z. H. Levinson, and R. Mechoulam. 1958. The toxicity of Veratrum and Solanum alkaloids to housefly larvae. Journal of Insect Physiology 2: 162–177.

Charters, M. L. 2003–2009. "Veratrum." California Plant Names: Latin and Greek Meanings and Derivations. A Dictionary of Botanical and Biographical Etymology. http://www.calflora.net/botanicalnames/pageV.html (accessed 2010).

El Sayed, K. A., J. D. McChesney, A. F. Halim, A. M. Zaghloul, and M. Voehler. 1995. Two steroidal alkaloids from Veratrum viride. Phytochemistry 38: 1547–1550.

Freis, E. D., J. R. Stanton, and F. C. Moister. 1950. Assay in man of the chemical fractions of Veratrum viride, and identification of the pure alkaloids geritrine and germidine as potent hypotensive principles derived from the drug. Journal of Pharmacology and Experimental Therapeutics 98: 169–173.

Howard. L. O., and R. H. Hutchinson. 1915. House flies. USDA Farmers' Bulletin 679. Contribution from the Bureau of Entomology, pp. 15–17. U.S. Dept. of Agric., Washington, DC.

Kalm, P. 1966. Peter Kalm's Travels in North America: The English Version of 1770. Revised from the Original Swedish and Edited by Adolph B. Benson with a Translation of New Material from Kalm's Diary Notes. Dover Publications, New York. (Orig. pub. 1937, Wilson-Erickson, New York).

Letters, notes, and answers: Angostura bitters. 1928. British Medical Journal 1: 986.

Nathanielsz, P. W. 1996. The timing of birth. American Scientist 84: 562–569.

Natural Standard. 2008. "American hellebore (Veratrum viride)." Natural Standard. http://www.naturalstandard.com (accessed 2010).

Nuvo. 2009. "Native Americans and lice." Nuvo for Head Lice. http://www.nuvoforheadlice.com/Native_Americans.htm (accessed 2010).

Plant-names.com. 2006. "Veratrum." Plant Names. http://www.plant-names.com/plant_names_page_32.htm#V (accessed 2010).

Schaffner, U., D. Kleijn, V. Brown, and H. Müller-Schärer. 2001. Veratrum album in montane grasslands: A model system for implementing biological control in land management practices for high biodiversity habitats. Biocontrol News and Information 22: 19N–28N.

Schep, L. J., D. M. Schmierer, and J. S. Fountain. 2006. Veratrum poisoning. Toxicological Reviews 25: 73–78.

Starna, W. A., G. R. Hamell, and W. L. Butts. 1984. Northern Iroquoian horticulture and insect infestation: A cause for village removal. Ethnohistory 31: 197–207.

Taylor, C. A. 1956. The culture of false hellebore. Economic Botany 10: 155–165.

Tucker, A. O., and S. Belsinger. 2003. "Bitters: Beverages with moxie." The Herb Companion. http://www.herbcompanion.com/Cooking/Bitters-Beverages-with-Moxie.aspx (accessed 2010).

Wikimedia Foundation. 2010. "Gentiana lutea." Wikipedia. http://en.wikipedia.org/wiki/Gentiana_lutea (accessed 2010).

———. 2010. "House of Angostura." Wikipedia. http://en.wikipedia.org/wiki/House_of_Angostura (accessed 2010).

Zager, P. E., and C. J. Jonkel. Managing grizzly bear habitat in the northern Rocky Mountains. Journal of Forestry 81: 524–536.

Zomlefer, W. B., N. H. Williams, W. M. Whitten, and W. S. Judd. 2001. Generic circumscription and relationships in the tribe Melanthieae (Liliales, Melanthiaceae), with emphasis on Zigadenus: Evidence from ITS and trnL-F sequence data. American Journal of Botany 88: 1657–1669.

References

Featherfoil

Baskin, C. C., J. M. Basin, and E. W. Chester. 1996. Seed germination ecology of the aquatic winter annual Hottonia inflata. Aquatic Botany 54: 51–57.

Brys, R., H. Jacquemyn, and M. Hermy. 2007. Impact of mate availability, population size, and spatial aggregation of morphs of sexual reproduction in a distylous, aquatic plant. American Journal of Botany 94: 119–127.

Cholewa, A. F. 2008. Hottonia. In Flora of North America North of Mexico, ed. Flora of North America Editorial Committee, 8: 259. Oxford University Press, New York.

Copley, Georgianne. 1999. A life history study of Hottonia inflata. M. S. thesis. University of Connecticut, Storrs.

Darwin, C. 1877. The Different Forms of Flowers on Plants of the Same Species. John Murray, London.

Hawker, L. E. 1932. A quantitative study of the geotropism of seedlings with special reference to the nature and development of their statolith apparatus. Annals of Botany o.s. 46: 121–157.

McAvoy, W. A. 2008. "Featherfoil (Hottonia inflata Ell.) of the Primulaceae, the primrose family, is an obligate wetland plant with a curious appearance and a fascinating lifecycle." Plant Talk. http://www.delawarenativeplants.org/index.cfm?fuseaction=trees.pageDetails&p=225-4-470 (accessed 2010).

Prankerd, T. L. 1911. On the structure and biology of the genus Hottonia. Annals of Botany 25: 253–268.

Wijnands, Onno. 1994. Pieter Hotton and Hottonia. New Plantsman 1: 175–176.

Fire-pink

Antonovics, J., M. E. Hood, P. H. Thrall, J. U. Abrams, and G. M. Duthie. 2003. Herbarium studies on the distribution of anther-smut fungus (Microbotryum violaceum) and Silene species (Caryophyllaceae) in the eastern United States. American Journal of Botany 91: 1522–1531.

Antonovics, J., D. Stratton, P. H. Thrall, and A. M. Jarosz. 1996. An anther-smut disease (Ustilago violacea) of fire-pink (Silene virginica): Its biology and the relationship to the anther-smut disease of white campion (Silene alba). American Midland Naturalist 135: 130–143.

Brooks, C. P., J. Antonovics, and T. H. Keitt. 2008. Spatial and temporal heterogeneity explain disease dynamics in a spatially explicit network model. American Naturalist 172: 149–159.

Fenster, C. B., G. Cheely, M. R. Dudash, and R. J. Reynolds. 2006. Nectar reward and advertisement in hummingbird-pollinated Silene virginica (Caryophyllaceae). American Journal of Botany 93: 1800–1807.

Fenster, C. B., and M. R. Dudash. 2001. Spatiotemporal variation in the role of hummingbirds as pollinators of Silene virginica. Ecology 82: 844–851.

Larson, K. W. 2010. "Plant of the week: Fire pink (Silene virginica L.)." U.S. Forest Service: Celebrating Wildflowers. http://www.fs.fed.us/wildflowers/plant-of-the-week/silene_virginica.shtml (accessed 2009).

Fringed Polygala

Blanchan, N. 1900. Nature's Garden. Doubleday, Garden City, New York.

Ernst, E. 2005. Popular herbal medicines having effects on the central nervous system. In Nutritional Neuroscience. ed. H. R. Lieberman, R. B. Kanarek, and C. Prasad, 383–392. CRC Press,, Boca Raton, FL.

Greenish, G. 1920. A Text Book of Materia Medica, Being an Account of the More Important Crude Drugs of Vegetable and Animal Origin. J. & A. Churchill, London.

Gwilt, J. R., and P. R. Gwilt. Native North American medicines. Pharmaceutical Journal 265: 940–941.

Holm, T. 1929. Morphology of North American species of Polygala. Botanical Gazette 88: 167–185.

Lacaille-Dubois, M.-A., and A.-C. Mitaine-Offer. 2005. Triterpene saponins from Polygalaceae. Phytochemistry Reviews 4: 139–149.

Larsen, E. L. 1957. Pehr Kalm's account of the North American rattlesnake and the medicines used in the treatment of its sting. American Midland Naturalist 57: 502–511.

Mabry, C., and T. Korsgren. 1998. A permanent plot study of vegetation and vegetation-site factors fifty-three years following disturbance in central New England, U.S.A. EcoScience 5: 232–240.

Milby, T. H. 1976. Studies in the floral anatomy of Polygala (Polygalaceae). American Journal of Botany 63: 1319–1326.

Mohrs, W. B., et al. 2000. Plant natural products active against snake bite—The molecular approach. Phytochemistry 55: 627–642.

Muma, W. "Fringed polygala (Polygala paucifolia)." Ontario Wildflowers. http://ontariowildflowers.com/main/species.php?id=45 (accessed 2009).

Turcotte, C. 1997. Towards sustainable harvesting of Seneca snakeroot, Polygala senega L., on Manitoba Hydro rights-of-way. M.S. thesis. University of Manitoba, Winnipeg. http://mspace.lib.umanitoba.ca/bitstream/1993/752/1/mq23536.pdf (accessed 2011).

University of Wisconsin–Stevens Point. "Family Polygalaceae, Polygala paucifolia Willd." Plants of Wisconsin. Robert W. Freckmann Herbarium. http://wisplants.uwsp.edu/scripts/detail.asp?SpCode= POLPAU (accessed 2010).

Weed, C. M. ca. 1895. Ten New England Blossoms and Their Insect Visitors. Houghton, Mifflin, New York.

Wenzel, B. 2010. "Fringed polygala, gaywings, flowering wintergreen (Polygala paucifolia Willd.)." U.S. Forest Service: Celebrating Wildflowers. http://www.fs.fed .us/wildflowers/plant-of-the-week/polygala_paucifolia .shtml (accessed 2010).

Hepaticas

Anderson, E. 1936. Color variation in eastern North American flowers as exemplified by Hepatica acutiloba. Rhodora 38: 301–304.

Ashwood Nurseries. "Hepaticas." Ashwood Nurseries. http://www.ashwood-nurseries.co.uk/index .php?option=com_content&task=view&id=13&ltemid-8 (accessed 2009).

Baskin, J. M., and C. C. Baskin. 1985. Epicotyl dormancy in seeds of Cimicifuga racemosa and Hepatica acutiloba. Bulletin of the Torrey Botanical Club 112: 253–257.

Bernhardt, P. 1976. The pollination ecology of Hepatica acutioba DC (Ranunculaceae). Bulletin of the Torrey Botanical Club 103: 255–258.

Bryant, William Cullen. 1839. Poems. Harper and Brothers, New York.

Burroughs, J. 1887. Signs and Seasons. Houghton, Mifflin, New York. Available at http://books.google.com/ books?id=GdI-AAAAYAAJ&printsec=frontcover&dq= John+burroughs+Signs+and+Seasons&hl=en&ei= ilrkTfC3NMi4tweghpXeCQ&sa=X&oi=book_ result&ct=result&resnum=1&ved=0CC4Q6AEwAA#v= onepage&q&f=false (accessed 2010).

Coffey, T. 1993. The History and Folklore of North American Wildflowers. Houghton Mifflin, Boston.

Dutton, B. E., C. S. Keener, and B. A. Ford. 1997. Anemone. In Flora of North America North of Mexico, ed. Flora of North America Editorial Committee, 3: 139–158. Oxford University Press, New York.

Glass, B. 2002. Hepatica: An early bloomer. Chicago Wilderness Magazine. http://chicagowildernessmag.org/ issues/spring2002/hepatica.html (accessed 2009).

Grieve. M. 1995. Liverwort, American. A Modern Herbal. http://botanical.com/botanical/mgmh/l/livame36.html (accessed 2009).

Howard, D. F., and W. R. Tschinkel. 1976. Aspects of necrophoric behavior in the red imported fire ant, Solenopsis invicta. Behaviour 56: 157–178.

Lloyd, J. U., and C. G. Lloyd. 1884–1887. Hepatica–liver leaf. In Drugs and Medicines of North America. Available at Henriette's Herbal Homepage, H. Kress, 1995–2010, http://www.henrietteherbal.com/eclectic/dmna/ hepatica.html (accessed 2009).

Mark, S., and J. M. Olesen. 1996. Importance of elaiosome size to removal of ant-dispersed seeds. Oecologia 107: 95–101.

Milius, S. 1998. Eating seeds shifts ant sex ratios. Science News 153: 184.

Missouri Botanical Garden. "Hepatica americana." Kemper Center for Home Gardening. Plant Finder. http://www. mobot.org/gardeninghelp/PlantFinder/plant .asp?code=K440 (accessed 2009).

Murphy, S. D., and L. Vasseur. 1995. Pollen limitation in a northern population of Hepatica acutiloba. Canadian Journal of Botany 73: 1234–1241.

Plants for a Future. 1996–2010. "Hepatica nobilis Mill." Plants for a Future. http://www.pfaf.org/user/Plant .aspx?LatinName=Hepatica+nobilis (accessed 2009).

Scott, D. C. 1909. A Nest of Hepaticas. In Flowers from a Canadian Garden, ed. L. H. Burpee. Musson Book Company, Toronto, Canada.

Skidmore, B. A., and E. R. Heithaus. 1988. Lipid cues for seed-carrying by ants in Hepatica americana. Journal of Chemical Ecology 14: 2185–2196.

Jack-in-the-pulpit

Barriault, I., D. Barabé, L. Cloutier, and M. Gibernau. 2009. Pollination ecology and reproductive success in Jack-in-the-pulpit (Arisaema triphyllum) in Québec (Canada). Plant Biology 12: 161–171.

Barriault, I., M. Gibernau, and D. Barabe. 2009. Flowering period, thermogenesis, and pattern of visiting insects in Arisaema triphyllum (Araceae) in Québec. Botany 87: 324–329.

Bierzychudek, P. 1982. The demography of Jack-in-the-pulpit, a forest perennial that changes sex. Ecological Monographs 52: 336–351.

———. Life histories and demography of shade-tolerant temperate forest herbs: A review. New Phytologist 90: 257–276.

Braun, J., and G. R. Brooks, Jr. 1987. Box turtles (Terrapene carolina) as potential agents for seed dispersal. American Midland Naturalist 117: 312–318.

Clay, K. 1993. Size-dependent gender change in green dragon (Arisaema dracontium; Araceae). American Journal of Botany 80: 769–777.

Doust, L. L., J. L. Doust, and K. Turi. 1986. Fecundity and size relationships in Jack-in-the-pulpit, Arisaema triphyllum (Araceae). American Journal of Botany 73: 489–494.

Feller, I. C., H. Kudoh, C. E. Tanner, and D. F. Whigham. 2002. Sex-biased herbivory in Jack-in-the-pulpit (Arisaema triphyllum) by a specialist thrips (Heterothrips arisaemae). In Thrips and Tospoviruses: Proceedings of the 7th International Symposium on Thysanoptera, ed.

L. A. Mound and R. Marullo, 163–172. CSIRO Entomology, Reggio Calabria, Italy

Frankland, F., and N. Thomas. 2003. Impacts of white-tailed deer on spring wildflowers in Illinois, USA. Natural Areas Journal 23: 341–348.

Grayam, M. H. 1990. Evolution and phylogeny of the Araceae. Annals of the Missouri Botanical Garden 77: 628–697.

Gusman, G., and L. Gusman. 2002. The Genus Arisaema: A Monograph for Botanists and Nature Lovers. A. R. Gantner, Ruggell, Lichtenstein.

Hale, C. M. 2006. Ground flora reduced in diversity and abundance when alien earthworms invade. Ecology 87: 1637–1649.

Huttleston, D. G. 1949. The three subspecies of Arisaema triphyllum. Bulletin of the Torrey Botanical Club 76: 407–413.

———. 1981. The four subspecies of Arisaema triphyllum. Bulletin of the Torrey Botanical Club 108: 479–481.

Levine, M. T., and I. C. Feller. 2004. Effects of forest age and disturbance on population persistence in the understory herb, Arisaema triphyllum (Araceae). Plant Ecology 172: 73–82.

Miklos, T. 1980. Biosystematics of the Arisaema triphyllum complex. Ph.D. diss., University of Michigan, Ann Arbor.

Parker, M. A. 1987. Pathogen impact on sexual vs. asexual reproductive success in Arisaema triphyllum. American Journal of Botany 74: 1758–1763.

Payne, N. F., B. E. Kohn, N. C. Norton, and G. G. Bertagnoli. 1998. Black bear food items in northern Wisconsin. Transactions of the Wisconsin Academy of Sciences Arts and Letters 86: 263–280.

Quattrocchi, U. 1999. CRC World Dictionary of Plant Names. CRC Press, Boca Raton, FL.

Renner, S. S., L.-B. Zhang, and J. Murata. 2004. A chloroplast phylogeny of Arisaema (Araceae) illustrates Tertiary floristic links between Asia, North America, and East Africa. American Journal of Botany 91: 881–888.

Ruhren, S., and S. N. Handel. 2000. Considering herbivory, reproduction, and gender when monitoring plants: A case study of Jack-in-the-pulpit. Natural Areas Journal 20: 261–266.

Rust, R. W. 1980. Pollen movement and reproduction in Arisaema triphyllum. Bulletin of the Torrey Botanical Club 107: 539–542.

Schaffner, J. H. 1922. Control of the sexual state in Arisaema triphyllum and Arisaema dracontium. American Journal of Botany 9: 72–78.

Lady-slippers

Batty, A. L., K. W. Dixon, M. Brundrett, and K. Sivasithamparam. 2001. Constraints to symbiotic germination of terrestrial orchid seed in a Mediterranean bushland. New Phytologist 152: 511–520.

Bernhardt, P. 1983. Skipping over the lady's slippers. Garden, March/April.

Burroughs, J. 1894. Riverby. Vol. 9 of The Writings of John Burroughs. Houghton, Mifflin, New York. Available at http://books.google.com/books (accessed 2010).

Cameron, D. D., I. Johnson, D. J. Read, J. R. Leake. Giving and receiving: Measuring the carbon cost of mycorrhizas in the green orchid, Goodyera repens. New Phytologist 180: 176–184.

Cribb, P., and M. Fay. "Cypripedium calceolus (lady's slipper orchid)." Kew: Plants and Fungi. http://www.kew.org/plants-fungi/Cypripedium-calceolus.htm (accessed 2010).

Cullina, W. 2005. Understanding lady's slippers. Lecture at annual meeting of Connecticut Botanical Society. November 19.

Darwin, C. 1862. On the Various Contrivances by Which British and Foreign Orchids are Fertilised by Insects, and on the Good Effects of Intercrossing. Murray, London. Available at The Complete Works of Charles Darwin Online. http://darwin-online.org.uk/EditorialIntroductions/Freeman_FertilisationofOrchids.html (accessed 2010).

Eagle One Productions. 2007. "Lady slipper, pink–(Cypripedium acaule)." Voyageur Country. http://www.voyageurcountry.com/htmls/floweringplants/plants/ladyslipperpink.html (accessed 2010).

Edens-Meier, R. M., N. Vance, Y.-B. Luo, P. Li, E. Westhus, and P. Bernhardt. 2010. Pollen-pistil interactions in North American and Chinese Cypripedium L. (Orchidaceae). International Journal of Plant Science 171: 370–381.

Felter, H. W., and J. U. Lloyd. 1898. Cypripedium (U. S. P.)–King's American Dispensatory, The Ohio Valley Company. Available at Henriette's Herbal Homepage, H. Kress, 1995–2010, http://www.henrietteherbal.com/eclectic/kings/cypripedium.html (accessed 2010).

Foster, H. L., and L. L. Foster. 1990. Cuttings from a Rock Garden: Plant Portraits and Other Essays. Atlantic Monthly Press, New York.

Haines, A. 2001. Taxonomy of the Cypripedium parviflorum complex in Maine. Botanical Notes 6: 4–6. Available at http://www.arthurhaines.com/botanical_notes/BotNotes_N6.pdf (accessed 2010).

Kalm, P. 1966. Peter Kalm's Travels in North America: The English Version of 1770. Revised from the Original Swedish and Edited by Adolph B. Benson with a Translation of New Material from Kalm's Diary Notes. Dover Publications, New York. (Orig. pub. 1937, Wilson-Erickson, New York).

Keenan, P. E. 1998. Wild Orchids across North America. Timber Press, Portland, OR.

Lang. D. 2004. Britain's Orchids. WILDGuides, Maidenhead, Berkshire, England.

Marren, P. 1999. Britain's Rare Flowers. T & AD Natural History, London.

McGhan, P.J.R. 2010. "Pink ladies slipper (Cypripedium acaule Ait.)." U.S. Forest Service: Celebrating Wildflowers. http://www.fs.fed.us/wildflowers/plant-of-the-week/cypripedium_acaule.shtml (accessed 2010).

O'Connell, L. M., and M. O. Johnston. 1998. Male and female pollination success in a deceptive orchid, a selection study. Ecology 79: 1246–1260.

Primack, R., and E. Stacy. 1998. Cost of reproduction in the pink lady's slipper orchid (Cypripedium acaule, Orchidaceae): An eleven-year experimental study of three populations. American Journal of Botany 85: 1672–1679.

Shefferson, R. P., B. K. Sandercock, J. Proper, and S. R. Beissinger. 2001. Estimating dormancy and survival of a rare herbaceous perennial using mark-recapture models. Ecology 82: 145–156.

Shefferson, R. P., M. Weiss, T. Kull, D. L. Taylor. 2005. High specificity generally characterizes mycorrhizal association in rare lady's slipper orchids, genus Cypripedium. Molecular Ecology 14: 613–626.

Sheviak, C. J. 2002. Cypripedium acaule. In Flora of North America North of Mexico, ed. Flora of North America Editorial Committee, 26: 494–499. Oxford University Press, New York.

———. 2002. Cypripedium parviflorum. In Flora of North America North of Mexico, ed. Flora of North America Editorial Committee, 26: 500–505. Oxford University Press, New York.

Simon, H. 1975. The Private Lives of Orchids. J. B. Lippincott, Philadelphia.

Lesser Celandine

Brewer, E. C. 1898. Dictionary of Phrase and Fable. Available at Misnomers, Bartleby.com, Great Books Online, http://www.bartleby.com/81/11493.html (accessed 2009).

Guldberg, L. D., and P. R. Atsatt. 1975. Frequency of reflection and absorption of ultraviolet light in flowering plants. American Midland Naturalist 93: 35–43.

Halket, A. C. 1927. Observations on the tubercules of Ranunculus ficaria L. Annals of Botany 41: 731–753.

Hedgerowmobile. "Lesser celandine (Ranunculus ficaria)." Hedgerows, Hedges and Verges of Britain and Ireland. http://hedgerowmobile.com/lessercelandine.html (accessed 2009).

Marsden-Jones, E. M. 1935. Ranunculus ficaria Linn.: Life-history and pollination. Journal of the Linnean Society (Botany) 50: 39–55.

Marsden-Jones, E. M., and W. B. Turrill. 1952. Studies on Ranunculus ficaria. Journal of Genetics 50: 522–534.

Metcalfe, C. R. 1936. An interpretation of the morphology of the single cotyledon of Ranunculus ficaria based on embryology and seedling anatomy. Annals of Botany, o.s., 50: 103–120.

Pakin, J. 1928. The glossy petal of Ranunculus. Annals of Botany, o.s., 42: 739–755.

Palser, B. F. 1975. The bases of angiosperm phylogeny: Embryology. Annals of the Missouri Botanical Garden 62: 621–646.

Sephora. 1999–2010. "Murad." http://www.sephora.com/browse/product.jhtml?categoryId=C9382&id=P7366 (accessed 2009).

Simpson, B. B., and J. L. Neff. 1983. Floral biology and floral rewards of Lysimachia (Primulaceae). American Midland Naturalist 110: 249–256.

Swearingen, J. "Least wanted: Fig buttercup." Plant Conservation Alliance, Alien Plant Working Group. http://www.discoverlife.org/mp/20q?go=http://www.nps.gov/plants/alien/fact/rafi1.htm (accessed 2009).

Taylor, K., and B. Markham. 1978. Ranunculus ficaria L. (Ficaria verna Huds.; F. ranunculoides Moench). Journal of Ecology 66: 1011–1031.

Top Cultures. "Lesser celandine (Ranunculus ficaria)." Phytochemicals. http://www.phytochemicals.info/plants/lesser-celandine.php (accessed 2009).

Wikimedia Foundation. 2010. "Ranunculus." Wikipedia. http://en.wikipedia.org/wiki/Ranunculus (accessed 2009).

Yves Rocher. 1968. Pharmaceutical compositions and method of making the same. US Patent 3608074, filed Feb. 29, 1968, and issued Sept. 29, 1971. Available at http://www.freepatentsonline.com/3608074.pdf (accessed 2009).

Lousewort

Ashby, E. 1980. What price the Furbish lousewort? Enviromental Science and Technology 14: 1176–1181.

Ginn, W. 2005. Investing in Nature: Case Studies of Land Conservation in Collaboration with Business. Island Press, Washington, DC.

Han-bi, Y., N. Holmgren, R. R. Mill. 1998. Pedicularis Linnaeus. In Flora of China 18: 97. Available at E-Floras.org., http://www.efloras.org/florataxon.aspx?flora_id=2&taxon_id=124237 (accessed 2010).

Irwin. H. S. 1977. Miss Furbish's lousewort must live. Garden 1: 6–11.

References

Lackney, V. K. 1981. The parasitism of Pedicularis lanceo-lata Michx., a root hemiparasite. Bulletin of the Torrey Botanical Club 108: 422–429.

Laverty, T. M. 1992. Plant interactions for pollinator vis-its: A test of the magnet species effect. Oecologia 89: 502–508.

Lloyd, K., and A. Pipp. "Elephanthead Pedicularis, Pedicu-laris groenlandica." MT.gov: Montana Fish, Wildlife & Parks. http://fwp.mt.gov/education/youth/lewisAndClark/plants/elephanthead.html (accessed 2010).

Macior, L. W. 1968. Pollination adaptation in Pedicularis canadensis. American Journal of Botany 55: 1031–1035.

———. 1968. Pollination adaptation in Pedicularis groen-landica. American Journal of Botany 55: 927–932.

———. 1971. Co-evolution of plants and animals: System-atic insights from plant-insect interactions. Taxon 20: 17–28.

———. 1978. Pollination ecology of vernal angiosperms. Oikos 30: 452–460.

Moore, M.R.S. "Pedicularis (betony/lousewort)." Southwest School of Botanical Medicine, Bisbee, Arizona. http://www.swsbm.com/FOLIOS/PedFol.pdf (accessed 2010).

Musselman, L. J., and W. F. Mann, Jr. 1977. Host plants of some Rhinanthoideae (Scrophulariaceae) of eastern North America. Plant Systematics and Evolution 127: 45–53.

Pennel, F. W. 1935. Scrophulariaceae of Eastern North America. Academy of Natural Sciences of Philadelphia, Philadelphia.

Piehl, M. A. 1963. Mode of attachment, haustorium struc-ture, and hosts of Pedicularis canadensis. American Journal of Botany 50: 978–985.

Psychoactiveherbs.com. 2004. "Pedicularis groenlandica, elephants head." Psychoactive Herbs. http://psychoactiveherbs.com/catalog/index.php?cPath=123_125 (accessed 2010).

Schneider, A., and B. Schneider. "Pedicularis." Southwest Colorado Wildflowers, Ferns, and Trees. http://www.swcoloradowildflowers.com/Yellow%20Enlarged%20Photo%20Pages/pedicularis.htm (accessed 2010).

Stevens, O. A. 1957. Weights of seeds and numbers per plant. Weeds 5: 46–55.

Mayapple

Filyaw, T. 2005–2006. Podophyllum peltatum. Plants to Watch: Non-timber Products from Appalachian For-est and Field. http://www.appalachianforest.org/ptw_mayapple.html (accessed in 2009).

Braun, J. and G. R. Brooks, Jr. 1987. Box turtles (Terrapene carolina) as potential agents for seed dispersal. Ameri-can Midland Naturalist 117: 312–318.

Crants, J. and B. Rathcke. Floral neighborhood and polli-nation success in mayapple (Podophyllum peltatum L.), a nectarless herb said to deceive its pollinators. Abstract of paper presented at the Plant Biology and Botany 2007 Joint Congress, Chicago, IL. July 7–11, 2007. http://2007.botanyconference.org/engine/search/index.php?func=detail&aid=1797 (accessed 2009).

Eastman, J. 1992. The Book of Forest and Thicket. Stack-pole Books, Harrisburg, PA.

George, L. O. 1997. Podophyllum. In Flora of North Amer-ica North of Mexico, ed. Flora of North America Edi-torial Committee, 3: 287–288. Oxford University Press, New York.

Hanzawa, F. M., and S. Kalisz. 1993. The relationship between age, size, and reproduction in Trillium gran-diflorum (Liliaceae). American Journal of Botany 80: 405–410.

Kintzios, S. E. 2006. Terrestrial plant-derived anticancer agents and plant species used in anticancer research. Critical Reviews in Plant Sciences 25: 79–113.

Lata, H., R. M. Morales, A. Douglas, and B. E. Scheffler. 2002. Assessment of genetic diversity in Podophyl-lum peltatum by molecular markers. In Trends in New Crops and New Uses, ed. J. Janick and A. Whipkey, 537–544. ASHS Press, Alexandria, VA.

Missouri Botanical Garden. 2001–2010. "Podophyl-lum peltatum." Kemper Center for Home Gardening. PlantFinder. http://www.mobot.org/gardeninghelp/plantfinder/plant.asp?code=L800 (accessed 2009).

Sanders, J. 2003. The Secrets of Wildflowers. Lyons Press, Guilford, CT.

Stearn, W. T. 2002. The Genus Epimedium and other Her-baceous Berberidaceae Including the Genus Podophyl-lum by J. M. H. Shaw. Timber Press, Portland, OR.

Stone, M. D., and D. Moll. 2006. Diet-dependent differ-ences in digestive efficiency in two sympatric species of box turtles, Terrapene carolina and Terrapene ornata. Journal of Herpetology 40: 364–371.

Testicular Cancer Research Center. 1997–2007. "Lance's TCRC Page." http://tcrc.acor.org/lance.html (accessed 2006).

University of Texas–Austin. 1996–1998. Cyberbotanica: Plants and Cancer Treatments. http://biotech.icmb.utexas.edu/botany/ (accessed 2009; site now discontinued).

USDA, ARS, National Genetic Resources Program. Germ-plasm Resources Information Network (GRIN) [Online Database]. National Germplasm Resources Laboratory, Beltsville, MD. www.ars-grin.gov/cgi-bin/npgs/html/tax_search.pl (accessed 2009).

Volk, T. 1995–2009."Tom Volk's fungus of the month for May 1999." Tom Volk's Fungi. http://botit.botany.wisc.edu/toms_fungi/may99.html (accessed 2009).

Whisler, S. L., and A. A. Snow. 1992. Potential for the loss of self-incompatibility in pollen-limited populations of Mayapple (Podophyllum peltatum). American Journal of Botany 79: 1273–1278.

Miterwort

Beattie, A. J., and D. C. Culver. 1981. The guild of myrmecochores in the herbaceous flora of West Virginia forests. Ecology 62: 107–115.

Bratton, S. P. 1976. Resource division in an understory herb community: responses to temporary and microtopographic gradients. American Naturalist 110: 679–693.

Hilty, J. 2004–2010. "Bishop's cap." Illinois Wildflowers. http://www.illinoiswildflowers.info/woodland/plants/bishop_cap.htm (accessed 2010).

Iverson, L., D. Ketzner, and J. Karnes. "ILPIN information on Mitella diphylla." Illinois Plant Information Network. http://www.fs.fed.us/ne/delaware/ilpin/1929.co (accessed 2010).

Mabry, C., and T. Korsgren. 1998. A permanent plot study of vegetation and vegetation-site factors fifty-three years following disturbance in central New England, U.S.A. Ecoscience 5: 232–240.

Mosquin, D. 2007. "May 25, 2007: Mitella stauropetala." Botany Photo of the Day [blog]. http://www.ubcbotanicalgarden.org/cgi-bin/mt/mt-search.cgi?search=Mitella&IncludeBlogs=10 (accessed 2010).

Nakanishi, H. 2002. Splash seed dispersal by raindrops. Ecological Research 17: 663–671.

Okuyama, Y., M. Kato, and N. Murakami. 2004. Pollination by fungus gnats in four species of the genus Mitella (Saxifragaceae). Botanical Journal of the Linnean Society 144: 449–460.

Ruhren, S., and S. N. Handel. 2003. Herbivory constrains survival, reproduction, and mutualisms when restoring nine temperate forest herbs. Journal of the Torrey Botanical Society 130: 34–42.

Savile, D.B.O. 1953. Splash-cup dispersal mechanism in Chrysosplenium and Mitella. Science, n.s., 117: 250–251.

Soltis, D. E., P. S. Soltis, and K. D. Bothel. 1990. Chloroplast DNA evidence for the origins of the monotypic Bensoniella and Conimitella (Saxifragaceae. Systematic Botany 15: 349–362.

Spongberg, S. A. 1972. The genera of Saxifragaceae in the southeastern United States. Journal of the Arnold Arboretum 53: 409–498.

Tenaglia, D. "Mitella diphylla L." Missouriplants.com. http://www.missouriplants.com/Whitealt/Mitella_diphylla_page.html (accessed 2010).

Woods, K. D. 1963. Effects of invasion by Lonicera tatarica L. on herbs and tree seedlings in four New England Forests. American Midland Naturalist 130: 62–74.

One-flowered Cancer-root

Achey, D. M. 1933. A revision of the section Gymnocaulis of the genus Orobanche. Bulletin of the Torrey Botanical Club 60: 441–451.

Björkman, E. 1960. Monotropa hypopitys L.—An epiparasite on tree roots. Physiologia Plantarum 13: 308–327.

Borg, S. J. ter, ed. 1986. Proceedings of a Workshop on Biology and Control of Orobanche. LH/VPO, Wageningen, The Netherlands.

Collins, L. T., A. E. L. Colwell, and G. Yatskievych. 2009. Orobanche riparia (Orobanchaceae), a new species from the American Midwest. Journal of the Botanical Research Institute of Texas 3: 3–11.

Estabrook, E. A., and J. I. Yoder. 1998. Rhizosphere signaling between parasitic angiosperms and their hosts. Plant Physiology 116: 1–7.

Garman, H. 1890. The broom-rape of hemp and tobacco. Bulletin No. 24, Kentucky Agricultural Experiment Station, Lexington, KY.

Gomez, L. D. 1980. Notes on the biology of the Central American Orobanche. Brenesia 17: 389–396.

Heckard, L. R., and T. I. Chuang. 1965. Chromosome numbers and polyploidy in Orobanche (Orobanchaceae). Brittonia 27: 179–186.

Kreutz, C.A.J. 1995. Orobanche: The European Broomrape Species, A Field Guide. Natuurhistorisch Genootschap in Limburg, Maastricht, The Netherlands.

Lolas, P. C. 1986. Control of broomrape (Orobanche ramosa) in tobacco (Nicotiana tabaccum). Weed Science 34: 427–430.

Michigan State University Board of Trustees. 2004. "Orobanche fasciculata Nutt., fascicled broom-rape." Michigan Natural Features Inventory. http://web4.msue.msu.edu/mnfi/abstracts/botany/Orobanche_fasciculata.pdf (accessed 2009).

Molau, U. 1995. Reproductive ecology and biology. In Parasitic Plants, ed. M. C. Press and J. D. Graves, 141–176. Chapman and Hall, London.

Mosquin, D. 2009. "Orobanche uniflora." Botany Photo of the Day [blog]. http://www.ubcbotanicalgarden.org/potd/2009/05/orobanche_uniflora.php (accessed 2009).

Musselman, L. J. 1980. The biology of Striga, Orobanche, and other root-parasitic weeds. Annual Review of Phytopathology 18: 463–489.

———. 1982. The Orobanchaceae of Virginia. Castanea 47: 266–275.

———. 1996. Parasitic weeds in the southern United States. Castanea 61: 271–292.

Nickrent, D. L. 1997–. "Orobanchaceae." The Parasitic Plant Connection. http://www.parasiticplants.siu.edu/Orobanchaceae/index.html (accessed 2009).

Nwoke, F.I.O., and S.N.C. Olonkwo. 1978. Structure and development of the primary haustorium in Alectra vogelii Benth. (Scrophulariaceae). Annals of Botany 42: 447–454.

Pscheidt, J. W., R. Halse, and K. Merrifield. 1996–2010. "Parasitic plants of Oregon." An Online Guide to Plant Disease Control, Oregon State University Extension. http://plant-disease.ippc.orst.edu/article_index .aspx?article_id=27 (accessed 2011).

Reuter, B. C. 1986. The habitat, reproductive ecology, and host relations of Orobanche fasiculata Nutt. (Orobanchaceae) in Wisconsin. Bulletin of the Torrey Botanical Club 113: 110–117.

Schneeweiss, G. M. 2007. Correlated evolution of life history and host range in the nonphotosynthetic parasitic flowering plants Orobanche and Phelipanche (Orobanchaceae). Journal of Evolutionary Biology 20: 471–478.

Schneeweiss, G. M., T. Palomeque, A. E. Colwell, and H. Weiss-Schneeweiss. 2004. Chromosome numbers and karyotype evolution in holoparasitic Orobanche (Orobanchaceae) and related genera. American Journal of Botany. 91: 439–448.

Thorogood, C. J., F. J. Rumsey, S. A. Harris, and S. J. Hiscock. 2008. Host-driven divergence in the parasitic plant Orobanche minor Sm. (Orobanchaceae). Molecular Ecology 17: 4289–4303.

Tomilov, A. A., N. B. Tomilova, I. Abdallah, and J. I. Yoder. 2005. Localized hormone fluxes and early haustorium development in the hemiparasitic plant Triphysaria versicolor. Plant Physiology 138: 14–1480.

USDA, NRCS. "Plants profile: Orobanche uniflora L." PLANTS Database. http://plants.usda.gov/java/ profile?symbol=ORUN (accessed 2009).

University of Texas–Austin. 2010. "Orobanche uniflora L." Native Plant Database. Lady Bird Johnson Wildflower Center. http://www.wildflower.org/plants/result.php?id_ plant=ORUN (accessed 2010).

University of Wisconsin–Stevens Point. "Family: Orobanchaceae, Orobanche uniflora L." Plants of Wisconsin. Robert W. Freckmann Herbarium. http://wisplants .uwsp.edu/scripts/detail.asp?SpCode=OROUNI (accessed 2010).

Voss, J., and V.L.S. Eifert. 1960. Illinois Wild Flowers. Popular Science Series, vol. 3. Illinois State Museum, Springfield, IL.

White, H. L., J. G. Sammon, W. C. Holmes, and J. R. Singhurst. 1998. Notes on the distribution of Orobanche ramosa L. and Orobanche uniflora L. (Orobanchaceae) in Texas. Phytologia 85: 121–124.

Wolfe, A. D., C. P. Randle, L. Liu, and K. E. Steiner. 2005. Phylogeny and biogeography of Orobanchaceae. Folia Geobotanica 40: 115–134.

Yokota, T., H. Sakai, K. Okuno, K. Yoneyama, and Y. Takeuchi. 1998. Alectrol and orobanchol, germination

stimulants for Orobanche minor, from its host red clover. Phytochemistry 49: 1967–1973.

Young, N. D., K. E. Steiner, and C. W. dePamphilis. 1999. The evolution of parasitism in Scrophulariaceae/Orobanchaceae: Plastid gene sequences refute an evolutionary transition series. Annals of the Missouri Botanical Garden 86: 876–893.

Zehhar, N., P. Labrousse, M.-C. Arnaud, C. Boulet, D. Bouya, and A. Fer. 2003. Study of resistance to Orobanche ramosa in host (oilseed rape and carrot) and non-host (maize) plants. European Journal of Plant Pathology 109: 75–82.

Zonno, M. C., and M. Vurro. 2002. Inhibition of germination of Orobanche ramosa seeds by Fusarium toxins. Phytoparasitica 30: 519–524.

Skunk Cabbage

Grayum, M. H. 1990. Evolution and phylogeny of the Araceae. Annals of the Missouri Botanical Garden 77: 628–697.

Grimaldi, D., and J. Jaenike. 1983. The diptera breeding on skunk cabbage, Symplocarpus foetidus (Araceae). Journal of the New York Entomological Society 91: 83–89.

Holdrege, C. 2000. "Skunk cabbage (Symplocarpus foetidus)." The Nature Institute. http://www.natureinstitute .org/pub/ic/ic4/skunkcabbage.htm (accessed 2009).

Ito, T., and K. Ito. 2005. Nonlinear dynamics of homeothermic temperature control in skunk cabbage, Symplocarpus foetidus. Physical Review E 72.051909:1–6.

Iverson, S. J., J. E. McDonald, and L. K. Smith. 2001. Changes in the diet of free-ranging black bears in years of contrasting food availability revealed through milk fatty acids. Canadian Journal of Zoology 79: 2268–2279.

Kalm, Peter. 1966. Peter Kalm's Travels in North America: The English Version of 1770. Revised from the Original Swedish and Edited by Adolph B. Benson with a Translation of New Material from Kalm's Diary Notes. Dover Publications, New York. (Orig. pub. 1937, Wilson-Erickson, New York).

Knutson, R. M. 1972. Temperature measurements of the spadix of Symplocarpus foetidus (L.) Nutt. American Midland Naturalist 88: 251–254.

McDonald, J. E., Jr., and T. K. Fuller. 2005. Effects of spring acorn availability on black bear diet, milk composition, and cub survival. Journal of Mammalogy 86: 1022–1028.

Nie, Z.-L, H. Sun, H. Li, and J. Wen. 2006. Intercontinental biogeography of subfamily Orontioideae (Sympolcarpus, Lysichiton, and Orontium) of Araceae in eastern Asia and North America. Molecular Phylogenetics and Evolution 40: 155–165.

Peterson, L. 1977. A Field Guide to Edible Wild Plants of Eastern and Central North America. Houghton Mifflin, Boston.

Prychid, C. J., J. S. Jabaily, and P. J. Rudall. 2008. Cellular ultrastructure and crystal development in Amorphophallus (Araceae). Annals of Botany 101: 983–995.

Prychid, C. J., and P. J. Rudall. 1999. Calcium oxalate crystals in monocotyledons: a review of their structure and systematics. Annals of Botany 84: 725–729.

Seymour, R. S. 1997. Plants that warm themselves. Scientific American 276: 104–109.

Seymour, R. S., and A. J. Blaylock. 1999. Switching off the heater: Influence of ambient temperature on thermoregulation by eastern skunk cabbage Symplocarpus foetidus. Journal of Experimental Botany 50: 1525–1532.

Small, J. A. 1959. Skunk cabbage, Symplocarpus foetidus. Bulletin of the Torrey Botanical Club 86: 413–416.

Thompson, S. A. 2000. Araceae. In Flora of North America North of Mexico, ed. Flora of North America Editorial Committee, 22: 132–133. Oxford University Press, New York.

Trelease, W. 1879. On the fertilization of Symplocarpus foetidus. American Naturalist 13: 580–582.

U. S. Department of the Interior. 2006. "Skunk cabbage (Symplocarpus foetidus)." USGS, Northern Prairie Wildlife Research Center. http://www.npwrc.usgs.gov/resource/plants/floramw/species/sympfoet.htm (accessed 2009).

Voss, E. G. 1964. Skunk-cabbage in Michigan. Michigan Botanist 3: 97–101.

Wen, J., R. K. Jansen, and K. Kiogore. 1996. Evolution of the eastern Asian and eastern North American disjunct genus Symplocarpus (Araceae): Insights from chloroplast DNA restriction site data. Biochemical Systematics and Ecology 24: 735–747.

Spring Beauties

Anderson, W. B., and W. G. Eickmeier. 2000. Nutrient resorption in Claytonia virginica L.: Implications for deciduous forest nutrient cycling. Canadian Journal of Botany 78: 832–839.

Dailey, T. B. and P. E. Scott. 2006. Spring nectar sources for solitary bees and flies in a landscape of deciduous forest and agricultural fields: Production, variability, and consumption. Journal of the Torrey Botanical Society 133: 535–547.

Davis, L. R., Jr., and W. E. Laberge. 1975. The nest biology of the bee Andrena (Ptilandrena) erigeniae Robertson (Hymenoptera: Andrenidae). Biological Notes No. 95. Illinois Natural History Survey, Urbana, IL.

Doyle, J. J., and J. L. Doyle. 1988. Natural interspecific hybridization in eastern North American Claytonia. American Journal of Botany 75: 1238–1246.

Ewan, J. 1963. A Virginia botanist. Review of John Clayton: Pioneer of American Botany, by E. Berkeley and D. S. Berkeley. Science, n.s., 141:1027–1028.

Farr, D. F., and A. Y. Rossman. 2010. Fungal databases. Systematic Mycology and Microbiology Laboratory, ARS, USDA. http://nt.ars-grin.gov/fungaldatabases/ (accessed 2010).

Handel, S. N. 1978. New ant-dispersed species in the genera Carex, Luzula, and Claytonia. Canadian Journal of Botany 56: 2925–2927.

Lewis, W. H. 1976. Temporal adaptation correlated with ploidy in Claytonia virginica. Systematic Botany 1: 340–347.

Lewis, W. H., R. L. Oliver, and T. J. Luikart. 1971. Multiple genotypes in individuals of Claytonia virginica. Science 172: 564–565.

Miller, J. M., and K. L. Chambers. 2006. Systematics of Claytonia (Portulacaceae). Systematic Botany Monographs 78: 1–236.

Motten, A. F., D. R. Campbell, D. E. Alexander, and H. L. Miller. Pollination effectiveness of specialist and generalist visitors to a North Carolina population of Claytonia virginica. Ecology 62: 1278–1287.

Natural History Museum. 2010. "The John Clayton Herbarium." Natural History Museum. http://www.nhm.ac.uk/research-curation/research/projects/clayton-herbarium/claytonialrg.html (accessed 2010).

Reynolds, G. 2009. Will drinking make you do it: What quercetin sports supplement enhances, and doesn't. New York Times Magazine. October 11, 2009, 24.

Schemske, D. W. 1977. Flowering phenology and seed set in Claytonia virginica (Portulacaceae). Bulletin of the Torrey Botanical Club 104: 254–263.

Wikimedia Foundation. 2010. "André Michaux." Wikipedia. http://en.wikipedia.org/wiki/André_Michaux (accessed 2010).

Witsell, T. 2007. Ozark spring beauty. Claytonia: Newsletter of the Arkansas Native Plant Society 27: 7.

Squawroot

Appalachian State University. 2003. "Squaw Root, Conopholis americana." Appalachian Cultural Museum. http://www.museum.appstate.edu/kimmem/2002/squaw_root/pages/squaw.shtml (accessed 2009; site now discontinued).

Baird, W. V., and J. L. Riopel. 1986. Life history studies of Conopholis americana (Orobanchaceae). American Midland Naturalist 116: 140–151.

Doak, K. D. 1929. Parasitism of Conopholis americana Wallr. on roots of Quercus bicolor. Phytopathology 19: 102.

Gomez, L. D. 1980. Notes on the biology of the Central American Orobanche. Brenesia 17: 389–396.

References

Hathaway, W. T. 2002. Squawroot. Danville Register and Bee, Danville, VA. April 28, 2002.

Heide-Jørgensen, H. S. 2008. Parasitic Flowering Plants. Koninklijke Brill NV, Leiden, The Netherlands.

Hendershot, D. 2004. "The naturalist's corner." Smoky Mountain News. http://www.smokymountainnews .com/issues/03_04/03_31_04/out_naturalist.html (accessed 2009).

Hilty, J. 2002–2009. "Cancer root." Illinois Wildflowers. http://www.illinoiswildflowers.info/woodland/plants/ cancer_root.htm (accessed 2009).

Johnson, A. S., P. E. Hale, W. M. Ford, J. M. Wentworth, J. R. French, O. F. Anderson, and G. B. Pullen 1995. White-tailed deer foraging in relation to successional stage, overstory type and management of Southern Appalachian forests. American Midland Naturalist 133: 18–35.

Light, K. "Squawroot." East Tennessee Wildflowers and Hiking Trails. http://www.easttennesseewildflowers .com/gallery/view_album.php?set_albumName= Spring-Flowers-Woodland-Yellow (accessed 2009).

Musselman, L. J. 1982. The Orobanchaceae of Virginia. Castanea 47: 266–275.

Percival, W. C. 1931. The parasitism of Conopholis americana on Quercus borealis. American Journal of Botany 18: 817–837.

Garner, N.P. 1986. Seasonal movements, habitat selection, and food habits of black bears (Ursus americanus) in Shenandoah National Park, Virginia. M.S. thesis. Virginia Polytechnic Institute and State University, Blacksburg.

Western New Mexico University. "Conopholis alpina Leibman var. mexicana (Gray ex S. Watson) Haynes (ground cone)." Vascular Plants of the Gila Wilderness. http:// www.wnmu.edu/academic/nspages/gilaflora/ conopholis_alpina.html (accessed 2009).

Wikimedia Foundation. 2009. "Conopholis americana." Wikipedia. http://en.wikipedia.org/wiki/ Conopholis americana (accessed 2009).

Trilliums

Bale, M. T., J. A. Zettler, B. A. Robinson, T. P. Spira, and C. R. Allen. 2003. Yellowjackets may be an underestimated component of an ant-seed mutualism. Southeastern Naturalist 2: 609–614.

Baskin, C. C., and J. M. Baskin. 2001. Seeds: Ecology, Biogeography, and Evolution of Dormancy and Germination. Academic Press, San Diego.

Berg, R. Y. 1958. Seed Dispersal, Morphology, and Phylogeny of Trillium. I Kommision HOs H. Aschehoug, Oslo.

Byers, D. 2003. Connections: The deer, the bumblebee, and the Trillium. Westmoreland Conservancy Newsletter, July 2003, 2–3.

Case, F. W., Jr., and R. B. Case. 1997. Trilliums. Timber Press, Portland, OR.

Choe, D.-H., J. G. Millar, and M. K. Rust. 2009. Chemical signals associated with life inhibit necrophoresis in Argentine ants. Proceedings of the National Academy of Sciences 106: 8251–8255.

Cullina, W. 2002. Propagation of North American trilliums. Native Plants Journal 3: 14–17.

Davis, M. A. 1981. The effect of pollinators, predators, and energy constraints on the floral ecology and evolution of Trillium. Oecologia 48: 400–406.

Foster, S., and J. A. Duke. 1990. Peterson Field Guides: Eastern/Central Medicinal Plants. Houghton Mifflin Company, Boston.

Gates, R. B. 1917. A systematic study of the North American genus Trillium, its variability, and its relation to Paris and Medeola. Annals of the Missouri Botanical Garden 4: 43–92.

Gunther, R. W., and J. Lanza. 1989. Variation in attractiveness of Trillium diaspores to a seed-dispersing ant. American Midland Naturalist 122: 321–328.

Hanzawa, F. M., and S. Kalisz. 1993. The relationship between age, size, and reproduction in Trillium grandiflorum (Liliaceae). American Journal of Botany 80: 405–410.

Irwin, R. E. 2000. Morphological variation and female reproductive success in two sympatric Trillium species: Evidence for phenotypic selection in Trillium erectum and Trillium grandiflorum (Liliaceae). American Journal of Botany 87: 205–214.

Jules, E. S. 1998. Habitat fragmentation and demographic change for a common plant: Trillium in old-growth forest. Ecology 79: 1645–1656.

Kalisz, S., F. M. Hanzawa, S. J. Tonsor, D. A. Thiede, and S. Voigt. 1999. Ant-mediated seed dispersal alters pattern of relatedness in a population of Trillium grandiflorum. Ecology 80: 2620–2634.

Knight, T. M. 2003. Effects of herbivory and its timing across populations of Trillium grandiflorum (Liliaceae). American Journal of Botany 90: 1207–1214.

———. 2004. The effects of herbivory and pollen limitation on a declining population of Trillium grandiflorum. Ecological Applications 14: 915–928.

Lubbers, A. E., and M. J. Lechowicz. 1989. Effects of leaf removal on reproduction vs. belowground storage in Trillium grandiflorum. Ecology 70: 85–96.

Mark, S., and J. M. Olesen. 1996. Importance of elaiosome size to removal of ant-dispersed seeds. Oecologia 107: 95–101.

Pellicer, J. M., F. Fay, and I. J. Leitch. 2010. The largest eukaryotic genome of them all? Botanical Journal of the Linnean Society 164: 10–15.

Sage, T. L, S. R. Griffin, V. Pontieri, P. Drobac, W. W. Cole, and C. H. Spencer. 2001. Stigmatic self-incompatibility and mating patterns in Trillium grandiflorum and Trillium erectum (Melanthiaceae). Annals of Botany 88: 829–841.

Vellend, M., J. A. Myers, S. Gardescu, and P. L. Marks. 2003. Dispersal of Trillium seeds by deer: implications for long-distance migration of forest herbs. Ecology 84: 1067–1072.

Trout-lily

Alan, G. A., and K. R. Robertson. 2002. Erythronium. In Flora of North America North of Mexico, ed. Flora of North America Editorial Committee, 26: 153–164. Oxford University Press, New York.

Bernhardt, P. 1977. The pollination ecology of a population of Erythronium americanum Ker. (Liliaceae). Rhodora 79: 278–272.

Bierzychudek, P. 1982. Life histories and demography of shade-tolerant temperate forest herbs: A review. New Phytologist 90: 757–776.

Blodgett, F. H. 1900. Vegetative reproduction and multiplication in Erythronium. Bulletin of the Torrey Botanical Club 27: 305–315.

Brundrett, M., and B. Kedrick. 1990. The roots and mycorrhizas of herbaceous woodland plants. II. Structural aspects of morphology. New Phytologist 114: 469–479.

Burroughs, J. 1884. Riverby. Vol. 9 of The Writings of John Burroughs. Houghton Mifflin, New York. Available at http://books.google.com/books (accessed 2010).

Kim, C.-S., T. Hara, P. K. Datta, E. Itoh, and M. Horiike. 1998. Insecticidal component in Thunberg spiraea, Spiraea thunbergii, against Thrips palmi. Bioscience, Biotechnology, and Biochemistry 62: 1546–1549.

Fackelmann, K. A. 1993. Unearthing the roots of tribal tradition. Science News 143: 207. March 27, 1993.

Felter, H. W., and J. U. Lloyd. 1898. Erythronium.—adder's tongue. In King's American Dispensatory. The Ohio Valley Company. Available at H. Kress, 1995–2010, Henriette's Herbal Homepage. http://www.henriettesherbal.com/eclectic/kings/erythronium.html (accessed 2010).

Glattstein, J. 2005. Bulbs for Garden Habitats. Timber Press, Portland, OR.

Handel, S. N., S. B. Fisch, and G. E. Schatz. 1981. Ants disperse a majority of herbs in a mesic forest community in New York State. Bulletin of the Torrey Botanical Club 108: 430–437.

Harder, L. D., and J. D. Thomson. 1989. Evolutionary options for maximizing pollen dispersal of animal-pollinated plants. American Naturalist 133: 323–344.

Harder, L. D., J. D. Thomson, M. B. Cruzan, and R. S. Unnasch. 1985. Sexual reproduction and variation in floral morphology in an ephemeral vernal lily, Erythronium americanum. Oecologia 67: 286–291.

Hjorth, N., and D. S. Wilkinson. 1968. Contact dermatitis IV: Tulip fingers, hyacinth itch and lily rash. British Journal of Dermatology 80: 696–698.

Lapointe, L. 2001. How phenology influences physiology in deciduous forest spring ephemerals. Physiologia Plantarum 113: 151–157.

Lapointe, L., and J. Molard. 2008. Costs and benefits of mycorrhizal infection in a spring ephemeral, Erythronium americanum. New Phytologist 135: 491–500.

Lerat, S., R. Gauci, J. G. Catford, H. Vierheilig, Y. Piché, and L. Lapoint. 2002. 14C transfer between the spring ephemeral Erythronium americanum and sugar maple saplings via arbuscular mycorrhizal fungi in natural stands. Oecologia 132: 181–187.

Parks, C. R., and J. W. Hardin. 1963. Yellow erythroniums of the eastern United States. Brittonia 15: 245–259.

Ruhren, S., and M. R. Dudash. 1996. Consequences of the timing of seed release of Erythronium americanum (Liliaceae), a deciduous forest myrmecochore. American Journal of Botany 83: 633–640.

Slob, A. 1973. Tulip allergens in Alstroemeria and some other liliiflorae. Phytochemistry 12: 811–815.

Stokes, R. and T. M. Culley. 2007. A novel approach to study gene flow between color forms of the tetraploid species Erythronium americanum. Abstract of paper presented at the Plant Biology and Botany 2007 Joint Congress, Chicago, IL. July 7–11, 2007. http://2007.botanyconference.org/engine/search/index.php?func=detail&aid=2150 (accessed 2010).

Thomson, J. D. 1986. Pollen transport and deposition by bumble bees in Erythronium: influences of floral nectar and bee grooming. Journal of Ecology 74: 329–341.

Thomson J. D., and B. A. Thomson. 1989. Dispersal of Erythronium grandiflorum pollen by bumblebees: Implications for gene flow and reproductive success. Evolution 43: 657–661.

Vezina, P. E., and M. M. Grandtner. 1965. Phenological observations of spring geophytes in Quebec. Ecology 46: 869–872.

Wein, G. R., and S.T.A. Pickett. 1989. Dispersal, establishment, and survivorship of a cohort of Erythronium americanum. Bulletin of the Torrey Botanical Club 116: 240–246.

Wikimedia Foundation. 2010. "Erythronium japonicum." Wikipedia. http://en.wikipedia.org/wiki/Erythronium japonicum (accessed 2010).

Twinleaf

Baker, D. G. 2007. Epimediums and Other Herbaceous Berberidaceae. The Hardy Plant Society, Pershore, England.

Baskin, J. M., and C. C. Baskin. 1989. Seed germination ecophysiology of Jeffersonia diphylla, a perennial herb of mesic deciduous forests. American Journal of Botany 76: 1073–1080.

Betts, E. M., ed. 1944. Thomas Jefferson's Garden Book, 1766–1824. American Philosophical Society, Philadelphia.

Board of Regents of the University of Wisconsin. 2007. "Jeffersonia diphylla." University of Wisconsin-Madison/Botany Plant Growth Facilities: Botanical Garden. http://www.botany.wisc.edu/garden/UW-Botanical_Garden/Jeffersonia_d.html (accessed 2009).

Coffey, T. 1993. The History and Folklore of North American Wildflowers. Houghton Mifflin Company, Boston.

Cornett, P. 2005. Inspirations from the woodlands: Jefferson's enduring ties to Philadelphia's botanical riches. Twinleaf, January 2005.

Dave's Garden. "PlantFiles: Twinleaf, helmet pod, ground squirrel pea, Jeffersonia diphylla." Dave's Garden. http://davesgarden.com/guides/pf/go/2728/index.html (accessed 2009).

Foster, H. L., and L. L. Foster. 1990. Cuttings from a Rock Garden: Plant Portraits and Other Essays. Atlantic Monthly Press, New York.

George, L. O. 1997. Jeffersonia. In Flora of North America North of Mexico, ed. Flora of North America Editorial Committee, 3: 291–292. Oxford University Press, New York.

Hamel, P. B., and M. U. Chiltoskey, 1975. Cherokee Plants and Their Uses—A 400 Year History. Herald Publishing, Sylva, NC.

Hamilton, C., and R. Hamilton. 2005–2008. "American twinleaf." ScienceViews.com. http://www.scienceviews.com/plants/twinleaf.html (accessed 2009).

Heithaus, E. R. 1981. Seed predation by rodents on three ant-dispersed plants. Ecology 62: 136–145.

Herrick, J. W. 1994. Iroquois Medical Botany (The Iroquois and Their Neighbors). Syracuse University Press, Syracuse, NY.

Klingaman, G. 2005. "A botanical tale, or how Jeffersonia diphylla was named." University of Virginia, Inside UVA. http://www.virginia.edu/insideuva/textonlyarchive/94-04-22/5.txt (accessed 2009).

Massachusetts Historical Society. 2009. "Garden book." Thomas Jefferson Papers: An Electronic Archive. http://www.masshist.org/thomasjeffersonpapers/garden/ (accessed 2009).

McDonough, M. 2000. "Jeffersonia dubia." PlantBuzz. http://www.plantbuzz.com/RockGard/Woodland/Jeffersonia.htm (accessed 2009).

Missouri Botanical Garden. 2001–2009. "Jeffersonia diphylla." Kemper Center for Home Gardening: Plant Finder. http://www.mobot.org/gardeninghelp/PlantFinder/plant.asp?code=A409 (accessed 2009).

Moerman, D. E. 1986. Medicinal Plants of Native America. University of Michigan, Museum of Anthropology, Ann Arbor.

Monticello.org. "Twinleaf." Th. Jefferson Encyclopedia. http://wiki.monticello.org/mediawiki/index.php/Twinleaf (accessed 2009).

Schilling, E. E., and P. J. Calie. 1982. Petal flavonoids of white-flowered spring ephemerals. Bulletin of the Torrey Botanical Club 109: 7–12.

Smith, B. H., C. E. deRivera, C. L. Bridgman, and J. J. Woida. 1989. Frequency-dependent seed dispersal by ants of two deciduous forest herbs. Ecology 70: 1645–1648.

Smith, B. H., M. L. Ronsheim, and K. R. Swartz. Reproductive ecology of Jeffersonia diphylla (Berberidaceae). American Journal of Botany 73: 1416–1426.

Stanton, L. C. 1992. "A botanical anniversary." Twinleaf Journal. http://www.twinleaf.org/articles/jeffersonia.html (accessed 2009).

Stearn, W. T. 2002. Epimedium and Other Herbaceous Berberidaceae. Timber Press, Portland, OR.

Thomas Jefferson Foundation. "In bloom at Monticello." Th. Jefferson Monticello. http://www.monticello.org/site/house-and-gardens/in-bloom (accessed 2011).

University of Cincinnati. "The botany of the Lewis & Clark Expedition." University Libraries, Lewis & Clark. http://www.ucdp.uc.edu/lewisandclark/exhibits/botany/ (accessed 2009).

Wikimedia Foundation. 2010. "Jeffersonia." Wikipedia. http://en.wikipedia.org/wiki/Jeffersonia (accessed 2010).

Violets

Alexander, E. J., and C. H. Woodward 1941. The flora of the unicorn tapestries. Journal of The New York Botanical Garden 42: 105–122.

American Violet Society. 2000. "The violet in the art of painting." The American Violet Society. http://www.americanvioletsociety.org/Arts/Fine_Art.htm (accessed 2010).

Anderson, E. 1936. Color variation in eastern North American flowers as exemplified by Hepatica acutiloba. Rhodora 38: 301–304.

Andre, S. G. 1971. The Violet, Flower of Modesty: in History, Lore, and Literature. S. G. Andre, Canton, CT.

Baskin, C. C., and J. M. Baskin. 2001. Seeds: Ecology, Biogeography, and Evolution of Dormancy and Germination. Academic Press, San Diego.

Beattie, A. J. 1971. Pollination mechanisms in Viola. New Phytologist 70: 343–360.

Beattie, A. J., and N. Lyons. 1975. Seed dispersal in Viola (Violaceae): Adaptations and strategies. American Journal of Botany 62: 714–722.

Beredjiklian, N. 2000. The violets of Dutchess County. The Violet Gazette 1(4): 3. Available at The American Violet Society. http://www.americanvioletsociety.org/VioletGazette/VioletGazette_V1_4_P3.htm (accessed 2010).

Blanchan, N. 1999. Nature's Garden. Garden City Publishing, Garden City, NY.

Bois de Jasmin. 2005–2010. Sweet and powdery fragrance ingredients: Ionones. Bois de Jasmin. http://boisdejasmin.typepad.com/_/2005/11/sweet_and_powde.html (accessed 2010).

Bryant, W. C. 1855. The yellow violet. The Violet Gazette 1(4): 6 (2001). Available at The American Violet Society. http://www.americanvioletsociety.org/VioletGazette/VioletGazette_V1_4_P6.htm (accessed 2010).

Bryant, W. C., II, and T. G. Voss, eds. 1975. The Letters of William Cullen Bryant: Volume 1, 1809–1836. Fordham University Press, Bronx, NY.

Central Park Conservancy. 2010. "Shakespeare Garden." The Official Website of Central Park. http://www.centralparknyc.org/visit/things-to-see/great-lawn/shakespeare-garden.html (accessed 2010).

Coffey, T. 1993. The History and Folklore of North American Wildflowers. Houghton Mifflin, Boston.

Cross, H. 2010. "Shakespeare Garden in Central Park." About.com. New York City Travel. http://gonyc.about.com/od/photogalleries/ss/shakespeare_gar_4.htm (accessed 2010).

Culley, T. M. 2000. Inbreeding depression and floral type fitness differences in Viola canadensis (Violaceae), a species with chasmogamous and cleistogamous flowers. Canadian Journal of Botany 78: 1420–1429.

———. 2000. Why violets are so successful. The Violet Gazette 1(4): 7. Available at The American Violet Society. http://www.americanvioletsociety.org/VioletGazette/VioletGazette_V1_4_P7.htm (accessed 2010).

———. 2001. Natural pollination of Viola flowers. The Violet Gazette 2(1): 5. Available at The America Violet Society. http://www.americanvioletsociety.org/VioletGazette/VioletGazette_V2_1_P5.htm (accessed 2010).

———. 2002. Reproductive biology and delayed selfing in Viola pubescens (Violaceae), an understory herb with chasmogamous and cleistogamous flowers. International Journal of Plant Science 163: 113–122.

Farlex. 2010. "Violet." The Free Dictionary. http://encyclopedia2.thefreedictionary.com/violet (accessed 2010).

Foster, H. L., and L. L. Foster 1990. Cuttings from a Rock Garden: Plant Portraits and Other Essays. Atlantic Monthly Press, New York.

Freeman, M. B. 1983. The Unicorn Tapestries. E. P. Dutton, New York.

Ginsburg. E. 2009. The very fragrant Parma violet. The Christian Science Monitor, February 27, 2009.

Haines, A. 2001. The Genus Viola of Maine. V. F. Thomas, Bar Harbor, ME.

Hall, B. 1999. "Dear sweet violets." Suite101.com. http://www.suite101.com/article.cfm/weeds_and_wild_things/19688 (accessed 2010).

Hill, S. 2007. "Flower symbol in Christian art." Suite101.com. http://www.suite101.com/content/flower-symbols-in-christian-art-a11350 (accessed 2010).

Howard, M. 2007. "Violet: History and culture." Suite101.com. http://www.suite101.com/content/violet-history-and-culture-a20979 (accessed 2010).

Illinois State Museum. "State symbol: State flower—violet (Viola sororia)." Illinois State Symbols and Their History. http://www.museum.state.il.us/exhibits/symbols/flower.html (accessed 2010).

Internet Archive. Full text of "A handful of pleasant delight, containing sundry new sonnets and delectable histories in divers kinds of metre etc. 1584. (By) Clement Robinson and divers others. Edited by Edward Arber." Internet Archive. http://www.archive.org/stream/handfulofpleasan00robiuoft/handfulofpleasan00robiuoft_djvu.txt (accessed 2010).

Karlsen, K. 2010. "Mary garden flower symbolism. Heartsease (pansy) flower symbolism." Living Arts Originals. http://www.livingartsoriginals.com/infomarygarden.htm (accessed 2010).

Laufer, G. A. 2001. Shakespeare's violets. The Violet Gazette 2(2): 5. Available at The American Violet Society 2000–2007. http://www.americanvioletsociety.org/VioletGzette/VioletGazette_V2_2_P5.htm (accessed 2010).

Leadbeater, M. M. 2006–2010. "Violet Day." Adelaide Co-operative History. http://www.ach.familyhistorysa.info/ww1violetday.html (accessed 2010).

Lukes, R. 1996. Nature-Wise: Butterflies. Door County Advocate. September 6, 1996.

———. 2001. Nature-Wise: Butterfly with simple needs offers great rewards. Door County Advocate. August 3, 2001.

Malécot, V. T., Marcussen, J. Munzinger, R. Yockteng, and M. Henry. 2007. On the origin of the sweet-smelling Parma violet cultivars (Violaceae): Wide intraspecific hybridization, sterility, and sexual reproduction. American Journal of Botany 94: 29–41.

Martin, T. 1991. Gardening; It's raining violets. The New York Times, March 3, 1991. Available at New York Times Archive. http://www.nytimes.com/1991/03/03/news/gardening-it-s-raining-violets.html?pagewanted=1 (accessed 2010).

References

Metropolitan Museum of Art. 2000–2010. "Flowers, plants, and trees." The Unicorn Tapestries. http://www.metmuseum.org/explore/Unicorn/unicorn_flora.htm (accessed 2010).

New York University. Introduction to New York University. New York University. http://www.nyu.edu/nursing/bulletin/intronyu.pdf (accessed 2010).

Newman, C. 1998. Perfume: The Art and Science of Scent. National Geographic Society, Washington, DC.

Pearson Education. 2000–2010. "Violet." Dictionary of phrase and fable—V. Infoplease. http://www.infoplease.com/dictionary/brewers/violet.html (accessed 2010).

Perfect, E. J., trans. 1996. Armand Millet and his Violets: Including Violettes, Leurs Origines, Leurs Cultures. Park Farm Press, Whitstable, Great Britain.

Rice, A. 2000. Violets as state flower symbols. The Violet Gazette 1(4): 7. Available at The American Violet Society. http://americanvioletsociety.org/HistoryTraditions/Violet_State_Flowers.htm (accessed 2010).

Russel, N. H. 1965. Violets (Viola) of central and eastern United States: An introductory survey. Sida 2: 3–113.

Savage, F. G. 1923. The Flora and Folklore of Shakespeare. Ed. J. Burrow & Company. London.

Schneider, J. 1996–2010. "Chronology of Napoleon's life." Napoleonic Literature. http://napoleonic-literature.com/Chronology.html (accessed 2010).

Scott, E. 2000. Butterflies and violets. The Violet Gazette 1(3): 5. Available at The American Violet Society. http://www.americanvioletsociety.org/VioletGazette/VioletGazette_V1_3_P5.htm (accessed 2010).

Shakespeare, William. A Midsummer Night's Dream and King John. The Complete Works of William Shakespeare. http://shakespeare.mit.edu/ (accessed 2010).

Singleton, E. 1922. The Shakespeare Garden. Century Company, New York.

Slevin, J. 2009. "Violets in myth and legend: Spring's symbolic flower of renewal and love." Suite101.com. http://www.suite101.com/content/violets-in-myth-and-legend-a100682 (accessed 2010).

Smith, L. W. 1972. Violets are for Eating: Recipes, Facts, Fancies. Le Bouquet, Fort Lauderdale, FL.

Sothers, C. 2004. Violaceae (Violet Family). In Flowering Plants of the Neotropics. ed. N. Smith, S. A. Mori, A. Henderson, D. W. Stevenson, and S. V. Heald, 390–394. Princeton University Press, Princeton, NJ.

Tolley, E., and C. Mead. 1993. A Potpourri of Pansies. Clarkson Potter, New York.

University of Texas–Austin. 2010. "Violet reaction—spring 2009." Past issues of Wildflower magazine. Lady Bird Johnson Wildflower Center. http://www.wildflower.org/pastissues/?id=129 (accessed 2010).

Wikimedia Foundation. 2010. "Orris root." Wikipedia. http://en.wikipedia.org/wiki/Orris_root (accessed 2010).

———. 2010. "Roses are red." Wikipedia. http://en.wikipedia.org/wiki/Roses_are_red (accessed 2010).

———. 2010. "Viola (plant)." Wikipedia. http://en.wikipedia.org/wiki/Viola_(plant) (accessed 2010).

———. 2010. "Viola odorata." Wikipedia. http://en.wikipedia.org/wiki/Viola_odorata (accessed 2010).

———. 2010. "Viola sororia." Wikipedia. http://en.wikipedia.org/wiki/Viola_sororia (accessed 2010).

———. 2010. "Viola tricolor." Wikipedia. http://en.wikipedia.org/wiki/Viola_tricolor (accessed 2010).

Virginia Bluebells

Earle, A. Scott. 2008. Borage family (forget-me-not family): Boraginaceae. In Idaho Mountain Wildflowers: A Photographic Compendium. Larkspur Books, Boise, ID. http://www.larkspurbooks.com/borage2.html (accessed 2010).

Hilty, J. 2002–2010. "Virginia bluebells." Illinois Wildflowers. http://illinoiswildflowers.info/woodland/plants/bluebells.htm (accessed 2010).

Hyam, R., and R. Pankhurst. 1995. Plants and Their Names: A Concise Dictionary. Oxford University Press, New York.

Ingen, G. V. 1887. Bees mutilating flowers. Botanical Gazette 12: 229.

L'Oreal, B. Belcour-Castro, and H. Burgaud. 2003. Use of a Mertensia maritime extract on oxidation dyeing of keratinous fibers. Intl. Patent PCT/FR2002/003829, filed November 7, 2002, and issued May 15, 2003. World Intellectual Property Organization. Available at http://www.wipo.int/pctdb/en/wo.jsp?wo=2003039500 (accessed 2010).

Macior, L. W. 1978. Pollination ecology of vernal angiosperms. Oikos 30: 452–460.

NOAA, Office of Ocean Exploration and Research. 2010. "Mertensia ovum." Ocean Explorer. http://oceanexplorer.noaa.gov/explorations/02arctic/logs/aug31/media/mertensia.html (accessed 2010).

Schneck, J. 1887. How humblebees extract nectar from Mertensia virginica DC. Botanical Gazette 12: 111.

Tenaglia, D. 2007. "Mertensia virginica (L.) Pers." Missouriplants.com. http://www.missouriplants.com/Bluealt/Mertensia_virginica_page.html (accessed 2010).

Texas AgriLife Extension Service, Texas A&M System. "Oyster plant." Aggie Horticulture. http://aggie-horticulture.tamu.edu/ornamentals/cornell_herbaceous/plant_pages/Mertensiamaritima.html (accessed 2010).

University of Alaska–Fairbanks. "Mertensia ovum (Fabricius, 1780)." Arctic Ocean Diversity. http://www.arcodiv.org/watercolumn/ctenophores/Mertensia_ovum.html (accessed 2010).

University of Wisconsin–Stevens Point. "Family Boraginaceae. Mertensia virginica (L.) Pers. ex Link." Plants of Wisconsin. Robert W. Freckmann Herbarium. http://wisplants.uwsp.edu/scripts/detail.asp?SpCode=MERVIR (accessed 2010).

W. J. Beal Botanical Garden. "Virginia bluebells." Plant of the Week. http://www.cpa.msu.edu/beal/plantofweek/plants/mertensia%20virginica_20080428.pdf (accessed 2010).

Wikimedia Foundation. 2010. "Mertensia." Wikipedia. http://en.wikipedia.org/wiki/Mertensia (accessed 2010).

Williams, L. O. 1937. A monograph of the genus Mertensia in North America. Annals of the Missouri Botanical Garden 24: 17–159.

Wild Ginger

Bergeron, C., A. Marton, R. Gauthier, K. Hostettmann. 1996. Screening of plants used by North American Indians for antifungal, bactericidal, larvicidal and molluscicidal activities. Pharmaceutical Biology 34: 233–242.

Bramlage, G. A. 2010. "Wild ginger (Asarum canadense) VaNPS 2010 wildflower of the year." Suite101.com. http://www.suite101.com/content/wild-ginger-asarum-canadense-vanps-2010-wildflower-of-the-year-a219773 (accessed 2010).

Cain, M. L., H. Damman, and A. Muir. 1998. Seed dispersal and the Holocene migration of woodland herbs. Ecological Monographs 68: 325–347.

Debelle, F. D., J.-L. Vanherweghem, and J. L. Nortier. 2008. Aristolochic acid nephropathy: A worldwide problem. Kidney International 74: 158–169.

Heithaus, E. R. 1981. Seed predation by rodents on three ant-dispersed plants. Ecology 62: 136–145.

Kelly, L. M. 2001. Taxonomy of Asarum section Asarum (Aristolochiaceae). Systematic Botany 26: 17–53.

Liang, Y., and I. Stehlik. 2009. Relationship between shade and herbivory in Asarum canadense (wild ginger). University of Toronto Journal of Undergraduate Life Sciences 3: 30–32.

Lu, K. L. 1982. Pollination biology of Asarum caudatum (Aristolochiaceae) in northern California. Systematic Botany 7: 150–157.

Lewis, M., and W. Clark. 1806. The Journals of the Lewis and Clark Expedition, ed. G. E. Moulton. June 27, 1806. University of Nebraska Press, Lincoln. http://lewisandclarkjournals.unl.edu/read/?_xmlsrc=1806-06-27.xml&_xslsrc=LCstyles.xsl (accessed 2010).

Mussulman, J., and J. L. Reveal. 2005. "Wild ginger." Discovering Lewis & Clark. http://lewis-clark.org/content/content-article.asp?ArticleID=2534 (accessed 2010).

Peattie, D. C. 1940. How is Asarum pollinated? Castanea 5: 24–29.

St. Olaf College. 2003–2010. "Wild ginger." St. Olaf College Natural Lands. http://www.stolaf.edu/academics/naturallands/woodlands/ephemerals/wild-ginger.html (accessed 2010).

Stritch, L. 2010. "Plant of the week: Wild ginger (Asarum canadense L.)." U.S. Forest Service: Celebrating Wildflowers. http://www.fs.fed.us/wildflowers/plant-of-the-week/asarum_canadense.shtml (accessed 2010).

Wildman, H. E. 1950. Pollination of Asarum canadense. Science 111: 551.

Index

virus, 185
voles, 5

Waller, Donald, 53
Wallroth, K.F.W., 173
Washington, George, 199
Washingtonia, 199
wasp(s), 18, 166–67, 179, 186–87, 211
    sawfly larva, 41
    yellow-jacket, 186
water lettuce, 101

water-violet, 79
weevils, 4–5
wet-dog, 184
wild ginger, 228–33
    long-tailed, 231
windflowers, 96
wintergreen, 87–89
    flowering, 87–88
wood-betony, 128
wood-poppy, 30
worms, 109
    alien, 109

Xanthotype sospeta, 57
Xylocopa, 226

Zingiber officinale, 232